Orientation to Inquiry in a Reflective Professional Psychology

SUNY Series, Alternatives in Psychology
Michael A. Wallach, editor

Orientation to Inquiry in a Reflective Professional Psychology

Lisa Tsoi Hoshmand

STATE UNIVERSITY OF NEW YORK PRESS

Published by
State University of New York Press, Albany

Printed in the United States of America

For information, address the State University of New York Press, State University Plaza, Albany, NY 12246

Production by Christine Lynch
Marketing by Bernadette LaManna

Library of Congress Cataloging-in-Publication Data

Hoshmand, Lisa Tsoi, 1947-
Orientation to inquiry in a reflective professional psychology / Lisa Tsoi Hoshmand.
p. cm. — (SUNY series, alternatives in psychology)
Includes bibliographical references and index.
ISBN 0-7914-2115-5 (alk. paper) — ISBN 0-7914-2116-3 (pbk. : alk. paper)
1. Psychology—Practice. 2. Psychology—Research. 3. Inquiry (Theory of knowledge) I. Title. II. Series
BF75. H67 1994
150′.72—dc20 93-39602
CIP

10 9 8 7 6 5 4 3 2 1

Contents

To my parents

Leon and Lillian Tsoi

Preface

This book is written with the aim of providing a broad perspective on inquiry in professional psychology. The ideas for the book emerged at a time of conceptual and methodological diversity within our discipline as well as changing discourse in the philosophy of knowledge for the human sciences. It is also a time when our profession is faced with increasing demands for service and socially relevant inquiry that can contribute to solving complex human problems. Questions are raised about the usefulness of psychological knowledge and the viability of a scientist-practitioner model. New efforts are needed in professional education and training to respond to the presenting challenges.

The teaching of inquiry approaches in the professional practice of psychology has been separated historically by curriculum structures from the teaching of standard research methods. Clinical inquiry and research methods are often taught as subsets of skills with either a presumed commonality of philosophical foundations or without sufficient integration. It is my intention as author to bridge the domains of research and practice by providing students and their instructors with an integrative base for examining psychological inquiry. This will be accomplished by examining the models and methods of inquiry in research and practice together and by providing a framework for linking common issues of inquiry to the special context and needs of professional psychology.

This project is guided by a vision of psychology as a reflexive discipline and a reflective profession. The development of the scientist-practitioner in such areas as clinical, counseling, school/educational, and consulting/organizational psychology is conceived in terms of reflective qualities of mind and the capacity to contribute to the professional knowledge base through the activities of research and practice. A pluralistic approach to knowledge is promoted, with an invitation to engage in thoughtful method choice and continual evaluation of our philosophical commitments. Researchers, practitioners, and methodologists may find in this treatise new grounds for collaboration. As we expand our professional worldview and acknowledge the continuity of our knowledge and practice with other areas of inquiry and cultural practices, we may claim our place among self-aware human disciplines and service professions.

In writing this book, I am indebted to many: my first psychology professor, Erik Kvan, who models the ultimate enquiring mind; other teachers and mentors, especially Michael Diamond, Ronald Gallimore, and Roland Tharp; colleagues and friends James Bitter, David Ho, and Mary Kay Tetreault for their support and interest during my work at the California State University, Fullerton; Jack Martin and Donald Polkinghorne, who have stimulated my thinking about many of the issues addressed here; Leo Goldman, who first suggested that I could write a book that includes alternative paradigms; and the hundreds of authors whose works have paved the way for this project. As a teacher of inquiry in both research and practice, I have benefited over the years from interacting with students and sharing in their experience of the search for knowledge. I am grateful for the freedom I was given in my own search by my parents, and for the love and encouragement of my husband, Reza, and my children, Anthony and Andrea.

Lisa Tsoi Hoshmand
June 1993

1

A Reflective Professional Psychology

PERSONAL REFLECTIONS ON THE PROFESSION

The first time I attended the American Psychological Association Convention (APA) as a graduate student, I was impressed with the vastness of the gathering and the variety and scope of the presented programs. These feelings have not changed after nearly twenty years in the field. I have worked in psychiatric hospitals and community mental health centers; I have also been in different academic settings, teaching doctoral students in clinical psychology as well as master's level students in clinical psychology and counseling. My various roles have allowed me to look at professional psychology from different angles. The conference attendance continues to be interesting, especially when I find myself involved in a truly meaningful conversation with participants who have a keen sense of a certain professional issue. As expected, groups with particular interests tend to huddle among themselves, though one may wonder how the profession would be if we could make it a habit to talk to colleagues from specialties other than our own.

When I read the *APA Monitor*, I am struck by the breadth of the field and the range of professional activities that require those who wish to keep pace with such developments to make a real effort at staying current. The job announcements reflect the great variety of work that psychologists do, from basic research to academic teaching, from private practice to policy research and the administration of programs. Then again, one never fails to find that very specific advertisement that reads: "Faculty position open. Clinical psychologists specializing in research on the behavioral treatment of anorexia are encouraged to apply." What has happened to the generalist in each of us? Have we become so specialized as a profession that we can afford to narrow down the field in our teaching? What kinds of messages, by the way we define ourselves and the types of knowledge we hold to be important, are we giving to those preparing for entry into the profession?

As a clinical psychologist by training, I was encouraged to follow a scientist-practitioner model. During my internship days, I experienced the clinical setting as a setting for research and met a number of research-oriented practitioners. Over the years, however, I have encountered varied reactions to research among fellow psychologists. Some practitioners support it in principle but not in terms of actual participation. Many do not read the professional journals where formal research studies are published. They prefer to read the works of master practitioners or descriptive information on particular populations and problems related to their practice. Some express the view that research reports in journals do not teach them how to become more effective practitioners. On the other hand, I have also known some psychologists in service settings who are clearly more interested in doing research than working with their clients. They long for the day when their employment contract could be modified to legitimize more time in research. My sense is that these varied attitudes toward research and practice are associated with different values and interests as well as academic cultures of origin. I have been fortunate to have encountered teachers and colleagues who seem to be as deeply committed to the advancement of knowledge as they are to the quality of their practice. There is much to be learned from these individuals who have managed to integrate the worlds of science and practice and to maintain high standards in both realms of activity.

It appears that the integration of science and practice is taken up with different approaches and degrees of commitment in the academic setting. Not being the typical academic who started a university career immediately after the completion of doctoral training, I probably had different expectations about professional education for the students. I found myself questioning whether the type of training I received, including the sequential introduction of academic coursework and practical experience, is the best way to prepare someone for professional practice. As a graduate student, I had performed well academically but found myself woefully unprepared for practice when I began my clinical internship. I saw the same struggles in the interns I supervised in the practice settings where I worked. In my subsequent academic positions, I have spent a great deal of time trying to identify processes of teaching and learning that would facilitate the integration of conceptual and practical skills in the student's development at every level of graduate education. I have listened to many opinions from colleagues and professional task forces on this matter, and I believe this is an area in need of our serious attention.

Conversations with colleagues involved in the professional education of scientist-practitioners have usually centered around issues such as what we should look for in those who seek to enter the profession; what kinds of knowledge, skills, and attitudes we should emphasize in professional education; whether there is valid support for the way we practice; and how we should evaluate professional competence or, better still, the attainment of professional wisdom. We become so immersed in these important issues that we sometimes forget to consider the societal trends and developments in the field that impact on the profession. I am aware of the concerns of practicing psychologists, having worked in mental health-service settings and continued to supervise students in field placements. There is a sense of awe that professional psychology is being pulled by forces larger than itself, such as political and economic forces behind licensing, accreditation, third-party payment, and the funding of systems of service delivery in which professional roles are sought. The complexity of issues and the heterogeneity of viewpoints and interests in the profession can be seen in the recent debates about health care reform in the United States as psychologists attempt to make a case for the profession.

It is not clear how the concerns that are discussed regularly by education and training committees in our professional organization are actually influencing the academic worldview or are considered in the day-to-day professional training provided by academic programs. By chance events, I found myself teaching in a graduate counseling program after spending many years steeped in clinical psychology. As it turned out, much of the professional worldview in counseling also fit quite well with my own. There seems to be a willingness to acknowledge the sociocultural context of professional practice and to view psychological knowledge from the standpoint of societal needs for a human-service profession. Yet I often question whether the program at my own university should continue to emphasize training in individual and family counseling in traditional facilities, when we can shift our focus to preventive interventions and program development such as in community-based integrative services. Universities, with their own institutional dynamics and constraints on teaching and curriculum, seem painfully slow in responding to societal needs.

Other types of conversations with colleagues took place by distant communication, through my writing and reading of others' reactions to my work. The latter have ranged from affirmation to surprisingly angry attacks. The attacks remind me of a debate I witnessed as a graduate student at a local professional meeting. It was between a therapist with a transactional analysis orientation and one of our own professors who represented the behavioral orientation. The arguments were sharp and the exchange unfriendly. We cheered for our own professor then, never stopping to question the completeness of the behavioral point of view in which we were so well indoctrinated. I find it discouraging when psychologists have difficulty talking to others in the profession who happen to hold different world-views. Without open listening and constructive dialogue, I am not certain how our profession can improve its vision.

Our mission as a profession has become a real challenge, with the growing complexity of human problems and the increasingly institutionalized role that society grants to psychologists. I wonder how many of us consider ourselves to be agents of social change. Being in midlife, I have to decide where and how I should make my own contributions. Someone once told me that he tried to find out who I am by looking up my APA division memberships, only to be unable to draw a firm conclusion. The fact is, I align myself broadly with the profession—no longer with the single division representing my original specialty training—and I lend support through dues, voting, and other means to those groups that represent social interests, populations, and issues about which I care. I do not feel strange about the fact that I am a clinical psychologist with an active membership in the counseling psychology division. I believe that boundaries can become barriers that only hamper us as a profession. They prevent us from seeing clearly the common causes to which we can contribute our varied training and experience.

As an educator, I naturally identify with those who are interested in teaching. I find it helpful to talk with others who are involved in designing graduate-level professional training in psychology. This does not mean that I have little to do with those who teach in other areas. As a practitioner, I have learned to work with members of other professions, such as psychiatry, social work, and nursing. As an academician, I find my interactions with colleagues from other disciplines to be especially enriching. People from philosophy, anthropology, and sociology, for instance, have much to say about the human domain and the social sciences. Others from education, social work, and human services share many of our professional concerns.

My students have also taught me a great deal about the profession by their questions and reactions to problem situations. A common question from entry-level students concerns how one is supposed to know that a certain way of responding to a problem of practice is the most appropriate action. Other questions are related to the overwhelming number of theories and therapeutic orientations from which to derive one's basis of working as a professional. Some students find the transition from theoretical studies to internship experience rather traumatic; something seems missing, and the luxury of theoretical speculations is replaced by the urgency of decisions and actions. The occasion of starting thesis and dissertation work brings about other types of dilemmas and distress. Should one conduct a simple survey study or a neatly controlled analogue experiment, or should one risk the "imperfections" of a clinical or applied study? Would the faculty committee find it acceptable if one were to conduct a case study, using qualitative, nonstandardized methods? Not infrequently, a student would start off with what seem to be available and acceptable instruments for measuring a certain construct rather than with a phenomenon of interest and the questions one wishes to ask. A similar restrictiveness is experienced in clinical and counseling work. Well-learned formulations tend to take over and dictate the observational lenses used. Certain technologies of assessment and intervention demand such procedural compliance that they leave little room for reflection. With some reluctance, self-doubts are expressed in the form of "Tell me what to do" or, more poignantly, "What can I trust so I know what I am doing?" At such moments, it is most helpful to stop and reflect—on the sources of our uncertainty, the way we have framed questions for ourselves, the underlying assumptions in what we think we know, and so forth.

Reflection as a self-directed activity must, at some point, come back to ourselves. This turning back to reflect on oneself, or the referring of one's experience to oneself, is called "reflexivity." In sharing some of my reflections on the profession, I should also share a little more about who I am. The fact that I am a woman, a wife, and soon a mother of two adolescents is relevant to my perspective, as is my Chinese heritage. Being a product of bicultural (and perhaps multicultural) socialization and having a husband with roots in the third world have a great deal to do with my worldview. I received my undergraduate education as a psychology major in a department that was once part of the philosophy department and was influenced by a European, historical point of view. Although I completed my graduate training in the United States and spent most of my professional life here and in Canada, I have always had the double vision of an outsider and one who has the benefit of immersion in American psychology. It has only been in recent years, however, that I have ventured to share my views on the profession.

I invite colleagues and students who will be reading this to reflect on the nature of our science and practice and the state of professional psychology. I believe that our self-understanding as a profession requires a reflexive study of the nature of the discipline and the foundations of its claims to knowledge and scientific practice. The reflexive approach to knowledge and our own ways of thought has been indicated by studies of the mind in relation to self and society (Mead 1962; Vygotsky 1978), the devices used in articulating knowledge and its context (Woolgar 1988), and the processes of systematic inquiry (Steier 1991c). Reflexivity is proposed here as a central concept in the reflective study of ourselves as a scientific and professional community, as much of self-understanding is held to be both social and personal.

SCIENCE, PRACTICE, AND PROFESSIONAL PSYCHOLOGY

The emergence of professional psychology has been linked to the development of psychology as a scientific discipline and the concept of a science-based practice. Most professional psychologists in this generation have been trained under some form of the scientist-practitioner model (Goldfried 1984; Shakow 1978; Raimy 1950). There are many issues surrounding the identity of psychology as a discipline. A prevailing definition is that psychology is a social science and, more specifically, a science of human behavior. Although this may be the accepted definition in most American academic departments, it should be recognized that the very nature of psychology and its autonomy as a discipline have been the subject of debate (for example see, Margolis, Manicas, Harre, and Secord 1986). One of the issues concerns the subject matter of psychology and how it is to be studied. If human behavior constitutes the subject matter of psychology, how broadly it is conceived and the extent to which human realities are studied in context would determine the scope of the discipline. Manicas (1986) expressed the opinion that much of Western psychology has been conceived at the individual level or reduced to biological terms and that this type of psychological science does not represent a complete study of human life in social context. A broadly conceived psychological domain would presumably call for an expansion of the prevalent approaches to knowledge in the discipline.

An issue central to the debates on the viability of psychology as a human science concerns the model of knowledge adopted by the discipline and how we choose to conduct inquiry. Cronbach (1986) questioned if psychology should aspire to be a theoretical science like physics, with a historical reliance on mathematical language and the logic of hypothetico-deductive theory testing. Others—notably Skinner (1987)—believed in psychology as an autonomous science of behavior modeled after the physical sciences. Skinner was criticized for encouraging scientism with his exclusively behavioristic stance (Mahoney 1989). The ongoing debates on the how psychology should define itself are captured, for instance, in the title of an article by Bunge (1990): "What kind of discipline is psychology: Autonomous or dependent, humanistic or scientific, biological or sociological?"

A fundamental point to be recognized is the reflexive nature of our discipline (Flanagan 1981). The fact that psychologists as humans are attempting to study humans means that the discipline must develop self-referenced knowledge and account for the contributions of the human observer in generating that knowledge. We are both the knowing subject and objects to be known. It is fortunate that, as humans, we are capable of reflexive understanding of the physical and social world in relation to ourselves. Reflexivity, which means referring back to oneself, requires stepping outside of the system we are part of (only in a manner of speaking) to study and reflect on our own involvement in it. Being reflexive involves reflecting on our accustomed ways of thought. This skill of reflection is one of the mature human abilities sometimes referred to as "metacognition." It enables us to evaluate our own condition and disposition, as well as our own ways of thinking.

What frame of mind should we use as we reflect on our science and profession? Disenchantment with our discipline's approach to knowledge and the profession's orientation to inquiry had been expressed by Koch (1981a) and Sarason (1981b), using criteria and standards that are not simply technological. Bevan (1986) commented:

> When we look at psychology and at ourselves as psychologists...we most certainly recognize that as we have advanced our academic enterprise we have also accelerated specialization and fostered a technological frame of mind at the expense of one that is broadly historical and philosophical. (393)

I agree with Bevan that to understand the evolution of the discipline and the current issues faced by the profession, we should turn to historical analysis of major trends, such as given in Koch and Leary (1985) and Leahey (1991). This is because questions about the identity of psychology and the persistent attendant philosophical issues have been variously framed and debated over time.

For example, one of the issues of contention has been the language we use for the description of human phenomena. Behavioristic emphasis in psychological science has confined description to the observer's standpoint, deemphasizing the experience and intentions of the actor. Some feel that this special use of everyday language in order to set psychology apart as a scientific enterprise is counter to a fully human discipline (Groeben 1990; Mischel 1969; Shotter 1975). If human action and human experience were considered to be the proper domain of psychology, psychology as a reductive science of behavior is called into question. Reductive methods of science require the operationalization of human events in simple, measurable, and observable units. Human intentions and experience are not readily reducible by such operational definitions and measurement or adequately described by language that is extensional rather than intensional (Margolis 1986b). If each of us were represented simply by personality traits and motivation as measured on an objective test, or described by others only with the language of a detached observer, it would not give a complete sense of who we are.

Reflexive analysis should include an examination of the interests and value orientation of psychology. Due to the very human nature of the discipline, it has the character of a normative or value-laden science rather than what is traditionally referred to as a "pure science." From a normative point of view, a scientific enterprise can be characterized by the type of interests and values it serves. According to the ideas of Habermas (1971), human knowledge interests can be distinguished into the technical (with application as goal), the hermeneutical (with understanding as goal), and the critical (with emancipation as goal). Using this typology of interests as a reference point, we can reflect on where our guild interests are directing the discipline and the profession. Among the three types of knowledge interests, the sharpest contrast seems to be between the conception of psychological science as one guided by technical rationality and the related goal of instrumental application and the conception of psychology as a human science of understanding and emancipation. For professional psychology, the concept of a science-based practice has been historically associated with a technological conception of science. It leaves those members of the profession who are involved in such areas as psychotherapeutic practice in a peculiar position of choosing among these varied definitions of our orientation. Some have argued that psychotherapy belongs with a hermeneutic and emancipatory human science rather than a rational, technical science of behavior (Kvale 1986; Lesche, 1985). However, many of the interventions used by practitioners also involve applications of behavioral technology. The particular type of interest we actually serve may become more apparent upon reflection.

The suggestion to scrutinize ourselves as a profession, however, may not be taken seriously as long as we continue to believe that psychology is an objective science and that we can be value-neutral as scientists. White (1983) argued that some psychologists,

> living in an ahistorical and unphilosophical era, have contrived to be unaware of their own intellectual and ideological commitments buried in their work and their theories... [in] seeking to be nonideological they have been ungovernably ideological. (6)

To be a reflexive discipline and a reflective profession requires that we become more historically and philosophically informed as well as ideologically self-conscious.

Questions about our profession's values and interests cannot be separated entirely from the model of inquiry we use in research and practice or from our assumptions about the subject matter of our inquiry. The evolution of our discipline and our professional identity involves epistemological, ontological, and axiological considerations and choices. *Epistemology* is concerned with the philosophy of knowledge that undergirds our approach to inquiry. *Ontology* refers to assumptions about nature, including our own place in it. *Axiology* involves values, social as well as cognitive ones associated with epistemic preference (Howard 1985b). The interplay of these three kinds of factors in the self-determination of professional psychology and our orientation to inquiry will constitute the underlying theme of this book. Reflections on our philosophical and historical foundations will begin in chapter 2, to be followed by a consideration of the sociocultural and ideological context of professional inquiry in chapter 3.

As will be explained in chapter 2, the dominant model of knowledge accepted by modern psychology has been premised on epistemological and ontological assumptions associated with *logical positivism* and *empiricism* (Ayer 1966; Hanfling 1981). It presumes an objective science capable of generating knowledge for technical application. This model of knowledge has been challenged as changes have come about in the philosophy of science. Increasingly, questions are raised about the philosophical assumptions underlying the methods of knowledge used by the discipline and whether they seem to be fitting with the human domain and the language-dependent nature of psychological inquiry. Epistemologically: "Is objectivity possible?" and "What types of language and tools should we use to describe psychological phenomena?" Ontologically: "What kinds of image of the human being are we promoting with our methods of knowledge?" and "Do we believe that humans act with intentions and free will?" These questions that are being raised in the changing discourse on the nature of psychological science should be of interest to those entering the psychology profession. As will also be explained in chapter 2, *social constructionism* as an emergent perspective on knowledge favors a science of understanding based on different methods of knowledge. This pluralistic view of knowledge allows us to be open to a diversity of conceptual frameworks and research orientations, the major examples of which will be described in chapters 4 and 5, respectively.

Psychology is now a highly differentiated field that is increasingly pluralistic in orientation. Pluralism is regarded by some theorists and methodologists as inevitable (Cook 1985; Cook and Campbell 1979; Royce 1985). One may consider each orientation to knowledge as having its particular niche by fulfilling particular missions (Howard 1991), the type of mission chosen being a function of our values and interests. An important fact is that every major system of inquiry (referred to as a *paradigm*) is associated with particular procedures and conceptual underpinnings as well as particular norms for judging knowledge claims. The existence of multiple paradigms means that researchers and practitioners have to conduct inquiry under different and seemingly incompatible rules and criteria of knowledge. Whether this engenders a healthy tension in the field and whether a divergent pluralism can bring about progress in psychological science and practice are open to question (Hoshmand and Martin 1992). Professional inquiry may be hampered by the lack of a common understanding about criteria and values that transcend our differences. Our profession needs to engage in open dialogue about our working theories of inquiry and evolve a shared conception of how our knowledge can contribute to progress in the human realm. Some philosophers are proposing a pragmatic reconciliation of the more relativistic views associated with a pluralistic orientation to knowledge and the philosophical orientation and methodology of the dominant scientific tradition (Margolis 1986b; Okrent 1988; Rorty 1991). The prospects for a second-order or metalevel framework, which may provide a common language and methodological guidelines for dealing with issues arising from our increasingly diverse orientation to knowledge, will also be discussed in chapters 4 and 5.

We are at a time when there are not only different perspectives on the nature of knowledge but different views on the relationship between our science and practice. Issues of an epistemogical, ontological, and axiological nature will continue to be debated as educators try to prepare the next generation of scientist-practitioners. This state of affairs can be confusing and unsettling, especially for those entering the profession. Although professional psychology has depended on the development of scientific psychology, professional practice has evolved mostly out of societal needs (Peterson 1991). The proliferation of psychological practice has, in a sense, outpaced the maturation of psychology as a scientific discipline (Sechrest 1992). This partnership of science and practice is at a critical point (see, for example, the discussion in Schneider 1990). There have been conflicts between scientific values and the values of professional practice (Garfield 1992). Our profession is continuously transformed as social changes and new challenges arise (Dorken and Associates 1986). The ability of psychological science to provide a sufficient knowledge base for solving the problems of practice and the relevance of academic research and theories to the purposes of practice are continuously questioned (Howard 1985a; Ross 1981; Sarason 1981a; Strupp 1981). As the proper role of inquiry in a practicing profession is debated, proposed revisions have yet to be implemented by the profession (Hoshmand and Polkinghorne 1992; Peterson 1985, 1991). The direction and outcome of this discourse remain to be shaped by the types of scientific worldviews and values adopted by future members of the profession. An open, reflexive stance may enable us to approach these issues and questions with thoughtfulness and to participate productively in their discussion.

A reflexive approach in this case implies self-scrutiny and awareness of the foundations and assumptive base of our discipline and profession. It involves a continuous questioning of our self-definition and professional interests. For the practicing members of the profession, a constant evaluation of our practice and how it contributes to a viable human-service discipline becomes both a challenge and a responsibility. A common ground on which to engage in such reflexive study consists in the models and methods of knowledge used by both researchers and practitioners. By examining the models and methods of inquiry shared by members of the profession (as we will do in this present volume), we can begin to understand our contradictions and congruities, our limitations and potentials. The vision of a science and practice that mutually influence and support each other may provide a general direction for a profession that is continuously evolving its identity.

ISSUES OF METHOD CHOICE

I would like to call special attention here to the question of method choice, by which I mean the choice of both conceptual and methodological means and frameworks. As stated earlier, a person entering the profession will be faced with a diverse range of methods and orientations. Due to differences of personal history, the role models and peers in one's educational setting would likely display varied commitments to conceptual models and methodologies that reflect their personal values and worldviews. An open attitude is necessary in order for one to appreciate the existing variety of models and methods. By learning about the full range of conceptual and methodological frameworks and their strengths and limitations, one may be in a better position to make informed choices. Further reflective study could reveal the diverse paradigms from which the available concepts and methods of knowledge are derived and the fact that they are linked to particular values and philosophical commitments. These are the reasons for the focus in this volume on our orientation to inquiry, and the invitation to make thoughtful evaluations of our methods.

Method choice needs to be guided by an understanding of the philosophical foundations of a given paradigm of knowledge, its conceptual and methodological implications, the type of problems or questions it is best suited to address, and the value orientation adopted toward the subject phenomenon. It is a process that is mediated by our personal values, worldview, and interaction with significant others in our environment. An articulation of our personal beliefs and values may help clarify the basis of our choices. Reflection on our experience with the use of theories and methods can further clarify the boundaries of their application. As practicing members of the profession, we have to consider additionally the special needs and purposes in the context of working with clients. Methods of information gathering used in the practice of psychology have varied effects on our relationship with clients and how they are led to feel about themselves. For instance, a client's need to make sense of his or her situation and to have someone empathize with the problem he or she is experiencing calls for a mode of interaction that would respond to such needs. These types of considerations make it necessary for us to be selective in our approach to professional inquiry.

It appears that there are certain parameters that would constrain method choice in psychological inquiry. One is that human phenomena, the subject matter of our science and profession, are always contextualized and unstable, if not indeterminate in meaning. Much of the data come in the form of natural language and cultural practices. Being so, they must be understood in context, using processes and means that are most conducive to such understanding. Similarly, professional inquiry is a social activity that is culturally situated and personally motivated. It, too, is embedded in context. As social agents, psychologists work within the settings and roles defined by society. As human beings, we are the products of our own culture and history, socialized by the institutions that grant us legitimacy as professionals. Our approach to knowledge must therefore account for our own embeddedness as well as the special nature of our subject matter. What this probably means in terms of method choice is that not all methods are possible or equally appropriate for a given task of knowledge. Not all paradigms could be co-equal in value in a given context. The crucial difference is in how one arrives at one's choices. The degree of critical self-reflection that accompanies a particular choice may determine our ability to continue to seek more viable options.

Of the many factors entering into method choice, the personal judgment of the professional plays a central role. For this reason, the rest of this chapter will touch upon personal knowing and the development of professional judgments and worldviews.

PERSONAL KNOWING AND PROFESSIONAL WORLD VIEWS

Surprisingly, the professional's personal approach to knowledge in general is seldom a subject of study. Similarly, professional worldviews tend to be taken for granted rather than subject to scrutiny. On the other hand, considerable attention has been given to the nature of professional judgment in research on cognitive factors in social information processing. This research has included studies of factors that influence social information processing (Cantor and Kihlstrom 1981; Fiske and Taylor 1984; Higgins and Stangor 1988), the heuristics employed in professional decision making (Kahneman, Slovic, and Tversky 1982; Nisbett and Ross 1980), and errors of professional judgment (Turk and Salovey, 1988). The lessons from these studies point to the fallibility of professional judgment and the need to guard against potential biases and errors. The implications of this area of research will be discussed in chapter 7. As a practicing profession, psychology must attend to the development of professional judgment in training as well as build in checks and balances in professional practice.

In attempting to improve on our professional judgment, there has been a tendency to look toward better instruments and procedures as an answer. Valid instruments of appraisal and reliable procedures of information gathering do contribute to the quality of information obtained by the professional psychologist. However, much remains to be processed and acted upon by the psychologist, based on experience and personal judgment. It is the personal knowing of the professional that is the determining factor in our judgments and actions. There is much that we need to learn about our own ways of knowing as a practicing profession. Due to the historical emphasis on formal research as a means of generating knowledge, there is at present no comprehensive framework for understanding the knowledge processes of practitioners. It is assumed that the professional psychologist trained with the scientist-practitioner model basically endorses the epistemological assumptions and practices of the academic psychologist and researcher. This seems to be true for behaviorally oriented psychologists (Krasner and Houts 1984). Yet many practitioners claim that their clinical ways of knowing are different from what they have learned in research training. Some experience a duality in their orientation to knowledge as researcher and practitioner.

The distinctive feature of the knowledge of practice is that it is interactive and contingent on the participation of both the professional and the client. The fact that the practitioner is always a participant observer makes it untenable to maintain the assumptions of a detached observer as in the traditional research setting. Kanfer (1990) identified several additional dimensions of difference between the functioning of laboratory researchers and practitioners that may have reinforced the division between science and practice. The possibility has been proposed (Hoshmand and Polkinghorne 1992) that alternative conceptions of psychological science and the knowledge of practice may overcome this division. The common thread between inquiry for research purposes and for practice is to be found in our ways of knowing or our applied epistemology (the subject of chapter 7). A working conception of how professional knowledge is tested and refined through application may be helpful in understanding our judgments and actions in practice.

Schon (1983) offered a conception of expert practice as reflective practice, in which knowledge is critically tested and revised in the light of experience. His conception is supported by the work of Dreyfus and Dreyfus (1986), who described the knowledge processes of practitioners at different levels of experience. An understanding of the knowledge of practice may enable us to place in perspective the respective roles and contributions of our academic theoretical knowledge, our experiential learning, and our practice-tested knowledge. As one undergoes professional training, it is important to reflect on one's native ways of knowing and how they evolve and change with education and the experience of professional research and practice. Due to the emphasis on objective methods and external criteria of knowing, however, there has been a relative neglect of the development of the enquirer and knower. This has been in spite of the fact that tacit dimensions of knowing are inevitably involved in all acts of knowing (Polanyi 1964, 1966). We shall therefore consider the place of personal knowing and how it enters into the development of professional worldviews.

There are several dimensions of personal knowing that are significant in the development of professional worldviews. First is personal epistemic style, which refers to one's preferred modes of knowing. Epistemic styles may be temperament based (Mitroff and Kilmann 1978) and/or a function of developmental stage (Salner 1988). Some of us learn from authoritative sources, and others, by personal experience. Some prefer working with ideas while others prefer learning by doing. Even as we reflect, the flow from question to answer and back to question varies for each person. Some of us need more time to pause at questions. Others reach out to question only after sufficient resting at answers. Epistemic orientation seems to affect scientists' choice of formal methods of knowledge (Kratwohl 1985). Thus, it is important to understand one's own epistemic style and to complement it with those method choices that would otherwise not be considered in inquiry. Epistemic style is probably related to one's preferred scientific worldview. Mitroff and Kilmann (1978) warned that favoring a single epistemic style would deprive a scientific discipline of alternative approaches to knowledge. Kratwohl (1985) and Salner (1988) speculated that there may be a developmental progression of epistemic styles, both for the individual and for the profession at large. The maturing of our discipline and profession could very well depend on the evolution of epistemic styles adopted by the members.

A second dimension concerns the use of self as a tool of knowledge. In professional inquiry, whether in research or in practice, the self of the professional can serve as an instrument for gauging human phenomenon in interaction (Baldwin and Satir 1987; Berg and Smith 1988; Kelly 1955). Professional training should provide opportunities for refining the use of self in inquiry. In Eastern ways of thought, the self as knower is given great emphasis (Paranjpe 1988a). The self becomes knowing through the dialectic interaction with one's environment, both external and internal. Knowing is thus synonymous with action and experience. The selfhood of a developing professional should be a central area of focus for the profession.

A third dimension concerns the influence of personal worldviews on our choice of professional paradigms. Personal beliefs and values influence our choice of conceptual models and methods of inquiry in that those consistent with our personal worldviews are more likely to be preferred. A study by Kimble (1984) on the epistemic values and scientific worldviews of different groups of psychologists revealed certain distinct differences. More deeply rooted metaphysical beliefs are probably involved in the way we conduct scientific inquiry and professional practice (O'Donohue 1989). Lyddon (1989a) pointed to the relationship between personal epistemology and preference for particular counseling approaches. Individuals entering the profession should take time to discover their implicit frameworks and evaluate how new ideas are assimilated and accommodated as they undergo their professional training experience.

Personal aspects of knowing therefore affect professional worldviews at several levels. The critical question is how personal knowing becomes integrated with the development of professional knowledge. It is important not to equate personal knowledge with total subjectivity. In its ideal form, this personal knowledge should be a product of experience that reflects the benefits of one's learning history and environment. Professional development does not occur in a vacuum. As members of a knowledge community, we participate in contributing to the knowledge claimed by the profession. Individually, we are each accountable to this community in our actions and practices. Collectively, we are engaged in a continuous process of shaping our professional worldview.

QUESTIONS FOR REFLECTIVE STUDY

The present chapter has touched upon many issues and developments in the field. In proposing a reflexive stance, I have organized this volume by two themes. One is a reflexive study of the models and methods of inquiry in our profession and their foundations. The other is a focus on epistemic skills and knowledge processes in the development of the professional psychologist. For the purpose of evolving an integrative understanding of the many topics we will examine in the coming chapters, I offer the following questions to guide the process of reflective study:

1. What are the forces that have shaped the models of knowledge and orientations to inquiry in our discipline and profession?
2. What are the persistent issues and problems in psychological inquiry?
3. What are the special needs in the professional context of practice and their implications for paradigm and method choice?
4. What kinds of assumptions and values should we adopt in professional inquiry?
5. What are the conceptual and methodological paradigms available for our use, and how are they related to particular perspectives of knowledge?
6. What types of epistemic skills and reflective habits do we need to develop as professional psychologists?

Question 1 will be addressed from a historical perspective, along with question 2, in chapter 2. Questions 3 and 4, the subject of chapter 3, will set the context for discussion throughout. Question 5 will be covered by a description of core ideas and conceptual systems in chapter 4 and major research paradigms in chapter 5. Question 6 is approached from several angles in the remainder of the book: in terms of methods of inquiry in chapter 6, knowledge processes in chapter 7, training in case study in chapter 8, and the development of reflective habits and research-practice integration in chapter 9. The overall question that should be kept in mind throughout concerns what kinds of models and methods of knowledge may serve professional psychology well as a human science and practicing profession.

At the end of each chapter, there are additional questions and learning activities suggested for readers who are current students and participants in professional training programs.

SUGGESTED ADDITIONAL LEARNING

Write an essay reflecting on your own epistemic beliefs and views on psychological knowledge. Include conceptual and methodological commitments, if any. Consider how these factors fit into your professional worldview and personal value system.

As you reflect on your own orientation to knowledge, try to identify those experiences that have contributed to your taking an open, as opposed to closed, stance on particular issues.

As a learner, when are you most certain of your grasp of knowledge? How do others respond to your preferred ways of knowing? What have you done about your ways of knowing around persons who differ in style and worldview?

2

Foundations and Issues of Psychological Inquiry

SETTING THE STAGE FOR AN OVERVIEW

The study of psychological inquiry can begin with a historical understanding of the foundations of knowledge in psychological science. As we examine models of knowledge and follow the changing perspectives on psychological knowledge over time, basic problems and issues of human inquiry will be identified. These problems and issues will provide the background for considering questions about the appropriate choice of concepts and methods in professional psychology. To accomplish this within the limits of this chapter, we need to build upon information and frameworks that are available. A review of major systems of thought in psychology may have been given in undergraduate courses on the history and systems of psychology. Depending on the scope of coverage and the inclinations of the instructor, there may have been some discussion of the history of ideas and the philosophy of science (at least in the Western intellectual tradition) as the larger frames in which to place psychological ideas and methods. Readers can familiarize themselves again with this information by referring to a number of sources (Koch and Leary 1992; Leahey 1991; Mahoney 1991; Rychlak 1988). Only a brief historical account of the development of the inquiry orientations in our profession will be given here.

It should be noted that just as perspectives on knowledge have evolved, the character of historical scholarship has also changed. Whereas the classic work of Boring (Boring 1950; O'Donnell 1979) gave a conventional account of the building of the discipline, recent historians of psychology have adopted a more critical approach that is sensitive to the sociocultural, political, and intellectual context of our development as a discipline and profession (Ash and Woodward 1987; Danziger 1987; Morawski 1988; Woodward 1980; Woodward and Ash 1982). This latter approach is consistent with a reflective orientation.

Contemporary historians of psychology are also of the opinion that the boundaries drawn between major systems in psychology and the shifts from one period of emphasis to another are less tidy and clear than have been assumed. Leahey (1992) noted, for instance, that in the early period of mentalism when psychology can be characterized primarily as a study of consciousness, there was no agreement about method (such as between the approaches of Wundt and James) or theory (in terms of physiological as opposed to phenomenological explanations). Although certain concepts and methods may be dominant at a given time and be considered representative of a major system of inquiry or paradigm, as discussed by Kuhn (1970), a continuum of concepts and methods existed in every historical period. Seldom is a clear break evident in the Kuhnian sense of a dramatic paradigm revolution whereby prior concepts and methods are rejected because of a radical change in ideas and methodological assumptions. Even as the discipline shifted its focus from consciousness to behavior and, later, back to a cognitive emphasis, a continuity of conceptual and methodological trends reflect persistent problems of inquiry framed and approached in different ways at different times. These differences represent major tensions that are still felt today. Leahey (1992) referred to such differences (as for example, the molar versus the molecular, and the structural versus the functional) as *themata* (following Holton 1973), or pairs of underlying philosophical commitments. We can regard these contrasting philosophical commitments as types of dialectical tension characteristic of our field. *Dialectics* is a way of understanding coexisting differences as complementary and potentially useful, rather than viewing them as opposing dichotomies in exclusionary terms. We shall utilize the metaphors of a *continuum of methods* and the *dialectics of knowledge* in our thinking about inquiry throughout this book.

I will first explain some terms that will be used in the description and discussion that follow. The word "foundation" as used in the title of this chapter refers to the underlying assumptions of systems of inquiry. It includes epistemological assumptions about the nature of knowledge and how we know, ontological assumptions about the world and human nature, and axiological assumptions about what are appropriate values to hold. This usage of "foundation" is to be distinguished from a particular meaning of "foundationalism" in the philosophy of science. *Foundationalism* refers to the assumption that cognitive certainty is possible in knowledge, as granted by a universal foundation of rationality. Philosophers of science had tried in the past to justify the nature of scientific knowledge by invoking the assumption of an objective reality independent of the enquiring mind (an ontological assumption about nature that is described as "realist"). *Realism* is the belief that reality has a truth status apart from the human mind. Under this assumption, insofar as scientists can demonstrate that their inquiry has followed procedural rules designed to guarantee objective knowing, accurate access to the world is assumed. Objective knowing is conceived as a particular way of knowing that involves the separation of the object and the subject in the knowing process (a position resulting from René Descartes's formalization of the mind-body distinction that is described as "dualistic"). This particular scientific worldview, associated with a realist ontology and an epistemological position of *dualism*, has historically constituted a *foundationalist* philosophy of science.

Foundationalism is exemplified by positivism, which was the prevailing philosophical foundation of the sciences from the mid-nineteenth century to the early parts of the twentieth century. Positivistic science is associated with realism and follows the basic tenets of objective knowing. The popular acceptance of this scientific world view led the philosopher Suppe (1977) to call it the "received view." As will be explained subsequently, the new philosophy of science of this century has moved away from the received, positivistic view that there could be a single, certain foundation for knowledge, to a more relativistic point of view. A different ontological and epistemological stance is taken by arguing that knowledge is a human construction influenced by sociocultural and historical context and the perspectives of the knower (thus referred to as "social constructionism"). Rather than being based on a universal foundation or guided by universal standards, different methods and products of knowledge are conceivable and can be understood in terms of their context and local norms. This point of view is shared to some extent by all who acknowledge social context and cultural differences in the study of human phenomenon. However, extreme *relativism* and *constructivism* (or a radical version of the social constructionist view) in current discourse about human inquiry have led to the characterization of this new-age thinking as "foundationless." A nonfoundationalist philosophy of science no longer assumes that we have any privileged basis for claiming certainty in knowledge (Margolis 1986a).

As we move from the historical evolvement of different perspectives on knowledge and the corresponding models of inquiry in psychology to the specific issues of psychological inquiry, we will be identifying issues of human inquiry that have continued to be the subject of debate among philosophers of science. Thus, the concepts and terminology used by philosophers in this regard should be learned as tools for helping us in our own conceptualization and discussion of the issues. Not surprisingly, from a historical standpoint, there are instances of time lag between developments in philosophical discourse and the inquiry practices in our field and their attendant views. In other words, psychology has not quite caught up with the latest thinking and discourse in the philosophy of science.

MODELS OF KNOWLEDGE IN HISTORICAL PERSPECTIVE

One of the ways of understanding the evolution of our discipline and profession is to examine the models of knowledge we have followed. A given model of knowledge can be identified with particular assumptions, methods, and standards, as well as the interests with which it is associated. As far as philosophical assumptions in psychological inquiry are concerned, it is important to realize that conceptions of knowledge and issues of epistemology in the human realm cannot be easily separated from ontological assumptions about the nature of the knowing mind and our place in the world. How we know is closely linked to what we assume we can know. It is also related to what we assume about ourselves as both knowers and human subjects. Furthermore, because we are human participants in a social world, the paradigms (or major systems of ideas and methods) of our profession are shaped by an interplay of these epistemological and ontological assumptions with other social values characteristic of the ideologies of our profession and our time. This last point will be elaborated in the next chapter.

As stated in chapter 1, the arguments in support of any given paradigm can be framed in terms of the three types of considerations: the epistemic, the ontological, and the axiological. This means that the language used in discussing issues of choice between paradigms should be understood in relation to the particular type of philosophical consideration involved. Furthermore, the arguments presented should be judged on the particular horizon that is indicated. In other words, two choices of theoretical models cannot be meaningfully compared if one were based on preference for a particular way of knowing (an epistemological consideration) and the other were based on value implications (an axiological consideration). For example, one researcher may have chosen learning theory to study self-control because its concepts are amenable to operationalization, whereas another may have preferred a humanistic theory because it holds humans to be agents with personal will, capable of self-determination. A more meaningful comparison would have been in terms of how the choices differ on the same horizon, using the same kind of consideration (epistemological, ontological, or axiological) to the extent that it is possible to distinguish them. In this case, we may ask which of the two choices will enable us to demonstrate empirically how self-control is possible with respect to a behavior of interest, a question posed at an epistemological level. This type of distinction of horizons should be kept in mind when we compare conceptual orientations as well as research paradigms in subsequent chapters.

"Method" is used here to refer to both conceptual and methodological approaches. The standards used to judge methods of inquiry are principles and criteria derived from the philosophy of knowledge associated with a given inquiry system or paradigm. Historically, the orientation to inquiry associated with the development of psychology as a science in the West was influenced by positivism. During the early to middle part of the nineteenth century, John Stuart Mill proposed a logical foundation for an empirical science with mathematical laws, and Auguste Comte founded the natural science model based on natural functional laws. The roots of this positivistic model of knowledge can be traced to an emphasis on sensory data and empirical methods in the late Renaissance period (as represented by the ideas of Galileo Galilei, Francis Bacon, and Thomas Hobbes) and the realist orientation of eighteenth-century British empiricism (as exemplified by John Locke, Isaac Newton, and David Hume). Due to these roots, the positivistic approach to knowledge is sometimes referred to by its Galilean mechanistic worldview or as a "Lockean paradigm". The experimental method associated with this tradition was further defined as a form of reductionism in the mid-nineteenth century (by Hermann Helmholtz). *Reductionism* is an approach to knowledge that involves seeking explanations for phenomena at a lower and simpler level. In this case, it reinforced the dualistic distinction between mind and matter by reducing observations of the world to physical evidence.

Just as the historical roots of positivism can be traced to early realism and empiricism, alternative views to positivism may be found in *rationalist* philosophies and *idealism* that grant the human mind an active role in knowledge. Rationalist and idealist views are represented in Immanuel Kant's ideas of an active mind that imposes its own structures on thought and perception. These views of knowledge that give primacy to human reasoning are referred to as the "Kantian perspective". It was followed by those who objected to the positivistic-realist portrayal of the human mind as a relatively passive receptacle of sensory knowledge. It is important to point out that early empiricism was a historical response to dogmatism in the Dark Ages when knowledge was dictated by authority such as associated with the doctrines of the church. During the Enlightenment, knowing by observation and verification through experience were conceived also as better ways of learning about the world than arm-chair philosophical speculations and argumentation such as practiced by the rationalist philosophers. (The issue of whether the mind shapes reality or reality determines the mind has been an underlying tension between those of an idealist-cognitivist orientation and those of a realist-behaviorist orientation. However, it can be reframed as a dialectical interaction of human consciousness and the world, with experience being coconstituted by the act of knowing and the context of knowing).

Although positivism was opposed in the period 1880-1920 by the neo-Kantian German intellectuals (such as Wilhelm Dilthey, Wilhelm Wundt, Franz Bretano, Edmund Husserl, and Max Weber) and the American psychologist William James, it revived in the 1920s and 1930s (Polkinghorne 1983). A formalized philosophy of logical positivism was developed by members of the Vienna circle, notably Rudolf Carnap, who viewed the work of scientists as being to uncover the logical structure of the world (Hanfling 1981). Science, according to the logical positivists, utilizes observational language that is distinguished from the theoretical by its truthful reference to the world and by its conformity to relational logic (as supported by the philosophical writings of Alfred Ayer, Ludwig Wittgenstein, Bertrand Russell, and Alfred North Whitehead). An objective science based on logical foundations and realist assumptions continued to thrive. Another significant contribution to positivistic methods of inquiry in the twentieth century was Percy Bridgman's *operationalism* of 1927, which defined concepts in terms of operations that can be objectively replicated and measured. Operationalism further consolidated the realist-dualistic emphasis on using an extensional language (for observation from a detached, outsider perspective) and the use of quantification in an attempt to describe an objective, extralinguistic, or language-independent world.

Thus, modern science was to be characterized by the use of objective methods involving the reduction of natural phenomena by operational definitions, detached observation, and quantification. It was to be judged by standards of precision, logical relationships, and correspondence to a reality assumed to be accessible with objective tools of knowledge. These methods and standards of knowledge constituted essentially the experimental tradition that was to prevail in psychology. Meanwhile, psychology was influenced by Charles Darwin's theory of evolution and the hypothesized continuity between animals and humans. From structuralism, there was a conceptual shift to functionalism and a psychology of adaptation and, finally, a behavioral emphasis that would allow animal and human behavior to be studied from a unified viewpoint. *Behavioralism*, as formulated by J. B. Watson at the beginning of the twentieth century, followed the positivistic emphasis by viewing psychology as an objective experimental branch of natural science. This turned out to be fitting with the intellectual climate and *zeitgeist* (or shared beliefs and interests of the intellectual community) in psychology after World War I. *Experimentalism* became a dominant force in psychology in Germany, where the founding members of American psychology were engaged in study and open to influence. Although German psychologists never tried to separate psychology from philosophy, and were more interested in the generalized human mind than the psychology of individual differences, this was not the case with American psychology (Manicas 1987).

There were many developments contributing to the rise of behaviorism and the positivistic worldview of psychology as a science in America. Among these were the professionalization of American psychology and the need of academic psychology to strive for institutional survival (O'Donnell 1985). Although few agreed with the simplistic and radical behaviorism of Watson, the profession shared the American culture's practical orientation in the desire for knowledge that would have practical utility, as promised by behavioral psychology. Psychology as a discipline also needed to establish its autonomy from philosophy and biology. The emphasis on experimental work legitimated its identity as a new science. The remaining development that should be mentioned is an interest in theory development during the first half of the present century, as exemplified by the work of Tolman and Hull (Leahey 1991). The hypothetico-deductive method had become necessary to account for unobservable forces that were theoretically invoked to explain phenomena in the natural sciences. Hypothetical constructs such as cognitive maps or motivation were used in psychology to explain learning and behavior. Experimental programs were designed to test hypotheses deduced from theories consisting of such constructs for the purpose of prediction. Philosophers such as Reichenbach (1951) and Popper (1962) highlighted the justification of theories as a critical feature of science. Thus, theory testing became the primary function of scientists. Psychologists engaged in theory development and theory testing while the discipline and the profession expanded.

The implications of these developments for psychological science and our approach to knowledge are profound. Due to the fact that scientific rationality is identified with the justification of theoretical propositions (as is true for other scientific disciplines), psychological research has been equated largely with theory testing. Theoretical research assumed a central place in the training of the profession and the admission of the results of inquiry into its formal body of knowledge, a state of affairs that is still true at the present time. Although the subsequent behavioralism of B. F. Skinner was intended to be distinct from behaviorism as a philosophy of science (Skinner 1963), the historical influence of positivism on psychology combined with the behavioristic emphasis of experimental psychology has led to a narrow conception of its scope and method. The term "methodological behaviorism", which has been used to characterize much of American psychology, refers to its continuing features of an objectivist, reductionistic science and the tendency of researchers to engage in restrictive forms of hypothesis-testing permitted by the behavioristic paradigm. A strong paradigmatic position results, which deems only certain methods of knowledge generation and testing as acceptable, that may be regarded as monolithic or "universalist" in its orientation to knowledge.

The positivistic paradigm and its behavioristic research methodology have continued to appeal to American psychology as it gains acceptance as a science-based profession and as psychologists define themselves as scientist-practitioners (Goldfried 1984; Strickland 1983). Meanwhile, the golden age of behaviorism seemed to have been replaced by a contemporary interest in cognitive science. The Lockean paradigm, with its mechanistic worldview, has been challenged by those who view the human observer as an active, self-interpreting agent with intentions and free will. By affinity with the earlier ideas of Kant and the German intellectuals, this contrasting view has been referred to as the "Kantian paradigm". (See Rychlak 1969 for a discussion of the implications of Lockean versus Kantian paradigms for our theories of causation and psychotherapy). The objectivity assumptions of positivistic science have been more recently questioned from a cognitive point of view (Gardner 1985; Sperry 1988, 1990; Mahoney 1988a; Weimer 1974). A central problem concerns how we investigate meaning in human thought and action. Internal tensions and challenges to methodological behaviorism are evident as many members of the profession share a disquiet about our orientation to knowledge and how we define the scope and method of the discipline (Leahey 1991). Other changes that are in process outside the discipline are beginning to have an impact on our field.

In spite of the influence of positivism on disciplines such as ours, philosophers of science have developed other views of knowledge that lend support to alternative models and methods (Bernstein 1986; Hesse 1980; Manicas and Secord 1983). Other social sciences have reacted to the positivistic research legacy by calling for alternative research paradigms (Brewer and Collins 1981; Dallmayr and McCarthy 1977; Lincoln and Guba 1985). These calls have come about with developments in the philosophy of science in favor of increasingly relativistic views of human knowledge. Foundationalism is being rejected along with the correspondence theory of truth, which assumed that objective knowledge mirrors or corresponds to an independent reality. The present era, which came about with a questioning of these modern-science conceptions of reality and the knowing mind, has been referred to as the "postmodern period" in the history of ideas (Connor 1989; Gergen 1991; Harvey 1989; Lyotard 1984; Silverman 1990). The most distinctive feature of *postmodern* thought is the rejection of a single authoritative model or universal foundation of knowledge that makes claim to certainty.

A prevalent view of knowledge in postmodern thinking is that of constructivism (Bruffee 1986; von Glasersfeld 1984; Mahoney 1988a). As mentioned earlier, under constructivism, knowledge is regarded as a social construction, dependent on the language and symbols of culture and the communal processes of meaning construction (Berger and Luckmann 1966; Bloor 1983; Geertz 1983; Pearce and Cronen 1980). Gergen (1985) proposed to use the term "social constructionism" to describe this movement. This view has brought a new perspective on the subject of psychological research (Danziger 1990). Our research subjects are no longer passive participants whose experience we can preplan and control entirely. In the psychological inquiry of practice, our data are regarded as coconstructed by us and the client. This conception supports interactive modes of knowing. It grants the human subject a greater voice. The psychologist George Kelly (1955) had anticipated this point of view with his theory of personal constructs. Kelly regarded each person as similar to a scientist, actively engaged in sense making or ordering experience with meaningful constructs.

A related assumption in the new philosophy of science is that knowledge is socially and culturally embedded or context bound. *Contextualism* (Sarbin 1977) can be regarded as the postmodern response to the problems of meaning encountered in inquiry in the human domain. In the contextualist view, knowledge is considered to be coconstituted by the act of knowing and its context. (For example, the meaning of anxiety to a person who has knowledge of it involves living and acting anxiously in a particular situation or relationship.) It is perspectival or dependent on the frame of reference used by the observer. (As another example, news reports on the same international event tend to differ especially across political lines.) Human inquiry and the knowledge enterprise must be sensitive to context in order to be meaningful. Taken together, postmodern constructionism and the emphasis on the social context of knowledge imply that self-reflexivity or our understanding of ourselves as human beings is very much a social process (Lawson 1985).

Constructivist and social constructionist perspectives can be found in recent psychological positions. The "self" has been regarded as a social construct (Harre 1984), and social construction, as the basis of personhood (Gergen and Davis 1985; Gergen and Gergen 1988). Human conduct has been studied as narrative truths constructed by observers (Polkinghorne 1988; Sarbin 1986b), similar to the way the actions of characters in a story or drama are interpreted by authors or playwrights. Social constructionist views of learning and cognition proposed by Vygotsky (1978) and expounded by Cole (1983), Wertsch (1986), and Rogoff (1990), have implications for the development of knowledge structures and the remediation of learning problems. Therapeutic orientations, such as certain forms of cognitive therapy (Guidano and Liotti 1985; Mahoney and Lyddon 1988), also reflect the constructivist view. These conceptual developments parallel the gradual adoption of methodological approaches consistent with a social constructionist perspective (Gergen 1985; Hoshmand 1989; Lincoln and Guba 1985; Neimeyer and Resnikoff 1982; Reason and Rowan 1981). Among the common characteristics of these alternative research paradigms are the attention to context-embedded meanings, acknowledgment of the contributions of the observer and the observed, utilization of tacit knowledge, and preference for interactive modes of knowledge construction. Holistic, interactive methods of inquiry can be found in research related to practice (Dokecki 1990; Gendlin 1986; Greenberg 1986; Mahrer 1970, 1978, 1979; Moustakas 1990). Organizational inquiry, for example, has witnessed what appear to be the beginnings of a paradigm shift (Lincoln 1985). A more pluralistic picture of how to generate psychological theories and knowledge has begun to emerge.

Before we consider the implications of these recent developments, we should take time to study the arguments for the change from a historically dominant universalist view of science to the new philosophy of science. In this connection, some of the persistent issues of human inquiry will be highlighted, with arguments presented from the different philosophical positions.

A SUMMARY OF RELATED ARGUMENTS AND ISSUES

We can study the arguments for alternative paradigms and models of knowledge in relation to epistemology, ontology, and axiology (Guba and Lincoln, 1990; Heron 1981; Hoshmand 1989; Lincoln and Guba, 1985). Many of the objections to positivistic science are concerned with its epistemological assumptions and conception of how we know. Positivistic science is associated with dualism, which assumes the separation of object and subject. It is also based on a realist ontology associated with an epistemological assumption of an enquiring mind independent of the objective world. Under these assumptions, the observer is supposed to be detached from the observed in order to achieve objectivity. The integrity of the stimulus properties of the observed is assumed to hold, apart from the influence of the observer or the context of observation. Using the example of an illusion such as the Muller-Lyer illusion (in which the presence of arrowheads pointing in opposite directions at the ends of two parallel lines of the same length gives the subjective impression of unequal lengths), we can in fact demonstrate that the objective stimulus (in this case, length of the lines) remains unchanged (or equal) after the context (of the arrowheads) is removed. On the surface, this example argues for the possibility of maintaining the objective integrity of the stimulus (pair of lines) by detaching it from its context (of the arrowheads, such as by erasing the latter). However, the more important point is that our perception and meaningful interpretation of the stimulus is dependent on the context. (In this case, the experience of the observer is that the lines are unequal.) Furthermore, if the same context stripping is applied to a human event (such as having a message delivered without tonal and nonverbal expression), we will be left with ambiguity. The assumptions of neutral observation and total detachment are counter to what we know from our own discipline's research about the embedded nature of perception—namely, that the observer takes an active role in the organization and interpretation of information.

The problem of meaning in the study of human phenomena is a central issue in psychological inquiry. Positivistic methods tend to isolate the object of study from much of its context, for ease of procedural control and measurement. The removal of context, as illustrated here, results in loss of meaning. This is especially true in the human domain. A verbal message delivered with a friendly smile, for instance, is interpreted differently from one that is stripped of the relational context. Human communication and human actions have to be interpreted in the context of social relationships and cultural milieus. *Finding the most appropriate unit of analysis for any given phenomenon without too much reduction or exclusion of context* remains a challenge for theorists and researchers. Whereas complex, holistic conceptual units may retain more of the contextual richness of a given phenomenon, they tend to present problems of reliability in observation and measurement. On the other hand, simpler reductionistic units permit greater reliability and ease of study but are often less able to capture contextual richness. For example, observing a therapist-client dyad as an interactive system is more informative and meaningful than monitoring discrete utterances by a client. Yet the former is a more difficult observational task than the latter. Parsimony becomes desirable when relatively manageable units of observation and analysis can account for a great amount of information in a credible way.

Opponents of behavioristic reductionism point out that methods and concepts that reduce complex problems to simple units of analysis and measurement often fail to capture the full meaning of human phenomena (Koester and Smythies 1969). Researchers, constrained by reductionistic concepts and methods, tend to select only those problems for study that are amenable to operationalization and measurement (McKay 1988). Practitioners, similarly constrained, tend to work with a narrow definition of complex problems (Schon 1983). When incomplete descriptions of the world result from our epistemological choices, they are said to have ontological implications. Some theorists object to the limited conception of reality that goes hand in hand with a particular approach to knowledge. The arguments against the traditional model of knowledge are thus framed in terms of the behavior of the observer-researcher as well as the manner in which we treat human phenomenon in our attempt to give it a manageable analysis and meaningful interpretation.

From a social constructionist perspective, the data we obtain are dependent on the informant's frame of reference. As is true for client assessment by a practitioner, the type of information given in response to a researcher's request is a function of the perceived relationship context and the nature of the interaction between the observer and the observed. The influence of context has been dealt with partially in research by planning for the phenomenon of interest to occur in controlled environments. Controlled experimentation, however, often involves reactive arrangements that produce unnatural responses from the subjects. Laboratory analogues and the requirement that subjects respond in a mode preplanned by the researcher do not guarantee the desired effect or allow subjects to respond in their native or natural modes. Reactive effects of standard research procedures and measurement had necessitated the search for less obtrusive research modes (Webb, Campbell, Schwartz, and Sechrest 1966). In participant modes of research, reactivity is presumed to be lessened by its naturalistic nature and longevity of relationship between the observer and the observed. Whether instructions are experienced by research subjects as intended by the researcher is an issue, though less for the participant researcher, just as it is questionable if clients can be assumed to respond to standardized testing items in terms of their intended meanings.

Accounting for the presence of the human observer is a problem of inquiry with which psychology has wrestled. Researchers have attempted, though not with complete success, to control for observer bias and experimenter bias by such means as keeping research assistants blind to the hypothesis (Rosenthal 1988; Rosenthal and Rosnow 1969). Psychological researchers, like other scientists, have had to acknowledge that research findings are theory-laden, or bound by the theoretical framework of the researcher (Hesse 1980). What is observed and how it is interpreted depend on the theoretical lenses used by the investigator. A learning theorist would see a behavioral event as a response to a particular stimulus, whereas a systems theorist would regard it as a part of a whole pattern of relationships. A person's anger response may be linked at one level to a preceding provocation by another, and considered at another level to be a function of the complex interaction between perceptual and self-evaluative processes and the relationship-meanings of the preceding communication. In participant observation (Spradley 1980), the contribution of the observer to the data is included and accounted for in terms of the personal and professional outlook of the observer and the relationship between the observer and the observed. A balanced perspective is possible only to the extent that the participant observer can set aside preconceptions, self-reflect on biases, and manage the researcher role effectively to gain trust and at the same time avoid excessive involvement.

Much of the dispute about the choice of methods stems from different views on *the role of language and judgments about language-mediated findings.* Human inquiry is uniquely mediated by the use of language. Research on persons cannot be separated from the use of language or the context that gives meaning as mutually experienced. Only cooperative inquiry would allow the enquirer and the human subject to clarify the rules of language and the cultural meanings to be shared (Heron 1981). When the human subject is treated as a collaborator in cooperative field inquiry, the interaction and reciprocity provide a context for learning about local meanings and verifying one's interpretations. This possibility is limited by detached modes of investigation. On the other hand, although there is no way of describing reality independent of language, researchers still hope to achieve "linguistically objective" means of description through replicable, intersubjectively validated observations. This practice is supported by those who argue for a *critical realism* under the new philosophy of science (Bhaskar 1989; Manicas and

Secord 1983; Greenwood 1991). No longer claiming a complete, accurate access to reality or a language-independent world, a new realism is proposed that concedes the influence of contextual factors and intersubjectivity in human knowing. Scientific rationality continues to be based on unbiased empirical observations as an epistemic ideal.

Inquiry in the human domain is complex because it requires *the interpretation and judgment of human actions and intentions,* involving ontological assumptions about human nature and beliefs about volition and free will. Depending on our ideology and value stances and the degree to which we regard human behavior as extrinsically determined relative to being volitionally controlled, we tend to make different attributions of a person's behavior. Even when we grant the image of the human as a self-determining free agent (Harre and Secord 1972), there are methodological difficulties in studying human agency (Howard and Conway 1986, 1987; Vallacher and Wegner 1987). Some feel that to demonstrate that human beings can self-control or self-predict, we should use first-person accounts of their actions framed in an intentional language rather than the extensional language of a detached observer (Harre, Clark, and DeCarlo 1985). It requires a different set of methods and standards than those associated with traditional methodology. This is because the latter utilizes controls and predictions introduced by the experimenter as well as third-person observations framed in an objectivist, extensional language. The proposal to study humans from an agential point of view has been aligned with the call for alternative research paradigms (Howard 1984b), at least in principle. A different view on this issue is that empirical research does not need to be totally deterministic, and that there are more ways than one of studying volition and its related phenomena (Borgen 1992).

Contrary to objectivist beliefs in the neutrality of science, psychologists as scientist-practitioners do not make neutral descriptions of people's behaviors any more than research scientists could make neutral theoretical statements (Homans 1978; O'Donohue 1989; Rose and Rose 1980). As stated in chapter 1, there is reason to believe that the theoretical and methodological preferences of psychologists are as much a function of their epistemological orientation as their value stances. Some have argued for alternative models of knowledge on the basis of beliefs in treating the human subject with greater dignity and as having agency and self-determination (Dana 1987; Howard 1984b; Rogers 1985). Others have argued from the point of view of the types of interest our inquiry should serve, that it should contribute to solving social problems (Argyris 1980; Sarason 1978, 1981b).

Given these various issues in psychological inquiry, what then, should we uphold as *the criteria and standards for valid inquiry in professional practice?* Psychological science has followed the concept of reliability and used several forms of validity in adjudicating knowledge claims (Brinberg and McGrath 1985; Campbell and Fiske 1959; Cook and Campbell 1979; Cronbach 1988). Internal consistency and agreement between occasions of observation or sources of information are generally appropriate standards. The traditional conception differentiated validity into *content*, *criterion*, and *construct* validation. Due to its claims as a theoretical science and a science-based profession, psychology has given much weight to "construct validity". The tools of inquiry developed for practice are expected to demonstrate the appropriate link to theoretical constructs or make theoretical sense. In professional practice, it is further important that the inference we make from inquiry would give useful information about the criterion behaviors and situations we consider relevant to a present problem or future practical purpose. These latter forms of validity, referred to as "criterion validity" and "predictive validity", respectively, are especially appropriate in professional inquiry. In chapter 6, we will examine issues of validity in relation to the various inquiry methods used in professional psychology.

Perspectives on validity in psychological inquiry have historically been influenced by the scientific emphasis on operationism in the measurement movement and the psychology of individual differences (Dawis 1992). Although recent discussions about validity have moved away from the traditional distinctions between the above-mentioned types of validity, concepts of validation are still influenced by the prevailing scientific practice. One proposal is to subsume all forms of test validity under the hypothesis-testing aims of the scientific method. This has been referred to as the unificationist view (Ellis and Blustein 1991; Forsyth and Strong 1986). It is argued that the issue of validity is ultimately a question of whether one can make valid inferences based on available evidence tested under conceptually relevant conditions. Because observations are interpreted with the help of constructs, meaningful inference has to involve construct validity. This point of view is based on the preeminence of theory and depends on the quality of the logic, method, and design in testing the relevant hypotheses. Whether one should equate the interpretive act only with the inferences made in formal hypothesis testing, however, remains an issue. Cronbach (1988, 1991) points out that validation is a continuous process of evaluation that requires multiple, cumulative testing and observations both within and outside of such testing.

It should be noted that the concept of validity takes on different meanings depending on the model of knowledge we use and its underlying philosophical assumptions. This point will be appreciated as we examine various conceptual and methodological paradigms in chapters 4 and 5. Construct validity, which has to do with theoretical meaningfulness, is highly relevant to the traditional experimental paradigm and its hypothetico-deductive approach. Measurement and hypothesis testing are the standard ways of establishing validity in this paradigm, as is control for the effects of factors extraneous to the theorized relationships. However, operationism that minimizes interpretation cannot adequately establish validity (Cronbach 1988). For example, a laboratory analogue of participation in a competitive game may not be a meaningful measure of a person's aggressiveness if the person interprets the moves as self-achievement rather than other-directed hostility. The scores on aggressive play in this case will not be a valid representation of the construct of aggressiveness.

From a constructionist perspective, meaningfulness and authenticity of a set of findings should be the primary criteria of interpretive approaches to inquiry. The inferences made in social constructionist approaches to inquiry are dependent on emergent dialogue and involvement outside of measurement. Recognizing the interactive nature of information gathering, "pragmatic validity"—in the sense of the participants finding the interpretations to be of value (Kvale 1987b)—has been proposed, for instance, as a criterion for evaluating the validity of interpretive findings. For example, a participant researcher can ask the interviewed subjects if they find the summary of interview findings to be useful. Relatedly, the confirmation of research conclusions by testimony of the subjects is considered to be one of several ways of gauging the value of research, under the assumption that human inquiry has catalytic or change-inducing effects (Stiles and Schneider 1992). This change applies also to the initial understanding of the researcher whose ideas and theories should be modified by the new findings.

If improved understanding is a goal in human inquiry, we have to include knowledge of the actor's internal frame of reference as well as consider the context of data generation and interpretation. What a client reveals to a therapist is a function of his or her self-system and world-view, as well as the perceived relationship with the therapist. Human intentions and actions cannot be detached from the social and cultural context in which they acquire meaning. The concept of "ecological validity", which requires the full consideration of context, seems all encompassing in this regard. It gives consideration to the personal and cultural meanings of all concerned parties and their interaction in the setting or milieu of investigation. In summary, any understanding or meaning derived from inquiry has to be communicated and clarified with feedback and further observed to have practical and contextual validity (Reason 1981). In subsequent chapters, we will continue to consider these various criteria for determining the validity of our inferences and our claims to knowledge.

The challenge of meaningful inquiry is *how we can obtain the authenticity of human responses without compromising the standards we use to guarantee valid knowledge.* This challenge has been posed as a conflict between rigor and relevance (Gelso1985). Some feel that methodological behaviorism has sacrificed meaningfulness for objectivist standards (Gendlin 1986; Goldman 1977). Precision of measurement and restrictive experimental operations that are designed to enhance the internal validity of an experiment often lead to less generalizability from laboratory to real life. Others do not have confidence in alternative methods of inquiry that they assume to have less rigorous standards. Recent discussions about models of knowledge and the increasingly pluralistic choices of methods of inquiry call for a new look at standards (Hoshmand and Martin 1992). There are two philosophical stances that represent attempts at *reconciling realist standards and the relativism associated with constructionist approaches to knowledge.* Though conceding contextualism and intersubjectivity in human knowing, the new realism (as referenced previously) continues to look for arbitration of knowledge claims at the level of veridical empirical observations. Recent formulations of *pragmatism* (Margolis 1986a) view human inquiry as particular ways of acting on the world for the purpose of problem solving. The test of knowledge is in action and application, as is true for our professional practice. Pragmatism may be reconciled with the new realism in that it regards the question of which inquiry practice would have the greatest pragmatic value as one that can be answered partly with empirical experience.

Which criteria to uphold and how one should apply standards usually depend on one's methodological commitments. Under a divergent methodological pluralism, researchers are faced with seemingly conflicting standards and warrants because paradigms are no longer commensurable, or governed by a single, universal set of standards. This incommensurability has led some to argue that paradigm choice is largely a matter of preference or convention (Feyerabend 1975; Kuhn 1970). However, it would not be possible for a scientific profession to achieve progress if there is no basis for judging the relative contributions of different inquiry practices to the common pragmatic purposes the profession is supposed to serve. A higher-order or metalevel reasoning is needed to guide the use of pluralistic methods. In chapters 4 and 5, we will consider some of the proposals for metalevel frameworks, including those based on pragmatism.

As an example of a possible response to the *problem of pluralistic standards,* Tharp and Gallimore (1982) illustrated a metamodel of methodological reasoning based on the experience of long-term field research and program evaluation in which different strategies and methods were used. In this case, certain research strategies and methods were found to be more useful for answering certain types of questions. Each has its place within the larger scheme of methodological reasoning derived from experience. The notion that the experienced knowledge of practicing inquiry can serve as a type of metareasoning in the selection of methods may be considered to be a form of pragmatism. A pragmatist conception of science may resolve some of the issues regarding standards of inquiry and provide a basis for a viable methodological pluralism. Pragmatism supports methodological pluralism by its emphasis on the heuristic aspects of method choice. It is congruent with the new realism in that the empirical test of experience is expected to provide answers to questions about what may constitute useful methods. Methodological pluralism would then mean that all methods are treated as potentially useful and to be evaluated through application over time. This reasoned application of pluralistic methods has the advantage that different perspectives are brought to bear on a given problem. The data generated with multiple means may also be more complete, based on convergent validity (Reason 1981). We can avoid ecological fallacies by using methods derived from different paradigms (that will be reviewed in chapter 5) to gather information at both the individual and collective levels in context (Brewer and Hunter 1989). The functional fit of our methods with the context in which we conduct our work is an important requirement in professional psychology.

PROFESSIONAL INQUIRY IN THE POSTMODERN AGE

We will next consider the implications of the historical developments and the identified issues for professional practice. Since the advent of the scientist-practitioner model of professional training in psychology (Frank 1984; Raimy 1950; Shakow 1978), professional inquiry in the context of practice has been presumed to follow the same model of knowledge as formal inquiry in the research domain. Many of the epistemological assumptions and criteria in the dominant model of knowledge are implicitly adopted by practitioners. It is assumed in standardized testing, for instance, that procedural uniformity and a detached stance by the examiner would help to produce objective and valid information. Instruments of client appraisal are expected to lead to good judgments so long as they have been demonstrated to be psychometrically sound. Although such assumptions and criteria are reflective of a historically dominant model of knowledge, the practicing members of the profession should continue to assess what kinds of model of knowledge will serve us well in the areas of practice.

In the relativistic context of postmodern discussions about the philosophy of knowledge, we are faced with more choices. Social constructionism brings a new perspective on science by regarding scientific theories and knowledge as human constructions, the means of which are expected to vary to the extent that they are culturally and historically embedded. There is a shift to discursive practices as a viable medium and means of knowledge construction (Kvale 1992). Positivistic science which has depended heavily on a hypothetico-deductive logic of verification and the use of an extensional language and quantitative methods may be viewed as one particular form of construction. It does not necessarily have cognitive privilege or epistemological superiority over other forms of construction. Alternative paradigms (such as described subsequently in chapter 5) that emphasize the use of natural language data, inductive processes, and qualitative interpretations represent other potentially useful methods of construction (Hoshmand 1989). As presented earlier, the historical account of the evolvement of models of knowledge confirms the co-existence of a continuum of models and paradigms.

The metaphor of a continuum in methods of knowledge reminds us that there are disciplines, such as in the humanities, that utilize other methods of inquiry that can potentially enrich those of our own discipline. Although the psychologist Kelly utilized the operationalized methodology of his time, the spirit of his constructive alternativism (Kelly 1970) may be interpreted as suggesting that professional psychologists should consider the full range of tools of knowledge construction in our inquiry practices. The range of conceptual systems in practice, as will be described in chapter 4, testify to our breadth of constructive possibilities. Practitioners and researchers of practice should become informed in different models and methods, as no one model or method seems complete.

Another feature of the new philosophy of knowledge is the recognition of both the tacit and the publicly explicated dimensions of knowing. Positivistic science has been biased toward publicly observable procedures of knowledge, relying on an extensional language of description and procedural adequacy for its knowledge claims. The primacy of the abstract and the tacit is now acknowledged in the psychology of science (Mahoney 1991; Weimer 1980). It directs us to consider personal and tacit forms of knowing as important ingredients in the creation and validation of knowledge (Polanyi 1964; Reason 1981). For the same individual conducting any form of inquiry, the dialectic of the participant mode and the rational objectivist stance may be involved in the process of knowing. Another dialectic could be the analytical and the intuitive, modes of knowing in which we are equally capable, the tension of which may be part of the nature of our knowing. These aspects of our applied epistemology will be further discussed in chapter 7.

Openness to alternative methods and modes of knowledge further allows the possibility that professional psychologists may develop a model of knowledge and epistemology of practice that will strengthen what is currently guiding research in the discipline (Hoshmand and Polkinghorne 1992). Professional psychology needs a model of inquiry in which the knowledge processes of practice are given a role complementary to the processes of research. A pluralistic view of knowledge can free the profession from the domination of hypothetico-deductive practices associated with the positivistic model, which has historically favored a linear, one-way conception of the relationship between theoretical science and psychological practice. Whereas in this traditional conception, only theoretical science informs professional practice, a pragmatically conceived science as a theoretico-practical enterprise requires a reciprocity of thought and action. Professional inquiry can reflect the mutuality of theory and practice as knowledge tested in experience becomes working theories upon reflection and revision. In chapters 5 and 9, we will take a closer look at research models that effectively link thought and action or theory and practice.

The issues of human inquiry discussed in the previous section have implications for professional psychology. The types of human inquiry conducted in psychological practice are not exempt from the problems of knowing encountered in research. As will be further discussed in chapter 3, the professional conducting such inquiry is always an embedded observer, influenced by his or her cultural and personal worldview as well as professional ideology. Although a detached stance can be taken to some extent, as in administering a standardized test or observing a child from the back of a classroom, this detached stance is more apparent than real. A multiplicity of factors that constitute the context of observation actually enter into the process of data gathering, interpretation, and subsequent decision making. The nature of the complaint, the cultural and linguistic background of the professional and the client, and the theoretical orientation of the practitioner are examples of some of the contextual factors. This embeddedness of the observer is definitely present in less detached modes of inquiry such as interviewing. Accounting for observer bias and, in broader terms, the contributions of the observer to the data becomes a critical aspect of inquiry in the context of practice, a fact to be kept in mind as we survey methods of inquiry in chapter 6.

The problem with meaning, which is one of the concerns with positivistic modes of knowledge, is particularly important in the professional inquiry of practice. The client's personal meanings are considered an essential part of the data sought in clinical and counseling inquiry. In human communication, however, there is seldom a one-to-one correspondence between message and meaning (Watzlawick, Beavin, and Jackson 1967). This is due to the constant shifting of context and the unstable nature of the personal experiences from which communication emanates (Gendlin 1978; Mahrer 1970, 1985). The challenge to valid interpretation becomes even greater when cultural differences are present (Sue and Sue 1990). The mode of inquiry we use should therefore be sensitive to contextual and cultural variations. In that professional methods and tools of inquiry are potentially culture bound and limited to particular contexts of usage, there is a need to find or create meaningful contexts and means of client assessment (Gardner 1988). One should ask, regardless of apparent cultural affinity, if a given mode of interaction and medium of information gathering are "native" to the client, or could be made sufficiently familiar to the client in order to obtain a meaningful response. These considerations will be further discussed also in chapter 6.

It appears that different rationalities and criteria may be involved in judging the application of a paradigm as it can involve conceptual, methodological, and practical-evaluative tasks. These different functions and tasks need to be coordinated such that there is communication between members of the profession who tend to be separated by a division of labor. Theoreticians and academic researchers who have predominantly been engaged in the first two tasks may be critical of practitioners who view their own role as undertaking the third task, and vice versa. Applying different rationalities and criteria, these groups lack a common base of discourse about paradigm choice. Semantics are involved in the choice of conceptual language associated with a given paradigm. The language of practice, once formalized and accepted, may hold fruitful ideas for theorizing. Syntactical and empirical concerns are involved in the choice of research tools for developing and testing a model. Practitioners immersed in the settings of practice can offer insights into the appropriate means for such testing. Pragmatics are involved in putting a paradigmatic solution into practical problem solving. For both researchers and practitioners, the pragmatist view suggests that the choice of a paradigm should be a function of the context of usage and the task of knowledge at hand.

An awareness of issues in human inquiry and existing perspectives on knowledge can help us question the philosophical assumptions of existing models of inquiry in professional psychology. Our philosophical commitments shape not only the questions we ask and the way we conduct our inquiry but also the priorities we set and the conclusions we draw (Guba and Lincoln 1990; Neimeyer and Resnikoff 1982; Rose and Rose 1980). *What kinds of direction and inquiry practices may ultimately contribute to progress* is a complex question at the heart of paradigm debates. Whereas constructionists would regard as valid those descriptions that are found to be truthful to the experience of the informant and enquirer, some researchers would venture further by proposing that descriptions are valid to the extent that they envision improved realities and useful courses of action (Argyris 1980; Sanford 1981a). Progress is defined by the human possibilities created in the process of our acting upon the world through inquiry.

It is on this last point, perhaps, that much of the purpose and value of professional inquiry depends. Progress in psychological science and practice involves not only epistemological and ontological concerns, but axiological considerations of a non-epistemic and moral nature. Professional inquiry should be informed by social values that can be justified by universal human interests. A fine line exists between the description of clients' problems and a prescriptive portrayal of such problems and their possible solution. Professional inquiry is by necessity socially and politically embedded. It is critically important for practitioners to ponder on questions of legitimacy, relevance, and personal values—as well as political and power issues—in their inquiry (Rosen 1981; Rowan 1981). Consideration of the prescriptive and reactive nature of professional inquiry should enter into our choice of professional paradigms. In the following chapter, we will further examine the context and embedded nature of professional inquiry.

SUGGESTED ADDITIONAL LEARNING

1. Review the terminology used in this chapter and clarify the meanings of unfamiliar concepts by questions and discussion.

2. Construct a timeline on the major historical developments in models of inquiry and perspectives on knowledge as they pertain to psychology.

3. Identify the methods and standards associated with the experimental tradition in psychology. Consider how they are related to the epistemological and ontological assumptions of positivistic science.

4. Identify some of the main issues in human inquiry, and evaluate the related arguments presented from different philosophical positions.

5. Identify a method of research that is premised on an objectivist and quantitative orientation to knowledge, and consider how you would *(a)* justify the approach and *(b)* critique it.

6. Discuss the implications of a social constructionist perspective for psychological research, such as presented in the following article by Gergen:

Gergen, K. J. 1985. The social constructionist movement in modern psychology. *American Psychologist* 40: 266-75.

What may be appropriate criteria for evaluating findings that are coconstructed by the researcher and the subjects, using interactive methods of gathering data that are in the form of natural language rather than measured behavioral responses?

7. Discuss the following article by Rychlak :

Rychlak, J. F. (1969). Lockean vs. Kantian theoretical models and the "cause" of therapeutic change. *Psychotherapy: Theory, Research and Practice,* 6: 214-22.

What are the respective difficulties faced by Lockean and Kantian researchers? What is your personal view on the suitability of either kind of paradigm for research and theoretical understanding in professional practice?

8. Consider the question of standards and the basis for justifying a given mode of professional practice. How would you argue respectively from a universalist and a relativist perspective?

9. Write a short essay on what you would propose as the criteria and manner by which we can assess whether psychological inquiry in research and practice has contributed to progress in knowledge of the human realm.

3

Professional Inquiry in Context

The previous chapter has provided a brief historical review of the foundations of psychological knowledge and the basic issues of human inquiry. Problems of knowledge are acutely felt in professional inquiry because of the context in which it occurs and the special societal role we assume. As professionals, we perform functions that are sanctioned by society based on our claims of expert knowledge. This knowledge is a function of our inquiry, the appropriateness of which depends on the kinds of values, interests, and purposes that it serves. These values, interests, and purposes are acquired by us as members of a larger society in which our profession is embedded. By adopting a reflexive attitude, we may be able to uncover the cultural, ideological, and sociopolitical dimensions of this embedding context and reflect on their impact on our knowledge enterprise and practices. The professional psychologist is in a unique position to view his or her discipline's science and practice in relation to the social order, through the interaction of scientific and professional worldviews with the social and personal perspectives of a citizen.

CULTURAL AND HISTORICAL EMBEDDEDNESS OF PSYCHOLOGICAL SCIENCE AND PRACTICE

The cultural orientation of American psychology cannot be separated from the way Western society takes consciousness of itself. A large part of this consciousness appears to consist in the image of the rational economic man driven by utilitarian individualism (MacIntyre 1988; Sahlins 1982). Individualism is reflected in psychological theories of the self (Cushman 1990; Sampson 1977, 1985, 1988) and the traditions and popular culture that shape American life (Bellah, Madsen, Sullivan, Swidler and Tipton 1985; Lasch 1979; Wachtel 1983). Autonomy and self-direction, for instance, are taken for granted in developmental and clinical theories of the healthy person (Goslin 1969; Loevinger 1976; Rogers 1961). Practitioners often assume that individuation is the appropriate norm for clients. Concepts of over-dependency and enmeshment are applied to relationships or family systems with the implication that lack of autonomy is detrimental to one's psychological well being. A certain degree of self-centeredness has been reinforced in therapeutic practice (Vitz 1977; Wallach and Wallach 1983), with themes of self-gratification and actualization that can be traced to beliefs and values shared by a culture of consumption (Jackson Lears 1983). Even problems of a macro nature, such as poverty and violence, are conceptualized by some at an individual level, resulting in blaming the victim (Ryan 1971). This is in spite of the likelihood that individualistic beliefs about the power of the isolated self may detract from sociological analyses of problems and collective efforts to seek social change (Caplan and Nelson 1973; Schur 1976).

The tendency to reduce social problems to individual differences in biology and behavior has been attributed to the influence of social Darwinism as represented in the ideas of Herbert Spencer (Prilleltensky 1989). Survival of the fittest, based on individual traits and abilities, complements the image of a competitive society. Psychological theories reflect this influence and portray what is valued by American society. For example, the theories of achievement motivation here are rooted in individualism and materialism (Spence 1985). In contrast, a holistic view of consciousness and techniques of meditation are the products of Indian psychology because its sociocultural milieu nurtures spiritual self-development (Paranjpe 1988b). Differing conceptions of the self in Eastern and Western perspectives have been linked to their respective cultural contexts (Marsella, DeVos, and Hsu 1985). For example, in many circles in American society, who you are amounts to what you do and what kinds of material success you have achieved. In Hindu thought, the real self is nonmaterial and to be achieved by religious transcendence of worldly behaviors. The Western empirical self embodied in social actions and achievements is at a lower level of meaning in the Hindu tradition. Our conceptual lenses and practices bear the stamp of the society and culture of which we are a part. In chapter 4, we will take a closer look at those core ideas and beliefs that have shaped professional practice and research in American psychology.

Like all professions and human enterprises, we are historically situated. The development of professional psychology has been affirmed by the contribution of psychologists during important events in history. The army's intelligence-testing program in World War I helped put psychology on the map (Samelson 1979). Subsequent growth of the profession was associated with postwar needs in the areas of clinical and educational services. The growth of the discipline was in part an adaptation to the social context, including the rise of professionalism to meet market needs (Danziger 1987). Concerns about maintaining a legitimate place in the academic world as well as among the professions led to psychology's choice of the scientist-practitioner model. It would allow psychologists to conduct research as well as demonstrate the social utility of research-generated knowledge. Historical context also influences the choice of problems for investigation. The Great Depression, social tensions, and group conflicts led to an interest in applied social psychology and several decades of research on the frustration-aggression hypothesis (Apfelbaum 1986; Lubek 1986). More recent economic changes and deinstitutionalization have presented the phenomenon of homelessness for current study (Jones, Levine, and Rosenberg 1991). The problems selected for attention by social scientists tend to be a sign of the times, as can be revealed by sociological and historical studies of a given area of knowledge (Buss 1975, 1979; Bronfenbrenner, Kessel, Kessen, and White 1986).

Thus, our profession has been shaped by cultural and historical contexts. To some degree, it has also contributed to shaping social and historical developments. The growth of developmental psychology, for example, was marked by the Child Study Movement at the turn of the century, the Child Development Movement of the 1920s and 1930s, and the period of developmental psychology in the 1960s, each associated with federal government funding, new programs, and supportive public action. The child and family court system evolved as a result of the child guidance movement and the mental hygiene movement (Levine and Levine 1992). As developmental psychologists reflect on their subject matter, it has become apparent that their work has been culturally and historically bound (Broughton 1987; Cirillo and Wapner 1986). The child and the roles given to members of the family and other institutions in human development are very much cultural inventions that took various forms over time (Edelstein 1983; Kessen 1983; Liljestrom 1983; Rogoff 1985). For example, images of the American father have fluctuated during this present century (La Rossa, Gordon, Wilson, Bairan, and Jaret 1991) from involvement to absence and perhaps back to involvement as epitomized by the single father with custody of his children. Even outside of the profession, the manner in which child psychology is given away reflects the times. The popular response in the 1950s and early 1960s to Benjamin Spock's prescriptions for child-rearing practices resulted in what is referred to as the "Spock generation". The same ideas and approach would not have fit with the depression years and may not apply as well to the present time.

Consistent with a social constructionist perspective, professional theory and practice in psychology bear the imprint of the culture and the historical period. Our conceptual and methodological tools tend to reflect culturally rooted images of the person and the particular society in which such images are dominant. An ahistorical and acultural approach to knowledge would only lead to the mistaken notion that our science has universal significance that transcends time and place. Individualistic conceptions in psychology have been challenged on both theoretical and empirical grounds (Gergen 1973; Hsu 1983). Some effort has been made toward a more anthropological approach to understanding human development, which undercuts the assumptions of individualistic theories of cognition (Cole 1983; Rogoff 1990). Theories of the self, when viewed in cross-cultural perspective, point to the individualistic and self-centering bias (Hsu 1985) as well as the positivistic, behavioristic bias (Smith 1985) of Western psychology. Methodological individualism in behavioristic research, with its focus on the individual in theoretical explanations of human behavior, is being rejected as a paradigm for the study of personality and relational orientation in Asian cultures (Ho 1991).

It is difficult, however, for any profession to overcome its own embeddedness. We have to be aware that in our continuing inquiry, information will always be gathered and interpreted according to our particular cultural perspectives and social values. Sandra Scarr (1985) pointed out that the shared beliefs and preferences for particular perspectives are unlikely to be challenged, because, as products of our own times and spaces, they tend to fit with the current ideology and cultural context. In professional practice, the effectiveness of the theory-spawned interventions will be judged by the same values and interests that shape the theories in the first place. Any conscientious critique will have to be highly self-conscious in nature, and must penetrate to the core assumptions of theories and practices. Vega and Murphy (1990), in analyzing the historical struggle of community-oriented theorists and community-based researchers, concluded that the social imageries and individualistic models of knowledge endorsed by psychology have been the major underlying constraints.

One may ask then, How would changes come about in our culturally encapsulated approach to knowledge? Howard (1991), taking a narrative approach to theorizing and knowledge construction, observed that we live by the stories we tell of our times and ourselves. On the one hand, it means that professional psychologists should be familiar with the folk culture and its diverse idioms. On the other hand, we have to be aware that the dominant subjective culture constituted by our social imageries and theoretical concepts is not easy to modify without an intentional empathic experiencing of other points of view. The socially conscious recommend that we attend to the changing social order so as to respond with sociopolitical sensitivity and assume an active role in the transformation process. Sampson (1989a) argued that the global social order demands that psychology modify its theory of the person into one that is socially constituted rather than rooted in individualistic assumptions. This view is supported by ecological perspectives (Bronfenbrenner 1979; Luria 1976; Vygotsky 1978), social constructionist theories of the self (Gergen and Davis 1985; Gergen and Gergen 1988; Harre 1984), and the European approach to social psychology (Parker 1989; Tajfel 1984). Whether mainstream American psychology would move in that direction remains to be seen. The new methodological trends and changing discourse about models of knowledge mentioned in the previous chapter may have a major role in this.

A move away from individualism to a more communal consciousness is considered to be necessary in order for psychology to serve the public interest (Sampson 1989; Sarason 1974; Smith 1990). Jason, Felner, Moritsugu, and Farber (1983) envisioned a preventive psychology based on interdependent social systems and a professional sense of community. Dana (1987) urged professional psychologists to adopt sociocentric values and to promote a service-oriented culture as a corrective to egocentric values. Sarason's (1985) discussion of caring and compassion in clinical practice supported the same notion of a service-oriented culture in balance of egocentric functioning. The socialization that graduate students and young professionals receive from academic settings and professional organizations has a significant role in shaping the culture of the profession and the values we adopt. Dana (1987) called our attention to the power structure of academia and the implicit lessons taught to members of the profession by the conventional scientific way of thought in our discipline. It would seem that our willingness to examine the academic culture and our professional rhetoric can provide a measure of self evaluation (Harriman 1989).

Encapsulation (Royce 1964) is a dilemma of any profession that aspires to a special knowledge of the human. It is also a problem in professional practice. Ivey (1993) recognized the importance of examining the European and American beliefs and values in Western counseling and therapy and the need to reconstruct cultural assumptions and related professional practices. A countermeasure to cultural encapsulation and ethnocentrism is to adopt a pluralistic approach to knowledge. Pluralism is needed in our sources of knowledge as well as our methods of knowledge. Pluralistic sources can consist in the contributions from individuals of different ethnic, gender, cultural, and socioeconomic backgrounds. Professional inquiry in our field should be informed by such a pluralistic community of practitioners and researchers. The study of cultures and subcultures in the form of indigenous knowledge and native practices (Ho 1988; Kim and Berry 1993) represents an additional way of balancing our own preconceptions and culturally bound interpretations. Semin and Gergen (1990a), coming from a social constructionist perspective, presented the case for placing everyday understanding on the same continuum as scientific ways of knowing. If scientism or an extreme scientific attitude is considered a form of professional encapsulation, our willingness to use everyday discursive practices as a means of understanding may prevent us from losing touch with certain social realities. In chapter 5, examples of research approaches that capitalize on native modes of knowledge generation will be given. The concept of indigenous knowing is related to the issue of giving voice to groups who have not been sufficiently represented. It has been proposed, for instance, that women's ways of knowing can enrich our knowledge of ourselves and the development of psychology as a discipline (Belenky, Clinchy, Goldberger, and Tarule 1986; Gilligan 1982; Ricketts

1989). The significance of native knowing and finding one's voice can be appreciated when we observe the participation of different types of knowers in learning situations that are collaborative in nature. As individuals with different worldviews and ways of knowing are given voice, a richer set of meanings begins to emerge as communally constructed knowledge.

In cross-cultural inquiry, where we are most at risk of the scientific imperialism of middle-class Western psychology (Ho 1985) and stereotypic conceptions (Triandis, Lisansky, Setiadi, Chang, Marin, and Betancourt 1982), an attitudinal set that goes along with self-reflection and psychological decentering may be helpful (Ho 1992). In other words, an intellectual attitude that is inclined toward dialectical thinking and openness to differences in meaning can help us understand ways of existence different from our own. In our professional inquiry and practice, consideration of cultural differences becomes paramount in importance. Counseling and therapy for culturally different groups (Atkinson, Morten, and Sue 1983; Atkinson, Thompson, and Grant 1993; Marsella and Pedersen 1981; McGoldrick, Pearce, and Giordano 1982; Pedersen 1985; Sue and Sue 1990) must be accompanied by culturally sensitive approaches to client assessment (Sue and Sue 1987; Westermeyer 1987). Similarly, critical evaluation of assumptions and methods in research on ethnic-minority populations is an ethical responsibility of the profession, its controversies notwithstanding (Atkinson 1993; Mio and Iwamasa 1993; Ponterotto and Casas 1991). Ethnic minority issues are to be addressed in policy, training, and research (Casas 1984; Myers 1992; Sue, Arredondo, and McDavis 1992). This consideration is to be extended to groups with lifestyles and social histories different from our own (Atkinson and Hackett 1988; Brown 1989). Culture learning in the broadest sense requires the open, reflective attitudes mentioned above.

Psychology as a human, social science is necessarily value laden (Howard 1985b). To acknowledge that we are part of the social system and relationships that we try to understand means that we cannot avoid social responsibilities and value stances. The problem of values has become critical in the postmodern age of relativism. Ravn (1991) questioned what types of values should guide our reality constructions when we consider human knowledge to be socially constructed. Those of a constructionist persuasion tend to emphasize diverse choices and options (e.g., Gergen 1982; von Foerster 1981). Others, notably Bellah and his associates (1985) stress the need for intentional commitment and unity of purpose. It has been suggested that diversity and unity of purpose may be possible through preserving the values of both liberation and commitment (Ravn 1991).

Diversity and unity may similarly be viewed as a useful dialectic in the approach to knowledge. Pluralism in theory and method permits greater latitude in the values and interests that can be served by a human science. This may be viable so long as we continue to have reflective conversations about our common purpose. In chapter 1, at least three types of knowledge interests were mentioned: the technical, the hermeneutic, and the emancipatory. In chapter 2, the changes in perspectives on knowledge from the positivistic to the constructionist were highlighted. In relation to knowledge interests, the positivistic paradigm and postpositivistic variants of the same paradigm are generally regarded as suitable for serving a technical interest because of the emphasis on the control, prediction, and manipulation of nature. The constructionist paradigm is associated with a hermeneutic interest because of its emphasis on understanding human experience and meanings. Hermeneutic interests will be served in the types of open inquiry into other cultural perspectives (including those that are antithetical to individualist, externalist, and objectivist views of the person) that are recommended as essential to countering cultural encapsulation (Paranjpe 1988b).

Emancipatory interests are addressed by those social theories that are critical of technocratic social practices and institutions that seem to be oppressive rather than enabling. The use of labeling and institutionalization by mental health professionals, for example, is considered from a critical perspective to be cultural practices for controlling deviancy in the interest of dominant groups (Scheff 1984; Scheper-Hughes and Lovell 1987). Critical theory aims to examine and question commonly held assumptions. Some, including feminists, regard critical theory (which we will examine further in chapter 5) as a distinct paradigm of knowledge (Guba 1990; Harding 1986). Besides feminist psychology, a critical-theory orientation can be found in social psychology (Parker and Shotter 1990; Sullivan 1984; Wexler 1983). In the critical perspective, self-reflection is both a means and an end in that it enables members of a scientific profession (or any social group) to identify the interests and value contexts presupposed in its scientific discourse (or social discourse). Blum and McHugh (1984), drawing on the ideas of Habermas (1973), explained that the ability to examine critically all claims to valid knowledge is emancipating and that dominant forces that limit our capacity to self-reflect as a community are oppressive. In regard to a reflexive study of the theories and methods of our discipline, critical theory reminds us that the knowledge we try to generate should be examined in terms of the interests and purposes that it serves. It also directs our attention to the ideological and value contexts in which knowledge activities are situated and their products are used by consumers representing various social and political interests.

THE SOCIOPOLITICAL CONTEXT OF PROFESSIONAL INQUIRY

The concerns of a critical perspective are largely related to the issue of power. The common saying that knowledge is power does not refer sufficiently to how power enters initially into the creation of knowledge, the negotiation for the resources needed to make it possible, or the subsequent decisions on its warranted use. A study of decision making by human-subjects review committees suggested that research proposals that are politically sensitive were more frequently rejected, apart from the level of ethical concerns (Ceci, Peters, and Plotkin 1985). The accountability of professional psychologists when conducting socially sensitive research is an issue that has received some attention (Scarr 1988; Sieber and Stanley 1988). Warwick (1983b) discussed the politics and ethics of field research, especially involving minority cultures and public policy. The sponsorship and auspices of research can influence the research process politically. We have obligations to the populations we study, not only in terms of protection of rights, but in avoiding biased conceptions of problems and other secondary effects of our inquiry activities. Although his examples are drawn from research in developing countries, their implications are relevant to the study of groups that are in less empowered positions. It is important to recognize that, irrespective of the topic and focus of inquiry, all knowledge activities have power implications (Rouse 1987). In our attempts to make sense of the world and to solve problems of living, we act on the environment in ways that are consequential. One needs only to consider the environmental impact of herbicides and insecticides to realize the effects of problem-solving knowledge made possible by modern science. That is why we, as social scientists who act on social realities in our inquiry, have to reflect on the social and political implications of our methods (Morgan 1983).

In recent years, feminists have attempted to engage the psychology profession in a conversation about the sociopolitical implications of our theories and methods of knowledge (Crawford and Gentry 1989; Hare-Mustin and Marecek 1988). Gender bias in the approach to psychological science and its theories presents problems of unequal power (Hare-Mustin and Marecek 1990; Lerman 1986). Burman (1991), for example, provided a feminist critique of developmental psychology for having used theoretical constructs of children and families that inadvertently maintain the power inequalities of existing social practices. Androcentric bias has been an issue with Freudian conceptions of family dynamics (Chodorow 1978; Gallop 1982). In therapeutic theorizing and practice, professional psychology has been criticized for not giving sufficient consideration to gender issues and the historical status of women (Avis 1985; MacKinnon and Miller 1987; Taggart 1985). Whether equal voice is granted in our inquiry and knowledge making to women as well as other social groups in less empowered positions is both a scholarly and sociopolitical concern. Sociohistorical studies of the participation of underrepresented groups, such as that undertaken by Laurel Furumoto on women in American psychology (1987), can place in perspective the status hierarchy that has affected the contribution of these groups.

From a feminist standpoint, simply including women as subjects in research does not solve the problem of androcentric bias (Grady 1981; Wallston 1981). The types of questions posed in psychological inquiry and the research process in the traditional paradigm are vulnerable to sex bias. For this reason, some feminist researchers have called for alternative methodologies. They challenge the basic premises of the scientific method (Harding 1986; Keller 1985). The nature of the proposed alternatives and the contribution of critical theory will be further discussed in chapter 5.

It was stated earlier that historical and ideological contexts influence the choice of problems for professional inquiry and the choice of theories for conceptualizing human problems. Psychology as a profession has been criticized for allowing its objectivist, experimental methods to dictate the choice of research problems, not sufficiently allowing the public interest to guide our selection of topics of inquiry (Sanford 1981b; Sarason 1981a, 1984). Although social scientists can only hold prudent aspirations for solving complex social problems (Cronbach 1982b), professional psychology must respond to the call to participate in action research and policy research (Argyris, Putnam, and Smith 1985; Masters 1984). Action research, as will be described in chapter 5, represents a model of inquiry that recognizes the social responsibility of psychologists as problem solvers and change agents. Policy research is a relatively new area of professional involvement for psychologists. The Task Force on Psychology and Public Policy (1986) concluded that greater involvement of professional psychologists in the public policy process will facilitate the growth of psychological knowledge and the application of our knowledge to society. Albee (1981, 1986) viewed the prospect of primary prevention in mental health, for instance, as further dependent on the ability of professional psychology to effect political action and social change. This view is echoed by DeLeon (1986), who outlined several areas of organized political action for psychologists, including child health issues, care for the elderly, functional illiteracy, criminal justice, and national health care.

Sociopolitical considerations include social as well as economic factors. The practice of psychological testing, for example, is shaped by the fact that test performance determines access to social opportunities. A state of inequity in access occurs when certain groups tend to show test performances that are consistently below what is required for admission to educational programs or selection for job opportunities. This has been true for certain minority groups in standardized testing, and has led to the call for the use of culture-fair and culture-sensitive tests. In one sense, culture-fair or culture-sensitive testing could be a professional means of guarding against inequity, such as in the allocation of educational resources. Testing, however, is viewed by some as a form of social control involving invasion of privacy. An antitest movement was seen in the mid-1960s when Congress investigated the use of personality tests by the federal government to screen job applicants, resulting in restrictions on their use. The legal system, following the Civil Rights Act of 1964, developed laws to regulate the use of tests that show different pass rates across social groups. These rules of thumb were summarized by the government as the Uniform Guidelines on Employee Selection Procedures (1978). Societal protection of disadvantaged groups is an ideological stance with political and economic implications.

The fact that the issues surrounding test usage represent a complex political, ideological, and economic matter probably explains the continued involvement of the judicial system with professional assessment practices (Lerner 1978). Disputes about whether I.Q. testing for school placement should be allowed with certain minority groups were settled by the legal process (Clune 1988; Gifford 1988; Karmin 1974; Linn 1986). The case of *Larry P. v. Riles* (1980), in which an African American student's special school placement on the basis of intelligence testing was contested, has been followed by a decade of continuing controversy. The fact is, the legal process is dependent on human judgment that can be influenced by political and economic factors. Jacobs (1985) illustrated how court reports on child assessment represent a negotiated reality that is not always in the best interests of the client. Dingwall, Eekelaar, and Murray (1983) showed how cultural relativism is sometimes invoked to justify inaction by child protective agencies in cases of abuse, such that their resources would not be overtaxed. Professional psychologists whose roles and participation in the political economy are significantly defined by assessment functions must be especially reflective on the above mentioned issues.

As another example of the influence of political and economic forces, shifts in professional identity and mode of practice have been observed as counseling practitioners move away from developmental and preventive functions toward clinical settings and roles more in keeping with medical schemes of reimbursement (Fitzgerald and Osipow 1986; Zimpfer and DeTrude, 1990). Third-party payment and licensure seem to have promoted a pathology orientation in the professional worldviews and theoretical perspectives of these practitioners (Steenbarger 1991). Sarason (1986) had cautioned that the public interest we choose to serve must not be mistakenly identified with individual and professional self-interest. Dana (1987) pointed out that societal needs for "quick fix" and services designed to ameliorate long standing dysfunction may detract from efforts in primary prevention. The relative emphasis on primary prevention as opposed to tertiary interventions becomes, in part, an ethical question for professional psychologists. As will be explained in the next chapter, our answer to this question is partly a function of our theoretical beliefs about the locus of responsibility for psychological dysfunction.

Patronage and resource allocation also affect our professional inquiry and practice. What types of research will receive funding depends on the political climate and societal values. For example, the community mental health movement in the United States has waxed and waned as a function of support from the administration and the dominant political party (Vega and Murphy 1990). The future of psychotherapy and its related research also hinges on society's willingness to invest in psychological well-being (Strupp 1986). It is important for us to be aware of the socioeconomic and political trends that affect the types of inquiry we conduct and the services we provide. There are new opportunities for a health care revolution that will affect professional psychology and public policy on mental health care (Kiesler and Morton 1988; Lorion 1991). Psychologists can play a role in the transformation process by conducting research on underserved populations, in the areas of needs assessment, program outcomes, service systems, and resource allocation. It means developing and adopting appropriate paradigms of inquiry and a range of methods that will enable us to do so.

Before leaving this topic area, we should consider the norms that govern us as a scientific community in sociopolitical terms. This is because science is a social institution with particular relationships to the larger society, just as scientists are human beings trying to fulfill particular needs in the social setting. Scientific rationality in its idealized objectivist form depends on the application of cognitive values and standards. Scholars and researchers presumably evaluate theories by their fit with the evidence obtained under controlled conditions of observation governed by procedural rules that are agreed upon by the knowledge community. The scientific community admits into its body of knowledge those theories that have been successfully tested in this manner. However, if we were to consider a controversial area such as parapsychology, it becomes apparent that some additional types of social negotiation and political activities are engaged in by its followers in their attempt to gain scientific respectability. Not only have some researchers of parapsychology tried to follow standard scientific methods, but they have solicited the endorsement of recognized professional groups (such as the Institute of Mathematical Statistics), published in recognized journals, and presented their work at meetings where mainstream psychology is discussed (Collins and Pinch 1982). Their minority point of view, which has been rejected on technical scientific grounds as much as social opinions of deviancy and cult-likeness, is being negotiated through informal social and political processes. Hence, the legitimization of knowledge involves cognitive as well as sociopolitical processes and standards.

If psychology as a human social science is no longer viewed as an objective science with a universal method, but rather a cultural construction embedded in historical and political context, we have to pay more attention to how our knowledge production is regulated and how our knowledge claims are justified by social and political processes (Mulkay 1979). The social orientation and political posture of professional psychology will have as much impact on our future as the knowledge we contribute. Recent observers of the social sciences have pointed to our dependence on language and rhetoric in persuading ourselves and the public of the knowledge we construct (Gross 1990; Nelson, Megill, and McClosky 1987). For instance, Wilkins (1986) discussed how rhetoric is used in conveying an impression of efficacy of behavior therapy. Language as a cultural product, however, is loaded with the baggage of social inequities and biases. Heelan (1989) argued that the justification of our science and practice should be set against the larger background of our cultural narratives. Scientific discourse is to be shaped not by the researcher's voice alone but also by what he considers to be the teacher's voice and the citizen's voice. Cultural critique in the form of deconstruction or the uncovering of seldom-challenged assumptions, such as applied to the social psychology literature (Parker and Shotter 1990), may reveal our inner contradictions, social biases, and the underrepresentation of certain voices. In sociopolitical terms, the credibility of a given knowledge claim is linked to the issue of who is given voice, and what types of interests are being represented. When a profession such as ours claims to serve the public interest, our relationship with the public should come under scrutiny.

OUR INQUIRY CONTRACT WITH HUMAN SUBJECTS

In professional practice, because the professional is given an expert status with power over the lay person and the public, there is a potential risk of abuse of power. Professional inquiry in research and practice requires the cooperation of human subjects and clients. This cooperation must not be obtained by coercion or under other ethically questionable arrangements. Formalizing the social contract for inquiry between the professional and the research subjects or clients is a way of protecting all parties from the transgression of rights. Protection of the rights of human subjects is an expected responsibility of researchers. Whereas the norms and rules governing the scientific community are fairly clear as far as defining roles in knowledge generation, they are more ambiguous for the practice community. That is why we need professional codes of ethics to provide broad guidelines. Even so, much ambiguity exists with respect to the ethical implications of the concepts, methods, and processes we use in carrying out societally sanctioned functions.

Principles of professional conduct and guidelines for research on human subjects are available in the America Psychological Association Ethical Principles and other sources (American Psychological Association 1982, 1992; Haas, Fennimore, and Warburton 1983; Jacobs 1983). Sieber (1992) provides practical guidelines for planning ethically responsible research, including risk/benefit assessment, particularly with respect to vulnerable populations. Guidelines for providers of psychological services further define the role of service providers and their accountability (Board of Professional Affairs 1987). Lest these guidelines not be sufficient in providing guidance and understanding, additional ethical principles and guidelines for inquiry with women and ethnic and other minorities have been proposed (American Psychological Association 1979; Davis and Proctor 1989; Fassinger 1991; Ibrahim 1986; Ibrahim and Arredondo 1986; Lerman and Porter 1990).

The basic question about the social contract we establish with the public is how psychology as a profession is treating its human clientele. The question has been raised as to whether our relationship with our human clientele has been beneficial or exploitative (Koch 1981b). The situation in traditional experimental research is one that changes the social identity of the participants in a way that creates an inherent power advantage for the researcher over the subject (Danziger 1988; Kelman 1972). Subjects may not exercise the option to refuse to participate even if they wish to do so. In spite of ethical guidelines, the practice of deception in social psychological studies has continued, and ethical compliance in published studies is probably still not uniform as reported (Adair, Dushenko, and Lindsay 1985). Clinical and psychotherapy researchers face ethical problems concerning placebo groups, inflexible treatment regimens, waiting periods, incomplete informed consent to participation, and insufficient debriefing and follow-up (Imber, Glanz, Elkin, Sotsky, Boyer, and Leber 1986; O'Leary and Borkovec 1978). In evaluating alternative method choices and designs, the professional psychologist has reasons to prefer those that will preserve the dignity of the subject or client and minimize the compromising of ethical principles.

Paradigms of knowledge that emphasize empowering relationships with our human subjects can be supported by the practice of reflexivity. Steier (1991b) explained that reflecting back on oneself and the social system in which one is embedded increases the researcher's accountability. Rather than being privileged knowers, researchers must face the possibility of asking the wrong questions or applying categories that do not fit the experiences and meanings of the subjects. Understanding is a social process that depends on relationship and the communication of meanings. Inquiry approaches that seek the voice of the subject in achieving understanding are necessarily more egalitarian.

SUMMARIZING THE IMPLICATIONS FOR PROFESSIONAL INQUIRY

The foregoing discussion has a number of implications for professional inquiry. The cultural and sociopolitical frameworks enable us to view knowledge production and justification as contextualized and involving symbolic formulations and social negotiations. They also provide an explanatory source for the cognitive and social values of professionals and scientists who are products of their own societies. Professional inquiry is subject to the forces of history while at the same time capable of shaping history. As a manifestation of human culture, it should reflect the diversity of our society and world order. The necessary tensions inherent in diverse human interests and worldviews will continue to be played out in social and political processes. In that our professional literature and other public statements represent our rhetoric, they should be subjected to cultural critique and reflective analysis.

As we set out in our inquiry, and during our encounter with our human clientele, many ethical questions arise. Ethical training of the professional psychologist, though available in graduate school, is mainly focused on compliance with ethical and legal standards. Given the ambiguities and complexities surrounding much of our interactions with the public we serve, discussions of cases involving ethical decision making in actual situations will be helpful. The American Psychological Association's *Casebook on Ethical Principles of Psychologists* (1987) illustrates the application of our professional code of ethics by presenting cases that were adjudicated. A source such as Austin, Moline, and Williams (1990), which presents case vignettes and questions on legal cases associated with issues involved in malpractice, can also be used for the discussion of ethical decision making. A number of models for ethical decision making have been described (Kitchener 1984; Paradise and Siegelwaks 1982; Stadler 1986; Tymchuk 1981). The general approach is to be able to identify the nature of the ethical issue in a given case, consider the relevant principles and values, generate alternative choices of action that may bring resolution of the problem, and evaluate the possible consequences of each choice of action. In other words, critical thinking and reflection are needed for the analysis of ethical issues and ethical decision making.

There is some research and support for the benefits of a problem-solving approach in ethics training (Gawthrop and Uhlemann 1992). However, we lack a data base and ongoing research on the ethical conduct of researchers. More fundamentally, there is a need for a conceptual scheme to guide research on professional ethics (Adair 1988) and discussions about psychology as a moral science (Morawski 1982; Prilleltensky 1990). Ultimately, appropriate professional conduct must extend beyond compliance with standards to enacting values and beliefs about what constitute a good society and measures of progress in our science and practice (Bellah, Madsen, Sullivan, Swidler, and Tipton 1991; Warwick 1980). We cannot shy away from such questions as what is virtue, what would constitute healthy relationships, what our responsibilities are for the human condition, and how we are to contribute to the common good. These axiological concerns are not to be obscured by ideological arguments or political rhetoric.

The societal role we choose defines the nature of our professional inquiry. The professional psychologist can be a problem solver and change agent, as attempted in the community mental health movement in the 1960s (Carter 1968). Professional inquiry is goal directed and action based. This has led to discussions about the treatment utility of professional assessments in clinical practice (Hayes, Nelson, and Jarrett 1987). In the research realm, the action research mode and an emphasis on implementation can be found in organizational inquiry (Hakel, Sorcher, Beer, and Moses 1982; Patton 1978; Lawler, Mohrman, Mohrman, Ledford, Cummings, et al. 1985). A significant function of the professional psychologist consists in testing the knowledge of the discipline in application and enriching our knowledge base with the knowledge of practice (Hoshmand and Polkinghorne 1992).

The recognition of context requires us to view our professional practice as culturally embedded activities within ongoing historical traditions and as reflecting particular kinds of values and local interests. This view is exemplified by recent models of evaluation that include the value component (Scriven 1986a; Shaddish, Cook, and Leviton 1991). In conducting program evaluation, questions are framed with particular interests in mind. Political pressures can be brought to bear on researchers and evaluators in ways that make it difficult to maintain the integrity of the process. The professional must be clear about his or her obligations, both scientific and social. Program evaluation research provides an excellent opportunity for learning about the context of professional inquiry and developing our sociopolitical sensitivity. It also places us in a position of pondering ethical questions. As professional psychologists, we need to have not only a theory of use in research and practice but a theory of valuing to guide and evaluate our actions.

Emphasis on the larger context of human behavior is beginning to find its way into psychological theorizing as well as practice. Moll (1990) described the cultural-historical approach of Vygotsky and its applications in education. Chaiklin and Lave (1992) presented various examples of professional practice in context. A contextualized conception of professional inquiry has profound implications for our knowledge activities. In a pragmatic sense, inquiry is our way of acting upon the world of which we are a part as self-interpreting beings. The collective historical impact of our profession's inquiry practices will transform not only the sociocultural and political environment that we try to understand but our understanding of ourselves in the process. Whether we adopt a technical interest, critical theory perspective, or a hermeneutic approach, an essential function we have with respect to social and psychological realities is to ask relevant and thoughtful questions. From the point of view of science, our professional inquiry may contribute best by the creation of new meanings and processes for communal discourse. As Cronbach (1986) stated, progress in psychological and social inquiry consists not so much in the determination of fixed answers to stable problems as in an open, creative process of understanding. It is through this continuous process of inquiry that psychosocial realities may be transformed.

SUGGESTED ADDITIONAL LEARNING

1. Identify examples of psychological theories that may represent forms of cultural encapsulation, and consider whether and how they need to be revised.

2. Reflect on your sources of knowledge and how they compare with the preferred sources of knowledge of your peers, instructors, and supervisors.

3. Discuss how the professional may benefit from the native ways of knowing of his or her clients and research subjects.

4. Debate on whether and how sociopolitical considerations should enter into professional research and the development of psychology as a science.

5. Select a journal article on a study in an area of your professional interest, and evaluate it in terms of how the human subjects were treated and what types of interests the study might have served.

6. Identify a situation in your area of professional practice that requires ethical decision making. Discuss the issues, choices, and consequences, and reflect on the process.

7. Identify the major social and political issues in the various areas of professional practice and discuss the types of action that may be required.

8. Read and discuss the following articles by Wrenn. What kinds of thematic concerns do you consider most pressing for the profession? What are your personal reactions to the author's self-reflection and portrayal of issues over time?

Wrenn, C. G. 1962. The culturally encapsulated counselor. *Harvard Educational Review* 32: 444-49.

Wrenn, C. G. 1985. Afterword: The culturally encapsulated counselor revisited. In *Handbook of cross-cultural counseling*, ed. P. Pedersen, 323-29. Westport, CT: Greenwood.

9. Read the following article by Caplan and Nelson, and evaluate the pros and cons of conceptualizing social problems in terms of individual factors:

Caplan, N., and Nelson, S. D. 1973. On being useful: The nature and conse quences of psychological research on social problems. *American Psychologist* 28: 199-211.

10. Read the following article by Albee, and discuss its implications in the light of current realities:

Albee, G. W. 1986. Toward a just society: Lessons from observations on the primary prevention of psychopathology. *American Psychologist* 41: 891-98.

4

Ideas, Conceptual Systems, and Core Beliefs

To understand the conceptual base of professional inquiry, we will consider the ideas and theories that have shaped our ways of thinking about psychological phenomena and our modes of practice. As indicated in the previous chapters, at the core of these ideas and conceptual systems are deep convictions and philosophical commitments. Altogether, they constitute the many layers of meaning through which we make sense of what we do and communicate among ourselves and with the public. Due to the richness of ideas in our field, it will not be possible to account for every major concept and theoretical belief prevalent in the profession. This chapter will only provide a framework for analyzing the conceptual underpinnings of professional inquiry and practice and the related issues.

FROM CONCEPTS TO SYSTEMS OF IDEAS

There are many ways of referring to ideas. Psychological concepts are ideas that have been framed as having characteristic meanings in our profession that distinguish them from the everyday ideas of the lay person. However, because we often use ordinary language in framing psychological ideas, our concepts are not entirely removed from commonsense narrative understanding. This has philosophical and practical significance for the nature of psychological knowledge. At certain times, psychological jargon requires translation into ordinary terms, thus involving a dual process of interpretation. At other times, our ideas and concepts seem indistinguishable from everyday understanding. These two possibilities are faced by the practitioner in working with clients. There is a constant translation and sharing of meanings in the reciprocal process of sense making. Professional ideas are imparted to the lay person, such as when a therapist teaches a client therapeutic concepts or particular ways of viewing problems. The professional depends also on the native knowledge of the lay person in interpreting human events. From a narrative standpoint, this communicative use of ideas and concepts takes place against the larger background of cultural meanings and practices that provide a commonality between professional uses of language and the everyday uses of language. As suggested in the previous chapter, therapeutic concepts (and narratives), for example, may be understood within the context of cultural narratives.

The term "variable" is used by the profession when an idea or construct is used in connection with research that involves quantification and measurement. It refers to something that can assume a range of values. Thus, when treated as a variable, a concept such as motivation takes on different magnitudes and levels as a function of the scale of measurement used. (A similar process occurs when the lay person speaks of different degrees of motivation based on qualitative judgment). However, there is no perfect way of measuring and defining any given construct. More than one operational definition may be proposed, especially for complex constructs such as intelligence. The construct meanings are not expected to be adequately represented in any single operational definition. If we take a construct such as anxiety, for example, it seems reasonable to apply not only a physiological language but a behavioral as well as phenomenological language. Each kind of description can be accompanied by a particular method of measuring anxiety, but will not be complete in representing the construct alone. We cannot assume that a given method of measuring a construct is the most valid. We can only speak of the relative validity of a construct with reference to a particular criterion and context of usage. This point will be expounded as we evaluate methods of inquiry in chapter 6.

Psychological variables are embedded in theory, which is a formal statement about particular relationships between entities that we describe with our concepts. In the experimental research tradition, theories are propositional statements that are testable and potentially admissible into the body of knowledge of the discipline. Yet, the term "theory" is sometimes used by members of the profession also to connote a tentative description of a phenomenon or a working hypothesis about a certain aspect of practice. Some of the "theories" used by practitioners are conceived at the level of ideological beliefs (such as associated with humanistic psychology), rather than generated by empirical research. These informal usages of the term should probably be distinguished from its more formal meaning by the level of discourse and the context of usage.

The varied uses of the term "theory" are perhaps reflective of the state of our field. There is no clear consensus on the theoretical status of psychology as a science (Cronbach 1986; Gergen 1973; Polkinghorne 1986; Skinner 1987). Some would like to believe that psychology should aspire to be a theoretical science like physics. Others assert that the effort to build general laws of behavior is misdirected because our social and cultural embeddedness means that there is always contextual variability in the meaning of behaviors. Still others feel that, except for the basic capacities such as learning and perception, for which we have relatively developed and tested theories, it is premature to refer to our ways of conceptualizing in psychology as theories. The proliferation of theories and terminology particular to certain schools of thought can become a problem if it means separate subcultures and groups of psychologists hardly communicating with one another or with the nonpsychology world. It has been suggested that we need to direct more attention to attaining agreement on the meanings of some basic concepts and to return to everyday observations, introspection, and commonsense thinking (de Groot 1990).

Professional psychology has, in addition, an abundance of ideas and postulated relationships that are rather loosely formulated and not subjected to formal testing in research. Many therapeutic concepts, for instance, represent the ideas of master practitioners that are not formally linked with the existing body of research. The fact that they have remained separate results in a more limited community of users and probably less potentiated value for the profession at large. This does not necessarily mean that they are not valid or useful, especially if they have been extensively tested in the experience of expert practice (Hoshmand and Polkinghorne 1992). Alternative terms such as "model" and "practical paradigm" (Van Strien 1987) have been suggested to represent the set of concepts used to describe the phenomena of practice, as in the case of a therapeutic model. A working model suggests something that is in the process of evolvement. It is developed in relation to a particular practical purpose. Similarly, the notion of a practical paradigm is based on problem solving. It represents our conceptualization of particular ways of problem solving. Although it is easier to place the practitioner in relation to working models and practical paradigms, the researcher may be regarded also as engaging in problem solving when testing the validity of ideas formulated as theories, and certainly when formally evaluating the utility of models. From this problem-solving point of view, the evaluation of practical working models and the testing of more formalized theories are no longer disparate activities. They dovetail in a common pragmatic goal of problem solving central to our profession.

Ideas and concepts are organized at many levels. When they are part of a network of ideas and meanings, they constitute a conceptual system. Theories and models represent conceptual systems with differing degrees of precision and formalization. It is important to note that the significance of a concept as well as of any theory depends critically on its relationship to an existing network of ideas. A concept in professional practice, such as "boundaries," is considered meaningful by those who understand it as one way of describing individual identities, relationships, and social systems. Furthermore, it has utility when understood as indicating a set of practices by which the professional defines a role in relationship to the client system and facilitates certain interactions conducive to individuals maintaining clear boundaries and so forth. On the contrary, holding an idea or hypothesis that has minimal conceptual linkage to other useful ideas and practices will probably not be too meaningful or productive.

There are many ways of comparing and grouping the existing conceptual approaches in professional inquiry. The question of what kind of conceptual category or unit will serve us best has been asked by those who tried to propose a particular classification of conceptual units (Allport 1958; Horley 1987). Differences between conceptual approaches are hinged on the nature of the unit of analysis, one of the most basic issues of inquiry mentioned in chapter 2. The "size" of the unit reflects the scope of one's conceptual focus. Small units that represent usually a low level of description or an analysis of a phenomenon by its component parts are referred to as molecular units. The simple activity of a neuron is an example of a molecular concept of behavior. Reductionistic conceptions of psychological problems tend to favor discrete, molecular units that are easy to define operationally. An example would be a discrete thought of craving as a unit of behavior that sets the condition for the appetitive response of consuming an addictive substance. On the other hand, units that are larger in scope or involve higher levels of description and analysis are referred to as molar concepts. For example, motivation conceived in terms of an interplay of attitudes, feelings, and one's evaluation of potential goal attainment would be a molar concept. In contrast to the reductionistic concepts, contextualist conceptions of an individual's problem such as in terms of the interrelationships between members of a family system, involve larger and more complex units of analysis. Similarly, an organic metaphor of higher psychological functions calls for units of changing quality and complexity that reflect processes of growth and differentiation over time. Narrow, behavioristic operational definitions of such units are seldom satisfactory. Thus, concepts such as cognitive style and conceptual-level functioning are not considered to be adequately represented by any particular form of psychometric measurement.

The issue of choosing an appropriate unit of analysis is faced by researchers of psychological practice, such as in trying to decide which level of analysis is most appropriate for studying therapeutic process (Greenberg 1986). Whereas it is easier to use simple units of analysis in a reliable fashion (such as in obtaining agreement between observers who use the same operational definition), the use of more complex units is expected to yield more meanings (thus enhancing internal validity). Methodologically, there is a kind of "trade-off" between reliability and validity in our choice of the unit of analysis. In the area of psychotherapy research, some researchers have conducted fine-grained analysis of therapist and client responses (Hill 1992) and specific sequences of acts (Martin, Martin, and Slemon 1989). Others have focused on more holistic events and change-related episodes (Elliott and Shapiro 1992; Mahrer and Nadler 1986; Rice and Greenberg 1984). It is possible that all levels of analysis can inform practitioners with their respective conceptual and empirical contributions. Similarly, in professional practice, it is appropriate to approach a problem with multiple units of analysis.

A client's interpersonal problems can be conceptualized in terms of particular deficits in communication skills as well as maladaptive relationship beliefs. Intervention can be guided by both formulations, and can consist of training in communication skills and the modification of relationship assumptions. The important question is whether the conceptualization leads to useful problem solutions.

Other dimensions of conceptual difference are related to ontological assumptions about psychological events and human nature. Weiner (1991) pointed to the historical shift in ontological conceptions of human motivation from machine metaphors to the person as a decision-maker and scientist. Concepts and theories based on particular ontologies are associated with particular research directions. When we conceive of the human domain as one that is saturated with personal and social meanings, we wish to find units of analysis that can capture the richness of such meanings. The assumption that humans are agents acting on their own free will and perceived social meanings calls for a conceptual language that refers to the actor's own intentions and the meaning of social actions. This is referred to as an "intentional language," in contrast to the use of an objective, "extensional language" whereby an individual's behavior is described from a detached observer's standpoint (Harre, Clarke, and DeCarlo 1985). If we also believe that human intentions and actions should be understood within the larger embedding context of entire systems of social practices and cultural meanings, we would require nonreductionistic units for their study. Mechanistic conceptions and molecular units of analysis usually go hand in hand with the use of objective language in the description of behavior. These uses of behavioristic concepts are not likely to be satisfactory to those who prefer an intentional language for the description and conceptualization of human agency in relation to social actions.

The ontological assumption of free will is usually held to be contrary to determinism that is inherent in most theoretical concepts in psychology, though some theorists have attempted to combine the two (Sappington 1990). Determinism has its limits in that the predictability of the phenomena we study is not always within our grasp; thus, we see the emergence of chaos theory (Gleick 1987; Wolf 1983). Scientists and mathematicians who came up with this theory have been puzzled by the fact that when predictable variables are combined, they produce complex systems that seem to behave in unpredictable ways—systems that contain patterns yet never quite repeat themselves. Researchers who use the chaos concept have argued that although chaotic systems may be derived from simple deterministic variables, they themselves are unpredictable. Nonetheless, deterministic worldviews are reflected not only in our conceptual approaches but in the manner in which researchers are expected to demonstrate free will. In the experimental tradition, research on human agency has involved demonstrating the portion of variance that is not explained by environmental determinants and sources of external control (Howard and Conway 1986; Howard, Youngs, and Siatczynski 1988). However, trying to prove a negative can never be conclusive. In reviewing concepts related to free will and their empirical demonstration, Sappington (1990) pointed out that while theories of free will can be compatible with the scientific tasks of prediction and control, the concept of free will is best treated as a metaphysical assumption.

The acceptance of a concept as well as a more elaborated theoretical system has much to do with the cultural meanings in which it is embedded, and its place in the history of ideas for a given community. Some psychological concepts seem to gain popular usage when incorporated into folk idioms and popular psychology, a confirmation of the affinity of psychological language and everyday talk. This is probably more so with the concepts used in professional practice, as shared in conversations with our clients. For example, a popular concept used by practitioners at the time of this writing is "codependency," which was used originally to refer to the psychological symbiosis between those who have an addiction problem and their significant others (Forward 1989). It has been extended in the self-help literature to dysfunctional relationships in general (Ackerman and Pickering 1989; Norwood 1985; Van Wormer 1989). It is not a concept connected with research on a formal psychological theory; yet its popularity among practitioners and their clients seems to be maintained by an increased sense in this society of the pervasive effects and emotional costs of psychological problems such as addiction and battering, against a background of cultural beliefs in individual responsibility and the care-taking role of women. On the other hand, a concept such as "learned helplessness," which is derived from research and used in theorizing on depression (Seligman 1975), has not pervaded the vocabulary of practitioners and their clients to the same extent as in the previous example. This is in spite of its conceptual link to formal theory and the practice-based observations that have helped in the clinical formulation of the phenomenon. One may speculate that its relative lack of use in the popular language of certain communities of practitioners is partly due to a cultural tendency to expect individuals to solve their own problems, even if a person is presumably the victim of the environment and learning history. Perhaps a reframing of the concept as "learned competence" would be better received. Parenthetically, one wonders how the new concept of learned optimism (Seligman 1991) may fare in the present climate of American society.

Chapter 3 has pointed to the historical and ideological influences on conceptual systems in psychology. Within the discipline itself, conceptual systems are judged by their linkage to the existing body of knowledge and the history of research and application. Though regarded differently and evolved through somewhat different routes, the conceptual systems used in research and practice respectively have been established by their history of application. While practice has depended on the research-tested theories of the profession, some of the conceptual systems used by practitioners have been derived from everyday observations and the knowledge of practice, and have been tested in practice. The coming together of these two sources of ideas and knowledge will require a reciprocity of theory and practice and a pluralistic conception of our professional knowledge (Hoshmand and Polkinghorne 1992). The professional psychologist of the future will have to find an open yet judicious way of selecting conceptual tools derived from diverse sources and contexts of application.

THE USES OF CONCEPTUAL TOOLS IN PROFESSIONAL INQUIRY

The preceding discussion is based on the perspective that concepts are meaningful (1) only in terms of their usage in particular contexts, (2) in relationship to other concepts that share a similar background of cultural meanings and practices, and (3) when employed with particular interests in mind. This is an important notion espoused by philosophers since the linguistic turn in the history of ideas (Malcolm 1967; Ossorio 1974; Wittgenstein 1968). If concepts or constructs are our means of making sense of the world, they can be considered to be tools applied with heuristic purposes. At a cognitive level, our ways of construing have been referred to by such terms as "schema" or "template" (Brewer and Nakamura 1984; Taylor and Crocker 1981). The metaphor of a map has also been used to refer to the meaning structure that we seem to impose on our experience of the world. Conceptual structuring occurs in everyday sense making as well as in professional inquiry. Concepts and theories structure our observations as we organize the perceptual information. It is in this sense that philosophers of science refer to observations as "theory-laden" (Hansen 1958; Hesse 1981). We always interpret information from a particular perspective, informed by our theories about the world.

There is also the saying that "one should not confuse the map with the territory." This could be taken as suggesting that our constructs could only approximate what is being described. The link between theory and observed facts is only tentative. Theories are continuously modified, just as cartographers find it necessary to update and revise maps. The distinction between map and territory also implies that there is no truth status to the constructs themselves. The notion of a map of reality tends to be associated with a representational approach to the world, whereby historically the empiricists have emphasized the role of sensory input, and the rationalists/idealists, the role of active ideation in gaining access to the world. The new philosophy of science has moved away from a mirror or map type of metaphor that had been used in the correspondence theory of truth. Current constructionist perspectives stress that it is not possible to describe the world independent of language. Our constructs are our means of social access to experience, to the extent that our language and conceptual systems are shared. The meanings we construct are psychologically real and have causal import when used. One need only observe the effects of our communication on interpersonal relationships to appreciate the psychological reality and impact of conveyed meanings. The philosophical implications of this will be discussed later in relation to the core beliefs of the profession and the search for a higher-order or metalevel framework for our conceptual applications.

From a personal, psychological standpoint, our conceptual system or template of the world is essentially our worldview. There are many facets to such a system, including the personal theories we hold about the phenomena studied by our profession. It is important for us to understand the relationship between the personal theories we hold and the formal theories of the profession (Martin 1988). It is also important for us to understand our own processes of concept formation and abstraction (Hunt 1970). Whereas professional theories are presumably used in guiding our approach to research and practice, the role of personal theories in professional functioning is less clear. The personal processes of knowing and formal judgments made by professional psychologists will be addressed in chapter 7. We cannot do without concepts and theories. Theory allows a researcher to select a focus and to make reasoned choices among a large number of ways of conceptualizing a phenomenon of interest. It makes inquiry more manageable on a practical level. Similarly for the professional in practice, a conceptual system helps direct attention to what is interpretable within an existing set of practices, and thus confer meaning on actions and events.

Our conceptual systems can also include ideas about the underlying causes of events. For those who subscribe to a hypothetico-deductive approach to research, a theory is a representational model of the forces posited to account for the phenomenon in question. For example, the psychologists Tolman and Hull posited theories of learning and motivation that involve hypothetical constructs. The function of research, then, is to describe and measure those observable events and elements that reveal this psychological reality that cannot be directly observed, and to test particular relationships between variables as predicted from the account. This is how causal theories are demonstrated and evaluated, based on assumptions of regularity and determinism. (For a discussion of ideas about causation, see White 1990). As can be expected, there are different accounts of any given psychological phenomenon. Psychologists may agree on the observable elements of a theoretical account but differ in their interpretations of them. How, then, do we reach agreement in regard to the value of our conceptual tools as used? The answer to this question is rather complex.

The appraisal of theory and the choice of conceptual orientation are regulated to some extent by the norms of the profession. Various kinds of criteria have been proposed for the evaluation of conceptual approaches (Royce 1978). As a professional community, we turn to the criteria of rationality that have been established for judging professional accounts. Theoretical statements as a professional account of a given phenomenon of interest are judged first of all by their clarity and internal coherence. Using common sense and thinking, we can further assess cognitively how the set of ideas involved holds against the internal consistency of other ideas. Parsimony is also valued when a conceptual system can accommodate a large set of meanings with a small number of concepts. Ultimately, if the theoretical account is presumed to have pragmatic value, it has to be demonstrated in application. Formal research is usually used to validate the predictive power of a theory, based on the demonstrated observed evidence. At other times, the testing may be done more informally, as when a practitioner evaluates the fit of a working theory or conceptual model with the field experience of practice. Finally, to complete the process of accountability to the community of users, a report is made and communicated through a professional forum such as a journal. An account of the assessment of the theory or conceptual system is given. This will be judged by the professional community for intelligibility and credibility, based on the clarity and cohesiveness of the arguments presented, the authority of the cognitive test involved, and the soundness of the methodology of demonstration. A theory or conceptual system that can stimulate new ways of thinking and future inquiry is considered to be fertile and potentially contributing to progress toward increased knowledge.

What should be recognized is that there are many steps and levels of evaluation, involving a number of criteria and standards. Common to all the processes is the use of human judgment in a way that is accountable to the professional community. The psychology and the sociology of knowledge (Mahoney 1976; Merton 1973; Mulkay 1979) are relevant to the processes involved. Evaluation of our conceptual tools and their value as used in inquiry is a very human, social process. Although there are standards of rationality upheld by the profession, the final authority rests with communal judgments. This point has been stressed by historians and philosophers of science, especially since the rejection of universal foundations and standards (Kuhn 1970; Gutting 1980). Theory choice and theory appraisal seem to be more guided by value judgment and less rule governed than had been assumed traditionally in the philosophy of science (Howard 1985b; McMullin 1984). It is the responsibility of those who claim the utility of a given conceptual tool to give intelligible, compelling accounts of its meaningful application. Many of the accounts written by master practitioners or passed on orally through the supervision of practice are found by their followers to be compelling. Their wider acceptance will depend on the extent to which these accounts are fitting with the experience of application and are intelligible to reason, as explained to the profession at large. There are a number of conceptual systems that have earned the confidence of professional psychologists. Learning theories, psychodynamic theories, and system theories have distinct bases of support and reflect different histories and processes of achieving acceptance by the profession.

Some of the theories believed to be promising have served as guides in research. To cite a few examples, clinical and counseling research has been fruitfully guided by social-learning theories of self-efficacy (Bandura 1989), cognitive-mediation models of personal change (Martin 1984; Toukmanian 1992), as well as social-psychological theories of interpersonal influence (Strong and Claiborn 1982; Strong, Welsh, Corcoran, and Hoyt 1992; Weary and Mirels 1982). However, there has been a continuing debate about the appropriateness of theory-driven research. In the area of research on therapeutic practice, Strong (1991) and Martin (1991) argued for the use of theory-based formulations of research problems and theory-guided research strategies. They pointed out that the inductive collection of facts not integrated with a network of systematically tested ideas is not likely to be useful. On the other hand, Mahrer (1988) and Hill (1990) were concerned that theoretical lenses could limit interpretive possibilities and prevent researchers from an open process of discovery and faithful description of phenomena that we strive to understand. McKay (1988) concluded that the negative attitude toward theory-guided research has stemmed from the narrow hypothesis testing in the field associated with the restrictive use of a behavioristic paradigm. A case can be made for research guided by sound theoretical understanding and conceptually interesting questions, apart from narrowly conceived research methods and strategies. As will be explained in the next chapter on research paradigms, theoretically informed inquiry does not have to be at cross-purposes with more exploratory forms of investigation.

The concerns expressed about the choice of theory and research strategy involve issues that are both conceptual and methodological. Our choice of theory is related to our choice of methodological approach in inquiry. A molecular view of behavior probably calls for the use of reductionistic and behavioristic research methods that will not be as suitable in a molar conception of psychological phenomenon. For example, frequency counts of operationally defined, discrete responses will be more feasible with an operant theory of behavior than a system's conception. It was suggested in the previous chapters that our profession's method choices may have limited our inquiry. At the same time, the quality of research has much to do with our conceptual practices. Rychlak (1988) is of the opinion that many of the shortcomings of psychological research may be traced to conceptual limitations. Like Gergen (1978) and McGuire (1973), who had expressed similar concerns about the need for theoretical training, he believed that conceptual improvements and more attention to the thoughtful derivation of research questions will lead to the appropriate choice of research methods and the production of more meaningful research. Kukla (1989) gave a helpful survey of the types of issues dealt with by theoretical psychologists, and discussed the relation between their work and empirical research.

In following the path of theoretical understanding, however, one has to come to terms with the conceptual diversity in the field. Psychological theories range from the highly reductionistic stimulus-response formulations of human behavior to holistic conceptions of complex social systems in interaction. It may be instructive to examine the basis of conceptual preferences in both research and practice. It appears that professional practice is open to the use of diverse conceptual systems. The implicit criteria for application seem less restrictive than for researchers engaged in formal theory-testing research. This diverse concept use also gives rise to patterns of shared meanings that seem to reflect relatively stable commitments. It is such commitments to which we now turn.

CORE COMMITMENTS AND ROOT METAPHORS IN PROFESSIONAL PSYCHOLOGY

Every profession shares certain core beliefs. Pepper (1942) described major beliefs as world hypotheses, each with a particular metaphor at it core. These root metaphors enable us to understand the basic premises of major systems of ideas in application. We can analyze our theoretical systems in terms of core beliefs and central metaphors. We can also think of different modes of psychological practice in terms of their core assumptions and the world views of those who follow the particular practice. We ask, What are the implications of these different root metaphors and core commitments for models of inquiry in professional practice?

Pepper (1942) distinguished major ways of thinking into the formistic, the mechanistic, the contextualist, and the organic. Formism relies on the categorization of events by their similarities and differences. Professional inquiry and practice that appear to follow a formistic core metaphor include the assessment of personality traits and the use of psychiatric classification and diagnosis. Mechanism has as its root metaphor the machine that operates on the basis of linear causal forces. As mentioned in relation to the choice of units of analysis, behavioristic models of determinism reflect a mechanistic core metaphor. Mechanistic and deterministic theories lead to the search for biological or environmental factors as the discrete causes of psychological problems. Contextualism, on the other hand, is the holistic view that emphasizes the dynamic interplay of forces that constitute a historically situated event. It is reflected in interactional models of practice and an interest in the study of psychological phenomenon in the context of its biosocial, cultural, and ecological environment. In the contextualist view, the professional conducting inquiry is embedded in the process of information exchange with others who are coproducers of the data. Finally, organicism differs from mechanism by its metaphor of a living, growing organism as opposed to a machine. There is an interest in the internal organization of self-interpreting systems and their transactions with the embedding systems. Inquiry involves understanding the parts in relation to the whole, with a possibility of progressive change. Developmental perspectives and professional practices premised on human growth and increased differentiation are organic in their core assumptions.

Depending on the conceptual unit that forms the base of a theoretical system, there are different implications for causality. According to a classification by Aristotle, formistic conceptions of causality, as when the functional capability of an organism is linked to its physical composition (such as mental functioning being explained in terms of brain tissue damage), are concerned with what is termed "material cause". By the same classification, when mechanistic, linear forces are invoked to explain a phenomenon (as in the direct reinforcement of a behavioral response), it is referred to as "efficient cause." The use of teleological explanations, such as intention and purpose, involves "final cause". A conception that takes into account the interrelationship and structural pattern of parts of a unit (such as a system's conception of a family unit), is referred to as "formal cause". Cybernetic concepts of causality further acknowledge the mutuality of causal processes in any given system and their effects on the system (Maruyama 1963). Such concepts of control have been applied at a cognitive level to the analysis of self-regulation in human functioning (Carver and Scheier 1981, 1982). Rychlak (1969) discussed these various forms of causality as applied to theories of psychotherapy. He pointed out that the Lockean paradigm (characterized by behavioristic conceptual systems) tends to be associated with material and efficient causes, whereas the Kantian paradigm (characterized by developmental perspectives and humanistic theories of free will or human agency) tends to be associated with final and formal causes. The criteria to be used for evaluating different kinds of conceptual approaches should take into account the fact that they imply different ontological assumptions and seem to serve different purposes.

In practice, conceptual orientation translates into different modes of working with clients and problems. Formistic conceptions tend to be static, whereas organic conceptions allow for dynamic change. Professional inquiry that is focused on the individual, such as clinical assessment involving standardized norm-referenced testing and diagnosis, is formistic in adhering to an assumption of individual-centered traits and problems. Mechanistic models of behavior tend to invoke linear causal explanations, whereas the contextualist and the organic are more inclusive and dialectical. Operant behavioral analysis and the assessment of discrete cognitive antecedents of problems are linear in nature and isolated from the complex internal organization of cognitions in interaction with affect and behavior. They tend to result in a search for narrowly identified agents or personal behaviors that contribute to a presenting problem. Environmental stressors and self-produced stimulus factors may be emphasized in such approaches.

By contrast, professional practice involving whole systems, such as family counseling and organizational consultation, have as their primary focus the social unit of which an individual is a part. The assumption is that the interrelationships of members of the unit and the events impacting on the system as a whole largely determine individual outcomes. Thus the family unit or the organizational unit is the client, as opposed to the individual. Problems presented by the individual are interpreted in transactional terms and placed in the context of the system(s) involved. Human systems conceived in terms of the psychological, biological, and environmental levels are subject to bidirectional control between the levels. There is a recursiveness and fluidity of influence among the subsystems.

Taplin (1980) discussed the implications of general systems theory for assessment and intervention. Professional practice that is based on a system's perspective can be found in communication theory approaches to family therapy (Haley 1976; Watzlawick, Beavin, and Jackson 1967; Watzlawick, Weakland, and Fisch 1974) and integrative models of intervention that stress the interrelationship between psychobiology and behavior therapy (Lang, Levin, Miller, and Kozak 1983; Schwartz 1982). Sundberg, Taplin, and Tyler (1983) combined the system's approach with a dynamic, developmental conception of change. Counseling and clinical practice that emphasize developmental and preventive interventions (Drum and Lawler 1988; Mahoney 1991) reflect organismic (holistic, growth-oriented) and contextualist (transactional) perspectives. Contextualist conceptual approaches are also found in environmental and health psychology (Cohen, Evans, Stokols, and Krantz 1986; McLeroy, Bibeau, Steckler, and Glanz 1988; Moos 1979; Stokols 1987; Winnett, King, and Altman 1989). For further discussions of these core metaphors in relation to conceptual orientations in psychology and professional practice, the reader may refer to Altman and Rogoff (1987) and Lyddon (1989b).

Although it is possible to adopt a variety of conceptual orientations in professional practice by conducting inquiry at the individual as well as the system level, the core commitment of the practitioner may steer his or her actions toward a particular mode of inquiry and problem solving. This commitment is not only intellectual in nature but a reflection of the personal worldview and beliefs of the practitioner. Personal values and ideology play a part in the perception of a client's violent behavior as being a function of socioeconomic background and personal victimization. Similarly, a practitioner who intends to be an advocate for a particular group of clients is emotionally committed to attributing problems identified in professional inquiry to the conditions and environments under which the clients live, so as to be able to place responsibility for change accordingly.

There are a number of shared professional worldviews associated with particular professional roles or models of practice. A strong orientation among professional psychologists is that of being a behavioral scientist. Krasner and Houts (1984) found great consistency among behavioral psychologists in their scientific worldviews and orientation to inquiry. The role of a behavioral scientist is broadly linked to the definition of the discipline as a science of behavior. As stated in the first chapter of this book, this definition varies depending on how we conceive of human behavior. A conception of behavior that includes not only the personal but the biological, sociological, and interpersonal levels allows us to focus inquiry broadly. Oftentimes, approaches to the study of behavior are deterministic in that biological and sociological factors as well as interpersonal environment are held to determine how the individual acts. Determinism is also implicit in the psychoanalytic orientation in the conception of biological impulses and the psychic impact of formative emotional experiences. A less deterministic view is shared by psychologists with a humanistic orientation or a cognitive-constructionist orientation. Rychlak (1988) portrayed humans as purposeful and able to generate more choices than they are granted by the environment. Bandura (1989) used cognitive concepts of self-generated proactive control and influence, while allowing for reciprocal causation with the environment. Psychologists' stances on the issue of free will versus determinism have ranged from the hard determinism of Freud and Skinner to soft determinism and libertarian views shared by researchers of human agency and personal control (Sappington 1990).

Obviously, these general statements about professional orientations are oversimplified. One should make in-depth studies of particular conceptual systems that may have been subsumed under a given orientation. For instance, not all psychoanalytic theories have the same conception of the self and the ability of the self to transcend deterministic forces (Young-Eisendrath and Hall 1987). There is a myriad of contributions to modern psychodynamic theories, reflecting significant conceptual developments and differences (Masterson and Klein 1988; Pine 1989; Straker 1987). As another example of a generalization that needs to be qualified, in considering humanistic and cognitive-constructionist orientations as supportive of a conception of the human as a free agent, we need to grant a certain degree of realistic constraints. A person's freedom to choose is limited by biosocial and environmental factors, as is our ability to construct effectively a meaningful existence. Even professionals who are philosophically committed to the importance of the personal phenomenology of our human clientele must take into account real-world constraints. Most practitioners utilize both intentional and extensional language in conceptualizing and describing the concerns of clients and their social situations. We derive information from both self-interpreted meanings and publicly shared observational knowledge.

It is generally true that differences in core commitment and conceptual orientation are reflected in how the professional psychologist evaluates clients and attempts to bring about problem solutions. In therapeutic practice, models of change are linked with particular conceptual systems and their tacit assumptions and worldviews. For example, a constructionist view of human change places great importance on the client's interpretations of experience and the active contributions of the client to the change process. This is reflected, for instance, in the rationale of asking a client to write a self-characterization and a future role sketch as ways of understanding the client's self-constructs and personal issues, and facilitating the process of change. The form of practice that is congruent with this conceptual orientation will not be a directive approach such as rational-emotive therapy, in which the professional takes an active, expert role in challenging the client's meanings and suggesting areas of change. Rather, it will be more consistent with a constructionist orientation to provide developmental counseling or epistemic therapy (Guidano 1987; Joyce Monitz 1985; Mahoney and Lyddon 1988). Similarly, a primarily agential conception of human nature (or the belief in humans as self-determining agents) means viewing the client as capable of choice. The client's intentions and actions will be the focus of problem discussions. The client, rather than other agents, is held to be primarily responsible for change.

Just as there are apparent differences, there are considerable areas of overlap among the diverse conceptual orientations in our field. The attempt to analyze theories and classify them is called "systematology" (Madsen 1985). Koch (1959-1963) is a classic example of work in the comparative study of psychological theories. The study of history and systems in psychology enables us to see trends and continuities as well as discontinuities in psychological theories and methods. Another level of analysis is to consider the underlying metaphysical assumptions of our conceptual systems (Stam, Rogers, and Gergen 1987). It is worth asking if it is possible to derive a second-order framework to account for the choice of conceptual systems by our profession. This is the domain of metathesis.

META-LEVEL FRAMEWORKS

A metathesis is a higher-order or metalevel conception that provides a frame of reference for our theoretical and methodological approaches. What has been termed "metaphysical" in philosophy belongs in the realm of metathesis. Madsen (1985) distinguished between ontological theses, or philosophical statements about the world, and epistemological theses, or the philosophy of science. Metatheory can therefore be either an ontological metathesis on the nature of our subject matter or an epistemological metathesis on the practice of our science according to particular rules, criteria, and standards. The former provides a frame of reference for our theories, and the latter, our research methodology, with reciprocal implications. A metatheoretical system may include a perspective and a methodology of its own. Systematology or the comparative study of theories is one such methodology that is involved in metatheoretical work. Metamethodological analysis, or the comparative study of methods and their application, is another. Madsen (1985) pointed out that epistemological theses or metatheories of science are contributed by the history of science, the sociology of science, and the psychology of science. He did not specify the sources of metathesis about the subject matter of psychology. One may regard the metatheories of our subject matter as contributed not only by the social science disciplines but also by the humanities, which have statements to make about human nature and the human condition (Krantz 1987). In this connection, the Latin word *scientia* referring to the sciences includes those fields that are under the humanities.

In terms of a metatheoretical framework that may constitute a metathesis on the human domain and psychology as a science, there are a number of proposals. They tend to be perspectives that involve a metathesis compatible with a family of theories that may have a shared core metaphor and similar metagoals. Such metatheoretical perspectives are of interest to professional psychologists in seeking, for instance, psychotherapy integration where apparent differences in language and technique make translation between orientations difficult, if not impossible (London 1986). Metatheoretical understanding is an important corrective to casual eclecticism that disregards epistemological incompatibility and other philosophical differences between theoretical systems (Neimeyer 1988b; Norcross 1986; Prochaska and Norcross 1986).

Metatheoretical advances are important to research and the development of methodological principles. Staats (1981) argued for unified-theory construction with the aim of resolving schisms and organizing the knowledge obtained in different types of psychological research. By proposing paradigmatic behaviorism as a unifying framework, he suggested (Staats 1983, 1991) that metatheoretical work can integrate diverse concepts and research in a particular area such as emotions (Staats and Eifert 1990; Staats and Heiby 1985) or behavior therapy (Eifert and Evans 1990), as well as bridge separate theoretical areas such as behavioral principles and developmental psycholinguistics (Staats 1971; Rondal 1985). Staats also proposed what he referred to as interlevel and interfield theoretical analysis, such as using cognitive psychology to examine behavioral biology and operant psychology (Robinson and Woodward 1989). Another metalevel task is setting standards for evaluating existing theories. Coupled with metalevel analysis of methodologies across research programs by their pragmatic yield (as will be explained subsequently), such efforts may enable the profession to identify those approaches to knowledge that are most effective and fruitful.

Constructionism has been proposed as a metatheoretical perspective for cognitive approaches to counseling and psychotherapy that challenge reductionistic conceptions of the relationships among thought, feeling, and action (Mahoney and Lyddon 1988). It has also been regarded as a common epistemological base for personal-construct theory and systemic theory in therapy (Feixas 1990). Loos and Epstein (1989) illustrated how the ideas of Kelly can be combined with constructionist ideas in identifying the target system for intervention, codefining problems with clients, and positioning the therapist in family therapy. Neimeyer and Feixas (1990) argued that constructionism can serve as an integrative framework for personal-construct approaches, contemporary psychoanalysis that rejects Freud's early physicalist concepts, schema models of cognitive therapy, as well as systemic family therapies that emphasize constructed meanings. Practical applications of this integrative perspective can be found in different therapeutic modalities (Kantor and Neal 1986; Landfield and Leitner 1980; Neimeyer 1988a). Mahoney (1991) provides an integrative perspective on human change processes in psychotherapy that is based on cognitive science, organismic-systemic developmental theories, and a critical constructivism. His view is that there are constraints on a person's capacity for interpreting and altering experience, and these constraints interact dynamically with any change process.

Many constructionists consider the narrative as the essence of human systems of construing and communicating, and that which enters into narration and text as constituting human knowledge (Bruner 1986; Goodman 1978; Howard 1991; Mair 1988; Polkinghorne 1988). This narrative perspective is based on the notion that human beings think, perceive, and act according to narrative structures or story-form plots, and that this ability is what distinguishes us as users of language. That our everyday understanding reflects this story-type metaphor is perhaps revealed by the saying that one could understand another person well if one is able to "read" the other person "like a book." The narrative as root metaphor for psychology (Sarbin 1986b; Gergen and Gergen 1986) has significant implications. It offers an alternative ontology to realism in that narrative discourse about the world is taken not as a representation of a world independent of such representation but as a product of communal interchange that has its own psychological import. In other words, narrative psychology does not claim to have access to a language-independent world. When applied to therapeutic conversations, the narrative focus allows us to identify the transformations that occur during such conversations (Sluzki 1992). The social roots of language as a medium of thought and action also suggest a priority of the social over the individual (Harre 1986), contrary to the individualism of American psychology that was mentioned in the previous chapter. Using the narrative as a core metaphor, Harre (1987) proposed a social, discursive base for the conception of self as an alternative paradigm to methodological individualism.

This metatheoretical position of social constructionism has also been considered in terms of the power of discourse over social relations and practices. It provides a philosophical base for certain critical theorists (Foucault 1980; MacIntyre 1981). It is recognized that a particular type of narrative can confer power on a group to have a special voice over the ordinary voice of the citizen, as scientific discourse does in elevating the researcher's voice over the lay person's (Semin and Gergen 1990b). Thus, narrative discourse as a core metaphor in the metathesis of social constructionism permits a radical reconceptualization of knowledge in the human realm. It solidifies the view of psychology as a human science that is bound by its cultural and social location, with a potential for diversity in its meaning systems.

The constructionist interpretation of theorizing in psychology regards psychological theories as the products of constructions that are socially and culturally located (Stam, Rogers, and Gergen 1987). Concept application and theoretical modeling are human activities that give rise to the meaning systems used in our profession. Ontologically, theoretical concepts are not to be taken as preexisting, naturally occurring categories. Epistemologically, constructionism suggests a reflexive study of the very meaning-making processes constitutive of the psychological realm. Like any metathesis, constructionism has not been uniformly accepted and has yet to be fully evaluated for its proposed utility as a metathesis. As a proposal for an overarching, superordinate epistemology (Morgan 1991), it has been challenged on logical grounds and on the charge of allegiance to a continuing desire for certainty as granted by a prior set of epistemological standards (Sugarman 1992). Although this criticism is not likely to be acceptable to constructionists, the discussion and evaluation of metatheoretical frameworks will probably continue as proponents become more explicit about the goals and functions of such metalevel frameworks and as their critics become more reflective about the values and standards used to evaluate these metalevel proposals. In the end, a fundamental question we should ask of any metalevel perspective is how it relates to the conception of progress in our discipline and profession. When examining the diverse orientations in our field, we can attempt a metalevel analysis only by identifying the underlying assumptions and meta goals.

Another metatheoretical framework is the transactional perspective, which uses an organic, ecological metaphor as previously explained (Altman and Rogoff 1987). With its organismic world view, it subsumes as a group of compatible theories general system theory (von Bertalanffy 1968), Piaget's (1952) theory of cognitive development, Heider's (1958) social-psychological balance theory, Barker's (1968) ecological psychology, Bandura's (1978) model of reciprocal determinism, and others. Primarily a contextualist perspective integrated with Dewey and Bentley's (1949) transactionalism, the transactionalist framework promotes holistic units of analysis such as psychological processes and environments, and emphasizes the changing relationship among aspects of the whole. As Margolis (1980) had argued, whereas neither a molar nor a molecular theory alone is sufficient for explaining psychological phenomena, a conceptual system that treats subpersonal factors as embedded molecular components-of-molar processes can serve as an integrative framework. Very importantly, the transactional framework is capable of integrating the biological with the social. It allows us to include neuropsychology and biological functions (Bunge 1990; Panksepp 1990) in a holistic understanding of humans. It also provides a continuum between environmental psychology and other areas of professional psychology such as the clinical and the educational in following contextualist principles of theory, research, and practice. Rogoff's (1990) transactionalist conception of human development, for example, has implications for education and human change processes.

In the area of organizational psychology, the human relations, political, structural, and system paradigms seem to be transcended by a cultural paradigm (Yanow 1987). This is perhaps another example of a contextualist perspective serving as the integrative base of other conceptual approaches. It is not hard to see in the cultural paradigm a connection to social constructionism as well, in its rejection of the four previous ontological lenses in favor of an interpretive logic that treats actions and events as symbols and artifacts of construction within a cultural community. It is worth noting that Freudian theory has also been regarded as a metatheory by those followers of Freudian thinking who argue that it provides a universal language of the human psyche (Lesche 1973, 1981; Radnitzky 1970). Attempts are made to reinterpret other psychological theories in psychoanalytic terms. They represent an example of how the meta-assumptions and worldview of a conceptual system can sometimes be applied as a metathesis to other conceptual systems. However, as stated earlier, there must be a harmony of values, ontological presuppositions, and metagoals in order for an approach to be evaluated by the guidelines and standards of another orientation. Psychoanalysis itself was previously subjected to evaluation according to the metascientific thesis of logical positivism (Shafer 1970) and the criteria and methodological standards of natural science (Eysenck 1952). This has been considered by some (e.g., Lesche 1962, 1978) as an inappropriate exercise because the meta-assumptions and -goals of psychoanalysis are different from those of positivistic, natural science.

Finally, a metalevel framework in the form of an epistemological metathesis may be evolved from a meta-analysis of methodologies. The empirical study of researchers' applied epistemology and method choice, such as attempted in Hoshmand and Martin (in press), can yield an understanding of pragmatically sound applications of methods. A metamethodology partly based on the naturalized or empirical study of models of inquiry in use can perhaps guide researchers in decision making during the process of inquiry. From a pragmatic perspective, this proposed metamethodological development, as mentioned previously, is a response by philosophers to the problem of criteria and standards in a relativistic age following the rejection of foundationalism. Through empirical study of researchers' judgments and inquiry practices, we may be able to identify principles of sound judgment and practices that hold across diverse research paradigms. The development of such metamethodological principles, based on how well certain inquiry practices work in solving research problems, requires simultaneous advances in the profession's metatheoretical perspectives in support of the pluralistic uses of research paradigms. Our conceptual systems and methodological approaches are so closely linked that they must have a common meeting place in the metathesis that we hold. In the following chapter, we will examine paradigms of research and consider issues of methodology and method choice.

SUGGESTED ADDITIONAL LEARNING

1. Identify the sources of ideas in professional psychology for conceptualizing psychological problems and our practice.

2. Find examples of psychological concepts that are derived from everyday narrative understanding.

3. Explain the issues pertaining to selecting the unit of analysis, and consider them in relation to research and practice.

4. Identify the conditions and criteria for choosing a particular set of concepts or a formal conceptual system, and compare them with your own basis of conceptual preference.

5. Explain the uses of theory and discuss whether psychology should be considered a theoretical science.

6. Discuss the problems with capturing meaning and accounting for human intentions in psychological theorizing.

7. Identify the major types of core commitments in professional psychology, and discuss the implications of different root metaphors.

8. Reflect on your personal theories and preferred language for describing psychological events. What kinds of worldview and meta-assumptions do they indicate?

9. Find examples from a program of research that illustrate how conceptual issues are related to questions of methodology such as the choice of research problem and method of inquiry.

10. Discuss the following article by Fine and Turner on the pros and cons in particular uses of theories and concepts in professional practice:

Fine, M., and Turner, J. 1991. Tyranny and freedom: Looking at ideas in the practice of family therapy. *Family Process* 30: 307-20.

11. Debate on whether causal theories are possible and useful in psychology, using the following article by White as a basis for discussion:

White, P. A. 1990. Ideas about causation in philosophy and psychology. *Psychological Bulletin* 108: 3-18.

12. Evaluate the proposals for metatheoretical integration given in this chapter, and discuss their relevance to the area(s) of your professional interest.

5

Paradigms of Research

UNDERSTANDING PARADIGMS

Research paradigms are conceptual and methodological frameworks for guiding systematic inquiry. As the basis of particular choices of concepts and methods, they can be considered supermodels or scientific worldviews. There are ongoing debates on paradigm choice. It is important to recognize that the discussion about research paradigms may involve any or all of a number of interrelated issues that represent paradigm differences. First, there is the issue of theory choice. The type of conceptual orientation chosen represents a paradigm difference, as in the case of reductionistic versus contextualist theory choices. For example, methodological individualism or a conceptual bias toward the individual as the explanatory focus of psychological and social phenomena (Bhaskar 1979; Manicas and Rosenberg 1985) is considered to be a paradigmatic characteristic of traditional reductive hypothesis-testing research. Second is the issue of method choice. Our profession has been divided on the choice of research methods, with a tendency to polarize quantitative and qualitative or narrative approaches. Although the nature of method choice is usually linked to our theory choice, method preference in research is often assumed to be the essence of paradigm differences. A third kind of choice that has been referred to at times as a paradigm difference concerns the research strategies we use. Based on relative emphasis in purpose, some researchers are divided on their preference for hypothesis-testing as opposed to discovery or hypothesis-generating strategies. They may also vary in their relative reliance on experimental analogue and naturalistic approaches. These various dimensions add to the sense of divergence in research approaches in our field.

Other, less apparent differences are concerned with the logic of inference and argumentation in our approach to knowledge. For instance, nomothetic or group-based research utilizes statistical sampling and aggregation as its logic. Inferences are made about the characteristics of populations based on observations of a sample. Statements are couched in terms of general tendencies in reference to a statistically constructed normative picture. On the other hand, actuarial and case study research utilize theoretical sampling and comparison to a prototype, or the logic of parts to a whole. Particular events and cases may be chosen for their unique characteristics or as hypothesized exemplars of a type of phenomenon. Information is contextualized within a given case by its relationship to a qualitatively constructed interpretive context. A holistic, gestalt type of logic is used to deduce patterns in single as well as multiple cases (for replication or contrast). Even if replication is involved in both nomothetic statistical research and actuarial case studies, the process of inference and argumentation are sufficiently different to require different kinds of evaluation.

Above all, philosophical differences, as discussed previously in terms of ontological and epistemological assumptions as well as value stances and ideological commitments, represent the underlying reasons for variation in research orientation. For some researchers, an assumption of human agency would require the use of an intentional language of description and a methodology conducive to the analysis of intentional action (Harre, Clarke, and DeCarlo 1985). Preference for particular guiding metaphors in research implies particular methodological orientations. The narrative as guiding metaphor calls for a holistic methodology consistent with the assumption of irreducible meanings (Barnes 1981). Data in the form of natural language are to be treated as meaningful patterns and integrated wholes. In the narrative view, the central role of language as a social activity that gives rise to meanings also means a rejection of methodological individualism and its doctrine that social phenomena can be explained solely in terms of facts about individuals. As another example, action research with its emphasis on the activist role of the professional requires collaborative relationships with our human clientele in problem solving (Argyris, Putnam, and Smith 1985). The purpose of this type of research is to point to useful action.

Paradigm differences have implications for our approach to inquiry, our conception of the inquiry process, and our relationship with the human subject (Hoshmand 1989). The above introductory comments are intended to call attention to the many dimensions of research paradigms that may be compared and evaluated. We should question what is at issue whenever there is a discussion about paradigm differences. The fact that the basis of comparison and evaluation is not always made explicit has resulted in much confusion and unproductive rhetoric in paradigm debates.

UNRAVELING PARADIGM DEBATES

How may one participate in a productive discussion about research paradigms? First, we have to avoid paradigm polemics, even if it is convenient to use dichotomies. On close examination, many dichotomies are forced or misleading. Take, for example, the distinction between discovery and hypothesis testing. This distinction comes from Reichenbach's (1938) differentiation between the context of discovery and the context of verification in science. Although it has some utility in setting the role of formal logic in relation to theory testing, it does not help us to understand the practical reasoning involved throughout inquiry. The traditional assumption is that there are only two phases to inquiry, corresponding to the contexts of discovery and verification, and that different cognitive processes are involved in each, with critical evaluation being more essential to testing the end products of science. This conception of the inquiry process has been questioned by those who observed that evaluative processes occur throughout inquiry, and that a two-phase distinction is an oversimplification (Gutting 1980; Nickles 1980). Methodological decisions are no less important in research that has discovery and hypothesis generation as a primary purpose than in research aimed at the testing of specific hypotheses. Research conducted in areas of professional practice typically requires the flexible use of both discovery and verification strategies, a point that we will further consider.

Second, it is essential for us to be clear about the issue or dimension of difference that is under discussion. This is not readily accomplished, because we have not been in the habit of making explicit our philosophical assumptions, the language and type of arguments we use, or the horizon on which we wish to judge a particular orientation. Not infrequently, an entire paradigmatic approach would be rejected on the basis of the problems resulting from a particular manner in which the paradigm has been used. For example, the experimental paradigm has been rejected by those dissatisfied with much of the psychological research conducted in the hypothetico-deductive tradition. It appears that the problem lies partly in the behavioristic conceptions of complex phenomena and with the narrow hypothesis testing restricted by operationalization (MacKenzie 1977). To those who find experimental hypothesis testing useful, the total rejection of the experimental paradigm would mean "throwing the baby out with the bath water." If we can accept that reductionism is involved to different degrees in most conceptual and research efforts, then we must keep in mind that "how" to study our subject matter does not entirely determine "what" it is. In other words, epistemological reduction (though closely related to ontological assumptions) is not completely identical with ontological reduction. Many upsetting arguments have arisen from concerns that reductive approaches to knowledge have dehumanized the domain of psychology. These concerns about our subject matter are ontological and metaphysical, and do not necessarily have to be leveled with epistemological reductions.

Third, we have to evaluate and compare paradigms on the same dimension, using criteria appropriate to the assumptions of each paradigm. This may require an openness to considering criteria other than those we typically associate with a preferred paradigm. For example, it will not be appropriate to confuse an ideological argument about free will with discussions about the empirical utility of deterministic concepts of causality, a point that was made in the previous chapter. Furthermore, if our conception of causality is the issue, it will not be appropriate to evaluate agential and narrative models of research (that are associated with final cause or intentionality) according to the linear conception of causality that is associated with reductive behavioristic research. (Recall Rychlak's discussion of concepts of causality in Lockean and Kantian paradigms in his 1969 article). It is only fair to use the language and criteria appropriate to a given paradigm for its understanding. This is a more productive way to begin a conversation about paradigms that are not our initial preference.

Until the profession can engage in paradigm discussions with clarity and common points of reference, paradigm debates will have a paralyzing effect that can impede progress. The thesis of this book is that different models and methods of knowledge serve different purposes and have their place on the continuum of knowledge. Our other guiding metaphor is that there is a complementarity or dialectical relationship between contrasting approaches. If we think of each paradigm as a different world hypothesis (Pepper 1942), each can be valued for its utility in giving us credible accounts of our phenomena of interest. Just as Newtonian mechanics can account for many aspects of the constancies in our physical world, quantum theory can present a credible account of dynamic processes at the subatomic level. The complementary use of alternative paradigms is implied in the following statement by Dewey and Bentley (1949):

> Our assertion is the right to see in union what becomes important to see in union; together with a right to see in separation what is important to see in separation—each in its own time and place. (112)

The empirically and pragmatically minded members of the profession will certainly view our research paradigms as hypotheses to be tested in time and in those contexts that we consider important. Others may set their preferences based on the personal appeal of the kind of account of reality afforded by a given paradigm, the same way that all humans choose particular stories to live by. Still others would construct grand stories that may capture the themes of the different accounts, such as in the form of metatheories that we examined in the previous chapter.

Before we address the question of paradigm choice in research, and the prospect of evolving higher-order methodological principles that may be useful for all systems of inquiry, I will comment on the potentials and contributions of each of the existing paradigms from the standpoint of research on professional practice.

CONVENTIONAL PARADIGMS AND EXTENSIONS OF EXPERIMENTAL METHODOLOGY

The conventional research paradigm in psychology has been the experimental paradigm. Its prevailing use is related to the historical developments and the prevailing values and sociopolitical context described in the previous chapters. As a scientific paradigm with the promise of rigor, it provided the means by which psychology could gain legitimacy as a science-based profession. In borrowing the methodology of the experimental sciences, psychology also subscribed inevitably to the objectivist assumptions of the positivistic paradigm. The experimenter tries to control the research situation in order to isolate the phenomenon of interest. Psychological states and meanings are operationally inferred from observable, measurable behavior. There is a reliance on mathematical transformation of the physical evidence presumed to reflect the psychological, and subsequent argumentation by statistical inference. Confidence in the research findings also depends on the statistical significance of the measured results, even though the latter does not guarantee substantive importance. The research process entails an elaborate chain of deduction by which psychological constructs related to a particular theory and its myriad of auxiliary concepts are translated into procedurally viable operations and measured observations are subjected to statistical interpretations that are linked to the original theory through a further chain of inferred correspondence with the psychological phenomenon of interest.

In general, the experimental research paradigm aims at the study of systematic relationships among targeted variables while eliminating sources of error and contamination. With the aid of operationalization and measurement, and numerical representation of the data, researchers attempt to determine the systematic variability of the factors under study by controlling for the influence of extraneous factors and minimizing error variance. The prototype research design involves comparison between experimental and control groups, in the testing of a hypothesis about differences between populations represented by the group samples. This design originated from early interest in measuring individual and group differences in psychological traits. Aided by the development of inferential statistics and sampling theory, this became the major approach in experimental research in psychology by the 1950s. Statistical thinking has since assumed an important role in the reasoning used by researchers, with the possibility of its own flaws and fallacies (Campbell 1974; Williams 1979). Violation of the assumptions in statistical tests (such as the independence of observations, or normality and homogeneity of variance in distributions) can lead to incorrect decisions in hypothesis testing (Darlington and Carlson 1987; Wilcox 1987). The practice of rejecting a null hypothesis as a way of corroborating psychological theories also tends to result in a proliferation of theoretical positions (Meehl 1978; Serlin 1987). Researchers have to be concerned with selecting designs and statistical tests of sufficient power and at the same time be able to specify the magnitude of effect that is sufficient to test a hypothesis (Serlin and Lapsley 1985). The question is raised as to whether single studies based on this type of statistical hypothesis-testing approach can contribute to knowledge in the profession.

In certain areas of inquiry into the problems of professional practice, adaptations of the experimental paradigm in the form of analogues have been found necessary. For example, a clinical or counseling analogue is used to simulate under controlled conditions the treatment process undergone by clients (Heller 1971; Munley 1974). This common practice in the 1960s and 1970s involved simplification and standardization of treatment procedures. Therapists followed procedures defined in standard treatment manuals compiled for research purposes rather than the natural interaction and problem solving necessitated by situational and client problems that arise. Analogue researchers find themselves invoking questionable assumptions of uniformity such as among treatment agents and clients (Kiesler 1966; Paul 1967). It was realized that we must ask, instead, which intervention by what type of therapist is most effective with a given type of client and problem. Due to the nature of treatment, observation, and measurement in analogue settings, reactivity has been a major limitation of experimental research on practice. Smith, Glass, and Miller (1980) in conducting a meta-analysis of studies on psychotherapy outcome, found reactivity ratings to be correlated more strongly with effect size than other variables. Findings such as theirs suggest that the effects of psychotherapy may have been consistently overestimated by reactive measures. Artifacts and biases in conventional behavioral research have always posed problems of validity (Rosenthal 1988; Rosenthal and Rosnow 1969). Generalization to naturalistic settings beyond the experimental situation is an issue for professional psychologists who are supposed to apply research-generated knowledge to situations of practice.

Concerns about the reactive effects of experimental analogues and the external validity of experimental studies of the phenomena of practice have led to an interest in alternatives within the scientific research paradigm. Quasi-experimental and time-series designs (Cook and Campbell 1979; Kenny 1975) and single-subject designs (Barlow and Hersen 1984; Barrios and Hartmann 1988; Kazdin 1982) provide an extended repertoire for the researcher of practice. Other possibilities include longitudinal studies of phenomena that have developmental characteristics, and modeling of change to approximate the dynamic nature of clinical phenomena (Collins and Horn 1991; Francis, Fletcher, Stuebing, Davidson, and Thompson 1991). New statistical methods, such as path analysis, have been developed to make causal inferences without using experimental designs that involve the manipulation of an independent variable (Patterson 1986). For examples of specific applications of experimental research and extensions of the experimental paradigm in the areas of professional practice, the reader can refer to a number of sources (Heppner, Kivlighan, and Wampold 1992; Kazdin 1992; Kendall and Butcher 1982; Stricker and Keisner 1985).

Developments in statistics, experimental designs, and computer programs have in recent years expanded the conventional research paradigm and equipped researchers with a variety of techniques. For example, factor analyses and regression analyses are combined in structural equation modeling, which enables researchers to measure latent variables and study the relationship between different constructs. In clinical practice, cluster analysis can be used to form diagnostic groups or other homogeneous groups. Methods of sequential analyses are developed to analyze social interactions (e.g., in family therapy) that are of interest to practitioners. In view of the complexity of phenomena encountered by the professional psychologist, the availability of multidimensional scaling and multivariate statistics and research designs would seem to have an intuitive appeal. Following a mapping metaphor, researchers hope to use these tools to chart the complex territory of policy research and practice.

The fruitfulness of experimental research on therapeutic practice has, however, continued to be questioned (Gendlin 1986). The central issue is that operationalism imposes constraints on the conceptualization of the phenomena of practice. In addition to disagreement about how best to define the relevant constructs, there is also an inherent limitation in any form of reductive experimentation involving operationalization and measurement. Any single operationalization of a construct will consist not only of the variance associated with the construct concerned but also error variance and other unique nonrandom variance or bias. In other words, no single measure can be a perfect representation of a construct. To remedy the shortcomings of operationalization, multiple operationalism and the use of multiple measures had been recommended (Campbell and Fiske 1959; Webb, Campbell, Schwartz, and Sechrest 1966). This multiplism was formulated by Cook (1985) as a critical multiplism. Experimental and quasi-experimental research are to be improved with the use of multiple methods, multiple stakeholders posing research questions to probe multiple issues, multiple modes of data gathering from different sources, and multiple agents using different theoretical and value frameworks to analyze the data (Chen and Rossi 1981; Cronbach 1982a; Cronbach, Ambron, Dornbusch, *et al.* 1980; Dunn 1982; Shadish 1986). The combined use of discovery and theory-testing strategies and the use of multiple methods in psychotherapy research are examples of multiplism (Angus 1992; Shoham-Salomon 1990). Another use of multiple strategies is to combine correlational and experimental approaches, such as in psychotherapy research, to derive empirically tested aptitude-treatment interactions and aptitude-outcome interactions (Shoham-Salomon and Hannah 1991) that take into account the reciprocal influence of clients on the process and outcome of therapy (Pinsof 1989).

It is clear that the profession cannot do without conventional research methods because of their utility in testing specific hypotheses particularly concerning technological and practical matters such as whether one form of intervention is more efficacious than another and whether an overall program of practice makes a difference that is not just a function of time and random events. There is a risk, however, of assuming that experimental methodology and statistics would automatically confer rigor and validity on our research efforts. Not only can generalizability or external validity be limited by experimental controls that are intended to ensure internal validity, but whether meaningful interpretation is possible in this type of research can be an issue because of the long chain of inferences involved. The overconfidence associated with the use of the experimental paradigm and statistical techniques in the so-called soft areas of psychology has been questioned by Meehl (1978, 1991). Researchers are beginning to appreciate the need to evaluate the cumulative progress of experimental inquiry into particular domains, such as with meta-analysis of a group of studies (Bangert-Drowns 1986; Glass, McGaw, and Smith 1981; Nietzel and Trull 1988; Rosenthal 1991), even though the individual studies are hampered by the kind of ambiguities of interpretation discussed by Meehl. Using examples from industrial-organizational psychology, Hunter and Schmidt (1990) and Schmidt (1992) argued for the use of meta-analysis as a means of correcting erroneous statistical conclusions from single research studies. Another proposed remedy is to apply Bayesian analysis rather than rely on statistical hypothesis testing with a single sample (Winkler 1972). Prior research findings are used in this type of analysis, and estimates of population values are adjusted on the basis of new evidence.

In addition to better ways of dealing with the errors of sampling and measurement, the shift from the misplaced confidence in individual studies to series of programmatic research (that can be subject to meta-analysis) is probably a more appropriate way of reaping the fruits of conventional paradigmatic research. One reason is that single criterion-behaviors observed on single occasions can only give low estimates of cross-situational behavior stability. Even with the help of multivariate models, it is costly and practically impossible to conduct a single experiment that will instantiate all possible variations of subjects, settings, observers, measures, and other temporal and contextual factors (Cronbach 1975). Multiple levels of analysis and heterogeneity of variables are more possible to achieve with a planned series of studies. It is recognized in philosophy of science that research programs, rather than an ideal crucial experiment, can test multiple rival hypotheses

(Popper 1972). Programmatic research provides more opportunities for the reasoned use of multiple methods to yield progressively useful findings (Lakatos 1978). The implications of multiplism and programmatic research will be discussed subsequently under methodological pluralism.

Professional psychology needs research that is relevant and sensitive to the realities of practice. To improve research in the areas of practice, there has been more attention to the social validity of measurement and the assessment of clinical significance (Elliott, James, Reimschueseel, Cislo, and Sack 1985; Elliott and Shapiro 1992; Jacobson 1988; Jacobson, Follette, and Revenstorf 1984; Jacobson and Revenstorf 1988; Jacobson and Truax 1991; Kazdin 1977; Mahrer and Nadler 1986; Wolf 1978). Some of the attempts at addressing the issue of practical significance have involved statistical procedures of gauging the amount of deviation from particular populations and estimating a reliable index of change. These statistical solutions, however, cannot be separated from normative or value-laden considerations of the criteria for clinical significance (Hollon and Flick 1988; Kendall and Grove 1988; Saunders, Howard, and Newman 1988; Wampold and Jenson 1986). Increased efforts have been made to draw upon the knowledge of practice to inform research as much as using the implications of research to inform practice (Elliott 1983; Hayes and Nelson 1981; Kazdin, Siegel and Bass 1990; Stricker & Keisner, 1985). Researchers are urged to pay attention to how clinicians derive understanding from their observations during practice, and to help operationalize and evaluate the ideas and models originating, for instance, from systemic family therapy practice (Eisler, Dare, and Szmukler 1988). There is a call for innovation in clinical research methods and the evaluation of experimental methodology among those committed to this paradigm (Morris, Turner, and Szykula 1988; Newman and Howard 1991). These various efforts to improve the profession's use of the experimental research paradigm are encouraging.

The movement toward multiplism has meant, to some researchers, extensions of methodology beyond the experimental and quasi-experimental paradigms. They feel that the conventional paradigms do not yield satisfactory answers to certain types of questions (such as about human volition and the meaning and quality of subjective experiences). It is also fair to expect professional psychologists to consider more naturalistic, field-oriented alternatives that are suited for investigating the phenomena of practice, especially if they involve the same modes of interaction and natural language data that we use everyday with clients in practice.

NARRATIVE AND HERMENEUTICAL APPROACHES

The clearest alternative to the more traditional research paradigms consists of those approaches to human inquiry that emphasize the use of natural language and the interpretation of meanings and experiences as narrated or found in text. They include ethnomethodology and other ethnographic and grounded-theory approaches, as well as phenomenological and hermeneutic orientations that follow the narrative as a guiding metaphor. Although they have different origins and somewhat distinct communities of users, these approaches share a number of common characteristics. It is assumed that knowledge is a social construction, and that inquiry is always embedded in a personal and cultural context. The human subject, as a coconstructor of the data in the dialogical exchange of meanings, is to be treated in an egalitarian manner. There is a greater reciprocity between the researcher and the other participants in a project. The process of inquiry tends to be relatively open, with an emphasis on intensive observations and thick description. For this reason, these paradigms have been viewed as more supportive of discovery than theory testing, even though it is not entirely true that they are not useful for theory testing.

The ethnographic paradigm has been a major force in what Lincoln and Guba (1985) referred to as naturalistic inquiry. It originated from anthropology as a discipline and shares with the phenomenological orientation an interest in the native experience and indigenous meanings of human subjects (Geertz 1973; Sanday 1983; Schutz 1970; Spindler 1970). It utilizes participant modes of data gathering and content analysis of natural language data (Altheide 1987; Jorgensen 1989; Spradley 1979, 1980). As with ethnomethodology that has been developed in sociology (Garfinkel 1967; Pollner and Goode 1990)), ethnographic inquiry is practiced by immersion in natural social settings (Filstead 1970; Rose 1990; Van Maanen 1983). It has been adopted in educational research, organizational studies, and program evaluation (Bogdan 1972; Bogdan and Biklen 1982; Goetz and LeCompte 1984; Patton 1978; Schwartzman 1992; Skrtic 1985), all of which relate to practice. Its application to research of relevance to therapeutic practice has been documented by Hoshmand (1989), and has included clients' experience of psychotherapy and the perceptions, life issues, and counseling needs of special populations. The ethnographic paradigm is highly appropriate for the study of groups, organizations and other natural units (Lincoln 1985; Patton 1990)). It also provides a useful means of understanding the overall organizational or program context in program evaluation. Combined with cultural and developmental perspectives, it has been fruitfully utilized in research in educational psychology and practice (Tharp and Gallimore 1988). Researchers are beginning to apply it to the study of family therapy (Kuehl, Newfield, and Joanning 1990).

Closely related to the ethnographic approach is the grounded theory approach (Glaser and Strauss 1967), which is also associated with symbolic interactionism (Blumer 1969). Originally used in sociology, it emphasizes thick description and participant observation procedures. Emergent patterns of understanding are evolved from descriptive data and framed in theoretical terms. The grounded theory approach is discovery oriented and intended to be a corrective to the over reliance on preconceived ideas and conventional hypothesis testing by grounding the generation of theories in observation. It is a systematic approach with built-in processes of internal validation and checks for contrary evidence such as negative case analysis (Conrad 1978). It has been used by psychotherapy researchers in discovering the meanings of therapeutic events (Angus and Rennie 1989; Rennie 1990, 1992; Rennie, Phillips, and Quartaro 1988).

The phenomenological paradigm has its origins in phenomenology as a philosophy and in the study of perception and consciousness (Giorgi 1985; Merleau-Ponty 1962; Misiak and Sexton 1983). It emphasizes the embedded role of the researcher and the dialogical relationship with the human subject in inquiry. It defines the researcher's attitude as open and atheoretical yet reflective and questioning (Giorgi 1983). Its concepts and procedures are designed to illuminate the structure and meaning of human experience as lived. Interview and textual data are utilized. Research findings are regarded as situated and validated by thematic convergence. The phenomenological mode of understanding (Kvale 1983) is distinguished by its departure from dualistic and objectivist assumptions. It emphasizes descriptive and interpretive procedures that would allow a phenomenon to reveal its essence (Valle and Halling 1989). Examples of phenomenological studies of relevance to therapeutic practice have been cited in Hoshmand (1989), including the study of self-esteem and the experience of victimization, anger, and tragedy. Other applications of the phenomenological paradigm can be found in organizational studies and experiential and personological inquiry into health-related conditions (Levy 1981; Montgomery 1982; Shontz 1985). The emphasis in these studies is on determining the essential structure of such psychological phenomena as experienced in contexts that permit as full an explication of the experience as possible (Van Maanen 1990).

Other narrative-hermeneutic approaches are also characterized by a focus on natural language data, especially as examined in terms of various aspects of "text" (Polkinghorne 1988; Ricoeur 1984). While classic forms of hermeneutic inquiry relied on written texts, contemporary hermeneutics and narrative approaches often treat human interaction and discourse as a type of "living text." Such approaches differ from the grounded theory orientation by being used sometimes in conjunction with a particular theoretical framework (Sarbin 1986b). History, interview, and archival methods may be used in these approaches (Bertaux 1981; Mishler 1986a). Narrative psychology has drawn upon the humanities and may provide an umbrella for such areas as discourse analysis, which has its own body of literature (Atkinson and Heritage 1984; Moerman 1988; Potter and Wetherell 1987a). It may be allied with the hermeneutic approach adopted by some phenomenological researchers in terms of a reliance on textual analysis. Despite differences in origin, most narrative and hermeneutic approaches share the constructionist assumptions of knowledge being experientially derived and socially constructed. Patterns of meaning are to be discovered dialogically by the researcher in transaction with other embedded participants or producers of the textual data.

Examples of hermeneutic investigation in psychology are reported in Packer and Addison (1989a). Of note is the use of narratives from open-ended interviews to discover different voices that speak from distinct perspectives, as illustrated by the study of moral conflict and choice (Brown, Tappan, Gilligan, Miller, and Argyris 1989). The narrative approach has been used in personological research and studies of life themes (Csikszentimihalyi and Beattie 1979; McAdams 1988; McAdams and Ochberg 1988; Levinson 1978; Rabin, Zucker, Emmons, and Frank 1990). The use of stories in organizational studies has also been reported (Martin, Feldman, Hatch, and Sim, 1983; Mitroff and Kilmann 1975). Interest in the application of qualitative research methods from the narrative-hermeneutic paradigm is becoming evident in the area of family therapy and research into the family (Gail and Newfield 1992; Gilgun, Daly, and Handel 1992; La Rossa and Wolf 1985; Moon, Dillon, and Sprenkle 1990, 1991).

One question that has been asked of the interpretive paradigms is whether such inquiry would result in useful action. Although the primary interest is that of understanding rather than a technological one, hermeneutic inquiry has been linked with praxis (Hollinger 1985; Packer 1985). In such cases, action and text are metaphorically connected as inquiry is guided by a practical concern. The narrative-hermeneutic approach is futuristic in the sense of anticipating meaningful action (Gergen and Kaye 1992; Ricoeur 1983, 1985). By reflectively explicating unquestioned assumptions and meanings, hermeneutics can also bring about new action with enhanced understanding. An example is found in Misgeld and Jardine (1989) who conducted a hermeneutic inquiry into the educational doctrine of elementary schooling. The study suggested that educational practice based on the taken-for-granted doctrine could be modified as its justification was found to be questionable. This study not only illustrates the utility of hermeneutic inquiry, but connotes a critical perspective.

CRITICAL THEORY AS A PARADIGMATIC VIEW

In chapter 3, the critical perspective was mentioned in relation to the questioning of commonly held cultural assumptions and institutions. What distinguishes critical theory as a paradigm position is its claim to a different epistemological stance from that of the received view. Rather than subscribing to a universalist foundation, critical theorists tend to be constructionist in perspective. They object to the power implications of the dominant discourse legitimated by traditional scientific methods of knowledge. As a social criticism of this and other institutions, it was articulated in the works of Karl Marx, Max Weber, and Emile Durkheim, followed by writers of the Frankfurt school, the French structuralists and literary poststructuralism, the sociology of knowledge, and feminist theory (Popkewitz 1990). Though less prominent as a different voice, critical theory is finding its way into American psychology, mainly in terms of feminist interests. The question of feminist contributions to psychological theorizing, research, and practice has been under discussion (Gilligan, Ward, and Taylor 1988; Hare-Mustin and Marecek 1990), and the potentials for shaping psychological inquiry and practice asserted (O'Connell and Russ, 1991).

Feminists in America consider the dominant paradigm of knowledge as European, male oriented and closed to the participation of women and other minority cultures (Gergen 1988; Gilligan 1990; Hooks 1984). By adopting a constructionist stance, alternative modes of knowledge such as women's ways of knowing are recognized (Belenky, Clinchy, Goldberger, and Tarule 1986; Salner 1985; Shrewsbury 1987), with implications for pedagogy. Developmental psychology has benefited from this influence (Gilligan 1982; Jacklin and McBride-Chang 1991), as have social and cognitive psychology (Lott 1991; Morawski and Agronick, 1991). New clinical understanding is beginning to surface in the professional psychology literature (Belle 1982; Jack 1991; Miller 1986), along with feminist counseling and therapy (Enns 1993). The influence of feminist thought on mainstream psychological research has not, however, been as extensive as some have hoped (Lykes and Stewart 1986; Walsh 1989).

Although some feminist writers have promoted the feminist perspective on knowledge as a new epistemology (Harding 1986; Harding and Hintikka 1983), there is no single methodology associated with feminist research and epistemology (Riger 1992). Ethnographic and narrative-hermeneutic methods such as oral history interviews are generally used in conjunction with this critical perspective (Gluck and Patai 1991; Neilsen 1990). When the hermeneutic approach is applied from a critical perspective to deconstruct or make visible that which has become invisible by training and custom, it is referred to as critical hermeneutics. Interpretive research of this nature has the potential to emancipate or free people through the new understandings that are transformative (Lather 1986). It is possible that the influence of feminist perspectives on psychology will be gradually realized. Deconstruction in the form of social and moral criticism, or the analysis of scientific discourse in terms of power implications, can have implications for theory construction and practice in professional psychology (Chodorow 1989; Enns 1988; Gavey 1989; Walters, Carter, Papp, and Silverman 1988). Gender bias in research practice is also an area that requires continuing professional attention (Denmark, Russo, Frieze, and Sechzer 1988).

Besides supporting feminist theory and research, critical theory has been used in the deconstruction of the psychology of the self and the politics of social identities (Sampson 1989b, 1993), as well as in social and developmental psychology (Broughton 1987; Parker and Shotter 1990). Its methodological approach is generally discursive. As emphasized in chapter 3, a critical perspective on our approach to knowledge should raise questions about how we depict social realities and whether biases due to gender, culture, social class, and worldviews are sufficiently acknowledged. It is in this sense that critical theory as a paradigmatic view can contribute to the development of reflexive knowledge and a reflective profession.

TRANSACTIONAL AND SYSTEMIC PERSPECTIVES ON RESEARCH

In the previous chapter, the transactional framework and its historical and conceptual roots were described. As a research paradigm, it shares a number of common methodological principles with the system's perspective (Bateson 1979; von Bertalanffy 1968), sometimes conceived in cybernetic terms (Keeney and Morris 1985a). Researchers and participants are considered to be an embedded part of the phenomenon under study. There is an emphasis on context and the cocontribution of all participants to the data. Dynamic change is assumed to be inherent in any system, not to be represented by standard measurement of fixed variables. Events as the confluence of temporal, contextual, and psychological processes must be studied in interactional terms and in naturalistic contexts (Bronfenbrenner 1979; Magnusson 1981). Whereas the transactional paradigm is regarded as favoring methodological pluralism (Altman and Rogoff 1987), the procedural characteristics of research from a system's perspective have yet to be articulated for popular adoption by researchers in professional psychology (Hoshmand 1989).

Applications of the transactional paradigm can be found in environmental psychology, health promotion, and policy research (Stokols 1992; Stokols and Altman 1987). It has implications for the study of the social development of the self (Rogoff 1990) and human change processes in psychotherapy (Mahoney 1991). Applications of the system's perspective to research in professional psychology is most evident in the family therapy area (Kantor and Andreozzi 1985; Keeney and Morris 1985b; Steier 1985). Applications of system's theory from a human science perspective has also been proposed (Krippner, Ruttenber, Engelman, and Granger 1985). The slow development of systemic methodology in psychological research relevant to professional practice may be reflective of methodological individualism and the behavioristic bias of mainstream psychology.

As stated in the previous chapter, the transactionalist paradigm may serve as an integrative or metatheoretical perspective. Transactionalist and systemic paradigms enable us to include the biological and the social-ecological in psychological studies of human functioning. It is consistent with holistic orientations in all areas of professional practice. Its significance consists in moving the profession away from methodological individualism.

OTHER GUIDING METAPHORS FOR RESEARCH IN PROFESSIONAL PSYCHOLOGY

There are two other important orientations to research that are distinguished by their guiding metaphors, perhaps more so than unique methodologies. One concerns the study of human actions as intentional and purposeful behavior. The other has action outcomes as a goal, following an activist ideology, and is often referred to as "action research."

The study of meaningful and intentional action is associated with axiological assumptions of our human capacity for choice and ontologically driven epistemological assumptions of the nonreducibility of holistic acts to isolated physical events (Gauld and Shotter 1977). It has not been distinguished, however, by a unique methodology. Methods of traditional experimentation have been utilized in some empirical research on volitional action (Howard and Conway 1986, 1987). More recently, self-experimentation has been used to demonstrate self-determination (Howard, Myers, and Curtin 1991). Intentionality has also been studied in the therapeutic context, using qualitative methods and a grounded theory approach. Rennie (1992) described a series of studies on the client's reflexivity as the fount of intentionality. It is suggested that in the state of reflexivity, the person creates the relevant covert experience and the intentionality behind the overt. Through clients' self-reflection, therapeutic change is understood at the level of intentional acts.

Much discussion continues regarding the conceptual implications of human agency for our understanding of cognition and behavior (Harre 1986; Margolis 1986a). Social constructionist approaches treat human agency as arising from one's concept of self that is socially and culturally derived (Bruner 1990; Hermans, Kempen, and Van Loon 1992; Williams 1992). Dialogical forms of research in professional psychology as promoted in constructionist paradigms, and the movement in personality and social psychology towards treating the human subject as a co-investigator, may be generally considered to be influenced by the human agency metaphor (Hermans and Bonarius 1991). Perhaps a transactionalist paradigm may be used to conduct research as guided by this sociocultural interpretation of the metaphor of human agency.

The action research mode, on the other hand, can be traced to the ideas of Dewey (1929, 1933) and Lewin (1948). Intervention on problems is conceived as an approach to theory building, and theory building, as a guide to intervention. In other words, knowledge is grounded in action, and action allows knowledge to be tested. Its contemporary advocates are Argyris and associates (Argyris 1982, 1993; Argyris, Putnam, and Smith 1985; Argyris and Schon 1978, 1989). As a research paradigm, it emphasizes collaborative inquiry that is empowering of the participants (Torbert 1976). Inquiry is aimed at the description of problems as well as finding solutions. For example, members of an organization can be helped to uncover their implicit theories of action and to modify them in order to bring about organizational changes. The researcher helps to evaluate an organization's capacity for learning and use the data on existing barriers and ineffective learning to design and implement interventions that would build trust, resolve conflicts, and enable innovations. With problem solving as a guiding metaphor, it offers a highly appropriate model for professional psychology. Research concerning needs assessment, program evaluation, and the testing of specific therapeutic and educational interventions may be subsumed under this action mode (Nuttal and Ivey 1978; Torbert 1981). In general, the field orientation of action research means that naturalistic methods are most appropriate. The use of ethnographic methods in program evaluation is one such example (Guba and Lincoln 1989; Patton 1978, 1980). Organizational studies that attempt to link research with practice are consistent with the action research mode (Lawler, Mohrman, Mohrman, Ledford, Cummings, *et al.* 1985).

The action research mode is a response to the call for socially relevant research. In the area of health psychology, researchers have been asked to consider the social significance of their methodological decisions, such as regarding the selection of target problems, populations, and health promotion strategies (Geller 1991; Winnett, Moore, and Anderson 1991). These types of considerations surrounding the social validity of research that is oriented to intervention can set examples for similar research in other areas of professional practice. The action research mode will be further considered in chapter 9 in relation to the integration of science and practice in the development of the professional psychologist.

Keeping in mind the range of available research paradigms and methodological options, we will next consider the issues of paradigm choice and the implications of methodological pluralism.

PARADIGM CHOICE, METHODOLOGICAL PLURALISM, AND THE EVALUATION OF METHODOLOGIES

Paradigm choice in psychological research has been restricted by the historical emphasis on experimental research in our discipline, as well as the cultural, sociopolitical, and value contexts of our development as a profession. With the new conversations about alternative models of inquiry, and under the intellectual climate of postmodernism, there is a greater latitude of choice. Although educational influences and professional-reward systems will continue to shape the scientific worldview of our students, commitment to the philosophical assumptions and practices of particular paradigms is additionally a function of personal factors. One's temperament, native ways of knowing, and personal worldview are likely to contribute to the epistemic style in use. On the other hand, there seems to be a human capacity to develop modes of learning that are new and unfamiliar, as long as we remain open to the full range of possibilities.

In psychological terms, different cognitive styles are favored in different research orientations. In postmodern opinions, the propositional way of thinking that is associated with most of our dominant conceptual and methodological paradigms is regarded as the "paradigmatic mode". In contrast, the "narrative mode" associated with more holistic and interpretive (rather than logico-analytical) approaches is considered to have been insufficiently emphasized (Smith and Heshusius 1986). This distinction between the two modes came from Bruner (1986), who conceived of different patterns of thought as representing different ways of constructing knowledge and worldviews. (We will further consider the cognitive aspects of epistemic styles and ways of knowing in chapter 7.) The contrast between these two modes was given an excellent illustration in the area of psychotherapy process research by Rennie and Toukmanian (1992a), who regard the tension as necessary. A pluralistic orientation to research that encourages multiplicity in modes of thought should regard differing cognitive styles as potentially complementary in utility. Whether the profession can make this dialectic a creative tension depends on our willingness to avoid hegemony and to engage in open dialogue.

The suggestion of treating all systems of knowing as potentially useful does not necessarily translate into a risky type of epistemological relativism in which rationality can no longer be defined. Regardless of our personal preferences, we should be able to articulate the basis of such preferences and to evaluate our working assumptions and methods in a reasoned fashion. Methodological pluralism does not mean a thoughtless eclecticism. In the previous chapter, we recognized the value of metatheory in psychotherapy integration and how it may counter thoughtless eclecticism involving orientations with incompatible philosophical assumptions. As a metalevel proposal, methodological pluralism means more than a simplistic, atheoretical application of diverse methods. There should be a higher-order rationale or metareasoning involved in the selective, syncretic use of multiple methods. The search for a metalevel framework as the rationale for the practice of pluralistic method choices seems to be best assisted by a pragmatic conception of science.

In essence, the pragmatist orientation to knowledge is that formal inquiry and all attempts at knowing are purposeful ways of acting upon the world. They are motivated by our practical and existential concerns. Research is therefore a form of human problem solving that improves with experience. In psychology, pragmatist views were expressed by James (1907) and Dewey (Dewey 1957, Schlipp 1951). Recent discourse in the philosophy of science has also taken a pragmatic turn (Bernstein 1986; Laudan 1990; Rorty 1991; Toulmin 1972, 1983). It is argued that pragmatism can reconcile social constructionist perspectives with the new realism in the postmodern age of nonfoundationalist science (Margolis 1986b). Rather than formal rules based on a particular foundation of knowledge, research methodologies are to be understood in terms of the logic in use that is functional from a heuristic point of view (Kaplan 1964). The pragmatic view of inquiry stresses, therefore, the actual practices and applied epistemology of researchers. Hoshmand and Martin (in press) offer metamethodological understandings derived from studying the research praxis and applied epistemologies of programmatic researchers in therapeutic practice.

Research as a form of problem solving requires that we make flexible use of a broad range of methods to meet the needs of a given problem context. The pragmatic orientation to inquiry involves syncretic strategies in which the complementary strengths of different methods are employed. Triangulation of methods is the attempt to maximize the yield of single methods by using several methods in conjunction (Brewer and Hunter 1989). Like fishermen casting nets of different mesh, researchers who utilize multiple concepts and methods in triangulation hope to obtain a better "catch." Proponents of a planned critical multiplism (Cook 1985; Shadish 1986) have a similar purpose in counterbalancing the limitations of single methodologies with the strengths of other approaches. Warwick (1983a) explained how extensive and intensive methods could be combined to enhance both generalizability and qualitative depth of meaning. When data generated with different methods show divergence or are inconclusive, it prompts the researcher to probe deeper into the problem at hand. This is another benefit of methodological pluralism.

Examples of multimethod research of interest to professional psychologists include the study of therapeutic practice (Angus 1992; Angus and Rennie, 1989; Martin & Stelmaczonek, 1988), psychological aspects of health problems (Gordon & Shontz, 1990), and families with various types of problems (Brody & Sigel 1990). In the last example, Brody and Sigel provide a rare collection of biographies of programs of research in the family area, in which the researchers explained their method choices and their implications for continuing inquiry. This is an excellent resource and represents the type of publication from which the practicing researcher can benefit. The fruitfulness of pluralistic method choices can be empirically evaluated in the context of programmatic research and illuminated by access to the researchers' rationale for their decisions, as attempted in Hoshmand and Martin (in press).

It is also instructive to examine how a particular topic or a domain of research has been investigated by a variety of research methods derived from different paradigms. For example, Toukmanian and Rennie (1992b) present a number of research programs in therapeutic practice that are based on different methodological paradigms. Stanfield and Dennis (1993) present both quantitative and qualitative approaches to cross-cultural inquiry. In chapter 4 of the present book, the cross-fertilization of theoretical concepts and methods from diverse areas was mentioned in relation to the development of metatheoretical frameworks.

The informed choice of any given model of inquiry and its methodology requires descriptive understanding of the paradigm in question and a certain degree of familiarity with its application. Thoughtful evaluation involves an awareness of the criteria we apply and how our judgments are justified. A pluralistic orientation has implications for the evaluation of methodological applications. The problem for the profession is that pluralistic methods also mean multiple and potentially different standards of evaluation. As explained previously, each paradigm is associated with particular ontological assumptions and epistemic, as well as other, values. A viable methodological pluralism will depend not only on our ability to communicate effectively over our differences but the development of a comprehensive system of intelligibility that includes the criteria and standards of the full range of research paradigms. In chapter 2, some of the traditional criteria for judging validity in research are mentioned. For the evaluation of nonexperimental and qualitative research, the proposals have ranged from applying standards similar to the traditional to alternative considerations based on radically different assumptions. Examples of these varied proposals are identified below.

In the area of hermeneutic inquiry, Hirsch (1967) argued that it is not sufficient for an interpretive account to be coherent, but it must also be an accurate portrayal of the meanings and intentions of the person who produced the original narrative data. LeCompte and Goetz (1982) and Firestone and Herriott (1983) proposed that alternative and qualitative forms of research should meet the same standards of reliability and validity as those used with traditional research in the behavioral sciences. Miles and Huberman (1984) expressed the view that qualitative inquiry is hampered by the lack of decision rules and norms of validity. Kirk and Miller (1986) defined validity in terms of the fit between an observation and the basis on which it is made. In the opinions of Packer and Addison (1989ab), these proposals represent an implicit agreement with the correspondence theory of truth underlying traditional, objectivist research paradigms. They seem to continue to appeal to a notion of interpretation-free standards or an ultimate criterion of truth. Atkinson, Heath, and Chenail (1991) expressed a similar nonfoundationalist view as that of Packer and Addison, on the evaluation of qualitative paradigms proposed for family therapy research. It may be argued that qualitative research can be compatible with critical realism, in aiming to provide a tentative understanding of human realities.

Even the criteria of faithful description and authentic representation of experience (Lincoln and Guba 1986; Fischer 1987) seem to depend on the actor or the source as the final authority. Whether the original source can be the authority is open to question, as people may not always be faithful reporters of their own intentions or have insight into their own meanings. Other criteria that have been proposed include that of pragmatic validity (Kvale 1983) and catalytic validity (Lather 1986). These concepts suggest that the value of the research findings is to be judged by whether they enhance the understanding of the participants and lead to useful action or psychological change. Based not so much on the assumption of having any external evidence of truth as on a pragmatic way of conceiving purposeful inquiry, these suggested criteria are more functional in nature than formal canons and scientific norms.

It appears that there is no interpretation-free standard, and no one type of criterion that can be appropriate for all times and purposes. Conventions of discourse developed by the professional community set the context for evaluation. As long as we are not claiming epistemological security with one set of standards, we should be able to have open discussions and reasoned disagreements. The relative utility of different standards of judgment may be an empirical question (Howard, Maerlender, Myers, and Curtin 1992), in the sense of certain ones being demonstrated by experience over time to have greater functional value than others. This way of viewing the issue of evaluation is consistent with a pragmatic orientation to inquiry (Hoshmand and Martin, in press).

In their more recent writing, Lincoln and Guba (1990) acknowledged that standards of coherence, clarity, writing power, elegance, and so forth are concerned with the rhetorical power of research reports. Firestone (1987) argued that all forms of research involve rhetoric in their presentation. The acceptance of the work of researchers depends on writing as a craft. For hermeneutic researchers (Packer and Addison 1989a), the writing process is part of the interpretive process and therefore an inherent aspect of judging the validity of a given piece of research. In addition to rhetoric as a criterion and resonance of the work with its underlying belief systems, Lincoln and Guba (1990) also proposed empowerment and applicability as criteria. These criteria entail egalitarian treatment of all informants' constructions, and assume a possibility for the findings to raise consciousness and facilitate action, as well as transferability of understanding if there is sufficient contextual similarity with the site of application. The value of a given set of findings is linked to judgments about applicability or usefulness. As with more conventional research methodologies, qualitative approaches such as ethnographic methods should be evaluated in terms of the purpose they are intended to serve. What sets them apart from the descriptions and interpretations by the non-professional is the level of methodological rigor and the disciplined manner in which the inquiry is conducted (Hammersley 1992). Thus, there are areas of agreement among those who propose criteria for evaluating alternative forms of inquiry.

From the standpoint of the communal negotiation of knowledge claims, as discussed in chapter 3, rhetoric is part of the social process of science. Research methodology and the arguments used to persuade us that the logic of inference is sound may be considered to be rhetorical devices. The rhetorical aspects of research presentation should probably be given more attention in our profession. Spence (1989) cautioned that the appeal to argument by authority and partial testimony in traditional rhetoric has its dangers, and should be replaced by more egalitarian forms of persuasion. Hermeneutic, cultural, and critical perspectives may serve as guides in our analysis of the character of our professional rhetoric and in identifying the researcher's voice and the citizen's voice in our research findings.

In summary, methodological pluralism has significant implications for our profession's approach to knowledge and how we may go about evaluating our choice of methodology. It appears that any metalevel analysis must take into account the social nature of knowledge and the contexts in which the discursive practices of the profession are evolved. Like many other professions, we have not engaged in systematic self-study or invited scrutiny by sociologists and philosophers of social science. The psychological and social study of our research practice and scientific discourse will be an acknowledgment of the historical and social embeddedness of our knowledge activities and ourselves as a professional community.

SUGGESTED ADDITIONAL LEARNING

1. Find a research report on a subject of interest that you consider to have significant findings. Read and evaluate the report with the following questions in mind:

a. What kind of language is used by the author(s) and what are the effects of the language (word choice, special terms, and style of communication) on you?

b. What kinds of assumptions are made in justifying the method used?

c. Is the rationale that links the findings to the conclusions acceptable to you?

d. Can you think of counterarguments or other types of reasoning that may apply?

2. Read and discuss the following article by Meehl :

Meehl, P.E. 1991. Why summaries of research on psychological theories are often uninterpretable. In *Improving inquiry in social science*, ed. R.E. Snow and D.E. Wiley, 13-59. Hillsdale, NJ: Lawrence Erlbaum.

Meehl questioned not only summaries of research but also the common assumptions of hypothetico-deductive research in which statistical inference is used. What are the implications of his criticisms for our use of the experimental research paradigm?

3. Read and discuss the following article by Gergen:

Gergen, K.J. 1989. The possibility of psychological knowledge. In *Entering the circle: Hermeneutic investigation in psychology*, ed. M.J. Packer and R.B. Addison, 239-58. Albany: State University of New York Press.

Gergen seemed to suggest that psychological phenomena are indeterminate and open to interpretation, thus making it impossible for researchers to be certain about inferences from the measurement tools and operations used in traditional research and professional practice. Can his arguments be disputed? What implications do they have for the various research paradigms?

4. Using the references cited in this chapter, find an example of research that is based on each of the available paradigms. Compare and contrast the studies in terms of the type of research questions addressed, the apparent methodological assumptions, and the merits and limitations of the approach used.

5. Identify a research topic of interest that has been investigated with an experimental approach. Consider how it may be further studied with alternative methods of inquiry. For an illustration, refer to the following:

Thomas, L. E., and Chambers, K. O. 1989. Phenomenology of life satisfac tion among elderly men: Quantitative and qualitative views. *Psychology and Aging,* 4: 284-89.

6. Review the following examples of multimethod research, and evaluate the conceptual and instrumental yield from using multiple perspectives and methods:

Deegan, P. E. 1981. An empirical phenomenological study of failure to learn. *Journal of Phenomenological Psychology* 12: 231-44.

Heppner, P. P.; Rosenberg, J. I.; and Hedgespeth, J. 1992. Three methods in measuring the therapeutic process: Clients' and counselors' constructions of the therapeutic process versus actual therapeutic events. *Journal of Counseling Psychology* 39: 20-31.

7. McFall (1986) introduced four examples of theoretical-methodological linkage, in which studies ranging from molecular to molar conceptual models are used with different methods of measurement. Read the McFall article and the cited studies, and evaluate how theory and method interact in each case in inquiry into the selected problem areas.

McFall, R. M. 1986. Theory and method in assessment: The vital link. *Behavioral Assessment* 8: 3-10.

6

Methods of Inquiry

In this chapter, methods of inquiry used in psychological research and practice are discussed together rather than separately. Although there are significant differences between the context of research and the context of practice, the separate treatment of methods in these two contexts tends to reinforce the research-practice gap and obscure the common processes and issues of knowing involved in all inquiry. Therefore, an integrative treatment of methods of inquiry is attempted here. The following overview is organized by the major modes of inquiry—namely, observation, interviewing, and testing and assessment. Variations in method and approach within each modality can be understood in terms of the philosophical assumptions and paradigm differences discussed in the previous chapters.

OBSERVATION

Observation is the most basic method of information gathering. Observation approaches vary by the role of the observer, the choice of the setting, the types of events to be observed, and the temporality and procedures of observation. There are different degrees of participation by the observer, from the highly detached (such as behind a one-way mirror) to immersion in the setting and direct interactions with the observed.This continuum of observer stances (Kidder and Judd 1986) reflects different assumptions about objectivity and the extent to which we can obtain authentic information as a function of the type of relationship we have with our human subjects and clientele. Given the dualistic assumptions of the experimental tradition, detached observation is made in controlled research settings for the purpose of maintaining objectivity. There is either a minimal relationship between the observer and the observed or a restricted relationship based on standardized experimenter behavior. The same assumptions are reflected in approaches to client assessment that involve a detached practitioner using a standard observation checklist or predefined category system. On the other hand, field research associated with alternative research paradigms that subscribe to social constructionist views involve participant observation in naturalistic settings where reciprocal relationships are maintained with the informants (Bogdan 1972; Bogdan and Taylor 1975; Jorgensen 1989; Spradley 1980). This practice can be paralleled by observations by professional psychologists in those community settings that are native to their clients, such as home or school (e.g. Montemayor & Van Komen, 1980). For the most part, the participant observer role is assumed by practitioners in relation to clients, with varying degrees of conscious commitment to an epistemological stance of reciprocal influence on the information being generated.

Settings of observation vary from the contrived research context to community situations that are more or less natural. Although professional practice involves naturalistic observation (e.g. Hawkins, Peterson, Schweid, and Bijou 1966; Haynes, Follingstad, and Sullivan 1979), it may be confined to a therapist's office or a treatment milieu such as a therapy group, day treatment program, or inpatient hospital setting. The inferences made in each case are local in character. While generalization to other life situations is desired, it is also important to recognize the realistic psychological impact of these observation settings. A client's behavior on a psychiatric ward is very much a function of the culture of the treatment milieu, just as a student's behavior is a function of the classroom climate. Intensive local observation can be useful in understanding problems in particular contexts.

The type of events to be observed depends on the unit of analysis chosen by the researcher or the practitioner. Units of observation and analysis, as explained in chapter 4, are a function of the conceptual lenses or interpretive framework used. The level of analysis involved in the observations we make in professional practice has implications for problem solving. For instance, observing the behavioral ecology and person-environment interaction surrounding a given problem implies that the person alone is not considered to be the locus of the problem. Interventions such as on a school-related problem may then involve modifying the classroom ecology and finding a more optimal fit between the student and the learning environment. The choice of units of analysis is based on potential value in guiding action. When observation is used to obtain research data on the phenomena of practice, such as interaction events during therapy, pragmatic criteria are also used in selecting the units of analysis. For example, observed sequences of therapist-client interaction in individual psychotherapy that can inform practitioners about what constitutes significant events in the therapeutic process (Greenberg 1986), and episodes or therapeutic tasks that can be linked to midlevel treatment outcome in family therapy (Friedlander and Heatherington 1989; Heatherington and Friedlander 1990), are considered to be of value.

Discrete response categories and simple marker events, when isolated from embedding interactions and social contexts, have not adequately served the purposes of practitioners and researchers of practice. This is in spite of the demonstrated success of behavior modification involving simple observed units of behavior and their environmental contingencies. In recognition of the limitations of reductionistic approaches, behavioral assessment in research and practice has become more contextualist in recent years (Barrios 1988). Observation in naturalistic settings and multiple levels of analysis are increasingly used. The issue of target selection and choice of the unit of analysis in behavioral assessment has been considered from a number of viewpoints (Jacobson 1985a; Kazdin 1985; Kratochwill 1985a; Mash 1985). It is suggested that units of observation should be chosen for their developmental and functional significance and relevance to personal adjustment. Target selection requires continuous evaluation of the entire constellation of behaviors in a manner of problem solving. Ultimately, the choice of the unit of analysis is a matter of clinical judgment, based on the heuristic criterion of means-end relationship to intervention (Evans 1985; Evans and Wilson 1983). The professional psychologist selects those units of observation that have useful links to intervention and problem solving (such as mentioned above in relation to the various therapeutic modalities).

Another significant difference among observation approaches consists in whether the categories are predefined or emergent from the context of observation. In general, observation units are theoretically preselected in experimental research, just as particular behaviors considered relevant from a given theoretical perspective are focused upon in certain situations of professional practice. The researcher who prepares a coding system that targets certain aspects of a phenomenon and the practitioner who looks for those events and behaviors deemed relevant in a theory of practice are both guided by theoretically preconceived units. These units allow the observational findings to be interpreted within an existing conceptual framework or network of ideas about the phenomenon or problem in question. The focused nature of this type of observation is necessary for testing specific hypotheses. It has the disadvantage, however, of losing information that is not readily interpreted with the observer's predefined categories.

In contrast, participant modes of research and phenomenological approaches to client assessment tend to utilize a more emergent method of deriving categories of understanding by immersion and interaction in the relevant settings. An effort is made to observe reactions to naturally occurring stimulus events, such as critical incidents (Flanagan 1954), as opposed to stimuli introduced by the researcher or practitioner. Those recurrent verbal and nonverbal behaviors that are emergent from the natural stream of behavioral interactions are selected for attention and analysis (Bakeman and Dabbs 1976; Knapp 1978). This use of emergent categories gives more emphasis to the emic or insider perspective. It reflects underlying assumptions about our inability to anticipate what are most relevant and meaningful from the standpoint of the subject or client. This mode of observation may be considered discovery oriented, as it is more open and useful for generating hypotheses. It complements the focused observation in hypothesis testing that calls for more systematic procedures. In both research and practice, the knowledge derived from participation and immersion can inform the selection of more focused units of observation, especially when emergent categories have been systematically derived in the manner of a grounded theory. Many researchers of therapeutic practice do, in fact, draw upon their clinical observations and experience of practice in deciding how to analyze therapeutic phenomena for research purposes.

Systematic observation requires not only predefined categories but standardized procedures and observer behaviors as well. Systematic observation in natural settings has been extended from research to professional practice (Bijou, Peterson, Harris, Allen, and Johnson 1969; Hutt and Hutt 1970; Sackett 1978; Slosson and Callisto 1984; Werry and Quay 1969). This has been aided by the development of observational instruments, behavioral rating scales, and recording technologies (Bellack and Hersen 1988; Ollendick and Hersen 1984; Simon and Bayer 1974). Although most detached forms of observation involve systematic procedures, whereas participant modes are generally less standardized in approach, it is possible to conduct systematic observation with participant observers (Hay, Nelson, and Hay 1977; Jacobson and Moore 1981; Margolin, Michelli, and Jacobson 1988). In such cases, the degree of interaction between the observer and the observed tends to be restricted or less natural than is found in ethnographic and other qualitative research. Where participant observers are used in systematic observation, there seems to be low agreement between their observations and those made by detached observers of the same phenomenon (Floyd and Markman 1983; Margolin, Hattem, John, and Yost 1985). The source of discrepancy has been attributed to observer skills.

Training in systematic observation has been skills oriented and procedural in emphasis (Boice 1983; Hartmann 1982; Kidder and Judd 1986). By contrast, there is more reliance on the sensitivity of the observer as a human instrument in participant modes of research and clinical inquiry (Baldwin and Satir 1987; Berg and Smith 1988; Jorgensen 1989). Self-scrutiny and -reflection to examine one's assumptions, biases, values, and interests become a necessary part of observer reflexivity. This emphasis on the human instrument in qualitative inquiry does not mean that procedural concerns of sampling and reliability are not considered (Kirk and Miller 1985; LeCompte and Goetz 1982). A participant field researcher has to account for possible bias in the selection of informants as a function of his or her own personal qualities and how he or she may be perceived. Reliability of the informants' reports is also influenced by the degree of trust in the relationship, a matter of concern to both researchers and practitioners.

The issue of sampling in observation has theoretical as well as practical implications. Theoretically, any time we treat an observation as a sample of a certain phenomenon, we are making an assumption about its manifestation and generalizability. In practice, the method of sampling in observation depends on assumptions about the base rate of a behavioral event (Lipinski and Nelson 1974). Frequently occurring events can be observed or sampled intermittently, whereas infrequent or less predictable events require more continuous and frequent observation. The goal is to establish a baseline that is descriptive of the natural occurrence of the event. In professional practice, the experience and knowledge of the observer enable such judgments about appropriate sampling to be made. Immersion in the relevant setting and prior understanding of the behavioral ecology involved are helpful in designing observation systems in both research and practice. Preliminary scanning and narrative recordings can help observers decide how to conduct more focused observation. The same types of skills used by participant researchers apply to situations of practice in which the psychologist may serve as a consultant in setting up an observation system for monitoring a target problem. Rapport with concerned parties (such as teachers and remedial agents) and understanding of their frame of reference and motivational context are essential to planning the observations. Similarly, in the case of helping a client design a system for observing self or others outside of therapy sessions, only extensive discussion and clarification of the observer's concerns and environment will produce a meaningful approach (Kratochwill 1985b). A holistic understanding of the client's presenting problem and the functional meaning of related events is necessary in selecting the appropriate targets of observation and deciding on how they can be interpreted.

Research on observation as a method of inquiry has addressed a number of issues, including observer bias and observation effects, the type of setting chosen, and other methodological problems. Observer bias has been linked to fatigue, expectancies, and knowledge of hypothesis (DeMaster, Reid, and Twentyman 1977; Kent, O'Leary, Diament, and Dietz 1974; Haynes and Horn 1982; Redfield and Paul 1976; Rosenthal 1988; Shuller and McNamara 1976; Taplin and Reid 1973). Global estimates and ratings are particularly susceptible to observer error and bias (Cunningham and Tharp 1981; Klonoff, Revis, and Tice 1985). Reactivity is found not only to affect the observed but to have a reciprocal influence on the observer (Ciminero, Graham, and Jackson 1977; Hay, Nelson, and Hay 1977). This issue of observer effects and reactivity of observation is approached differently depending on the observer stance and the epistemological assumptions that are maintained. In the detached, objectivist approach, it is assumed that observer bias can be reduced by proper training, and that reactivity can be similarly reduced with the use of unobtrusive measures (Webb, Campbell, Schwartz, Sechrest, and Grove 1966). In participant modes of observation, reactivity is presumed to lessen as a function of the longevity and quality of the relationship the observer maintains with the informants. Reciprocity is expected, and the motivation and needs of both the observer and the observed are entailed in the observation, as suggested by the research finding of reciprocal reactivity. The participant observer has to learn to manage the observer's role in order to balance both the outsider and the insider perspective. This is similar to the use of clinical observations in which the practitioner has to be sufficiently involved in order to have empathic understanding of the client, and at the same time be not so overly embedded as to lose one's professional identity.

Given the philosophical discussion in earlier chapters, it is appropriate to view observation as necessarily reactive and always socially and culturally embedded. The important question is how we are to interpret a given observed event and make sense of the changes resulting from the process of observing. In the case of self-observation, such as when clients monitor their own problem behaviors and private events, reactivity operates in the form of intentional choosing between possible ways of being and acting. Anyone who has tried to self-monitor a behavior such as food consumption for weight control can appreciate the role of desire and the internal dialogue about whether one should "cheat" in terms of eating and even in the recording of one's behavior. In such instances, the observational findings should probably be interpreted in terms of self-directed intentional actions in interaction with stimulus factors in the environment, rather than being placed in a purely objectivist context of unidirectional environmental determinism. (Recall the discussion in chapter 4 on assumptions about human agency.) Reports of self-observation to the psychologist are further to be treated as social communication embedded in the professional relationship. They are likely to be a function of reciprocal self-esteem and the nature of the interpersonal contract present between the practitioner and the client. For example, a client may choose not to report on poor performance on a self-control assignment so as to not reflect poorly on the therapist or disappoint the therapist.

The degree of naturalness of observation settings that is desired is also open to discussion. Although it is assumed that naturalistic settings will yield information more relevant to everyday life, the generalizability of a given set of observations still depends on the competence of the observer and the overall methodology (Dipboye and Flanagan 1979; Hay, Nelson, and Hay 1980; LeCompte and Goetz 1982). Technically, generalizability of observations is determined by variability in response, observer, setting, and time, as well as the amount of error involved (Ary 1984). In practice, reliability depends on observer skills, how well defined the target events are, and the method of sampling (Green, McCoy, Burns, and Smith 1982). Furthermore, consistency of observation is not always possible because of person-setting interaction and a certain degree of expected variation (Hayes, Nelson, and Jarrett 1986). A researcher can introduce systematic biases in the choice of persons and behavior settings, just as a practitioner can commit errors of selective observation and overgeneralization in clinical inquiry.

The validity of observation is not guaranteed by a given observer stance or type of setting *per se*. Nor can we assume that the use of a rating scale or other observational instrument will produce valid findings. As a matter of fact, practitioners and researchers have not been sufficiently critical in their evaluation of observation tools. Many behavioral rating scales have not had a rigorous background of development. Even if there is established reliability, the validity of a given instrument or set of procedures rests with the manner in which it is used in a particular context. It is misleading to consider validity to be a property of a particular tool or procedure apart from the context of usage.

Recent discussions of behavioral assessment are beginning to address the issue of validity of observation in terms that are equally relevant to other modes of inquiry (Barrios 1988; Cone 1988). Direct methods of observation should not be assumed to be inherently superior to self-report and other methods of inquiry (Howard, Maxwell, Weiner, Boynton, and Rooney 1980; Jacobson 1985b). The meaningfulness of observational data is equally subject to interpretation as any other form of data. Observation of private events in cognitive-behavioral assessment illustrates some of the problems of interpretation. Whether we are attempting to obtain identifiable units of thought with thought sampling, thought listing, or think-aloud procedures (Merluzzi, Glass, and Genest 1981), or trying to assess the interrelationship among core cognitions (Safran, Vallis, Segal, and Shaw 1986), the information is mediated by the motivational context of internal processing and verbal reporting. The implications of the latter for the validity of the data are yet to be fully understood.

The analysis of observation data that are readily quantifiable has involved mostly descriptive graphic displays and nonparametric statistics (Siegel and Castellan 1988). Participant modes of observation produce both behavioral descriptions and narrative data. Miles (1990) describes methods for qualitative data collection and analysis, using vignettes and cases. Qualitative treatment of narrative data tends to focus on the thematic recurrence of contents and meanings (Miles and Huberman 1994; Silverman 1993). In this respect, it overlaps with the procedures for analyzing interview data, and will be described in relation to interviewing.

INTERVIEWING

Interviewing as a verbal exchange for investigative purposes is used in survey research (Fowler 1984; Turner and Martin 1984) and as a clinical method in ethnographic and other qualitative research (Brenner, Brown and

Canter 1985; McCracken 1988). It is the major method of information gathering in clinical inquiry and most areas of professional practice. Oral history and personological inquiry also rely on the interviewing mode (Bertaux 1981; Runyan 1982; Thompson 1978). The research interview may be conducted individually or with a group (Morgan 1988; Stewart and Shandasani 1990), just as clinical assessment interviews may include individuals, couples, and families. Methods of interviewing fall on a continuum, from the highly structured survey interview (Fowler and Mangione 1989) and standardized clinical interview (Skodol 1987; Spitzer and Williams 1985; Spitzer, Williams, and Gibbon 1987) to the unstructured (Lofland 1971) and more open-ended phenomenological, hermeneutic mode of interviewing (Honey 1987; Kvale 1983; Van Maanen 1990). This continuum again reflects different beliefs about the extent to which the interviewer knows the questions that need to be asked and can anticipate the categories the respondent will use. Survey research interviews and standardized clinical interviews utilize predefined categories of questions, whereas qualitative and open-ended interviews allow for emergent questions and meanings from the interaction with the respondent.

The continuum of interviewing methods also corresponds more or less to two epistemological poles, the realist and the constructionist, with their respective assumptions about the nature of the data and the roles of the interviewer and the interviewee. The objective survey mode, similar to detached observation, emphasizes detachment and the reduction of interviewer bias so as to ensure the accuracy of responses. On the other hand, interview approaches that emphasize the participant role of the interviewer and the use of self as an instrument in gauging the interaction are regarded by field researchers as "clinical methods" (Berg and Smith 1988). It is no accident that many clinical modes of interviewing share with ethnographic and phenomenological research interviews the same epistemological assumptions of participant embeddedness and the social construction of meanings.

Empirical research on interviewing as a method of inquiry has pointed to a number of considerations. One is that respondents often do not understand survey questions as intended by the researcher (Belson 1968; Beza 1984) or the requirements of their role as respondents (Cannell, Fowler, and Marquis 1968; Cannell, Oksenberg, and Converse 1981). The perceived context of the interview definitely affects the responses in the direction of acquiescence (Lenski and Leggett 1960; Weiss 1968) or guardedness (Locander, Sudman, and Bradburn 1976; National Research Council 1979). Racial factors and social expectations also enter into the interviewing situation (Campbell 1981; Schaeffer 1980; Sudman and Bradburn 1974). Most of the research on survey interviewing has been done from the perspective of the researcher's need to obtain objective and verifiable knowledge, using proper question form and wording (Schuman and Presser 1981). It is recognized, however, that the formalism of survey questions posed in a context isolated from the respondent's personal life may create what Converse and Schuman (1974) referred to as a "bias of rationality." Trow (1981) pointed out that the parallel problem of stripping context from the presentation of information, such as found in mass media, can have an alienating effect on people's understanding of their experiences. The artificiality of decontextualized forms of research interviewing, besides posing problems of validity, leaves the interviewee with the burden of making sense of a depersonalized interaction. This problem is ameliorated to some extent by thoroughly debriefing subjects after a research interview.

Although the interviewer's behavior is one of the major determinants of the interviewing response (Barath and Cannell 1976; Rustemeyer 1977), the mixed evidence on this factor (Blair 1977; Dijkstra and van der Zouwen 1982; Presser 1983) suggests multiple sources of variability in the interviewing situation. It is an oversimplification to use a stimulus-response model to characterize the social psychological and cognitive processes involved in an interview (Turner and Martin 1984). This observation is consistent with an interactional, social constructionist conception of human inquiry. In the situation of professional practice, practitioners are well aware that in addition to their self-presentation, much depends on how they are perceived by the client as a function of the past experiences brought into the interaction by the client. The sociocultural context and identities of the practitioner and the client influence the type of interaction and the meanings attributed to the communication (Chaplin 1988; Ivey, Ivey, and Simek-Morgan 1993; Sue and Sue 1990). Both parties are embedded in their own worldviews, assumptions, and biases, and bring into the transaction their reciprocal needs and personal frames of reference. Research on interpersonal processes in the therapeutic context has added to our knowledge of social, perceptual, cognitive, and motivational factors in the interview (e.g., Martin 1992; Toukmanian 1992).

In terms of developing one's effectiveness as an interviewer, a number of areas are worthy of attention. All forms of interviewing are dependent on cooperation and therefore require the building of rapport and trust. The skills developed in professional practice are useful for interviewing in field research, because the same interpersonal considerations in the context of practice apply to the research setting. If the overall goal is to access the interviewee's personal frame of reference, it would be crucial to utilize a mode of information gathering and interchange that is native to the respondent. An interviewee who is used to storytelling should be encouraged to give information in the form of anecdotes and stories, just as a client who volunteers dream reports should be allowed to give accounts of dreams and related imageries. Rather than presuming that certain preselected categories of questions will be meaningful to the interviewee, we must allow for native meanings to emerge. Both researchers and practitioners have to learn to use the expressions and categories of meaning provided by the respondent. Even if the domain of inquiry is clearly defined and we are certain of the questions that need to be asked, it is important to flow with the dialogue and to keep the interview at least semistructured or sufficiently open to permit interviewees to interject topics considered relevant from their standpoint.

Without suggesting that interviewing should be a form of rule-governed inquiry, there are some guidelines that seem to apply to all interviewing. As a general principle, anxiety needs to be managed, and the sequencing of questions should be designed to maintain an optimal level of communication (Sullivan 1954). This often requires flexibility and the ability to monitor the interpersonal effects of the interviewing process. It is important to ask open rather than closed questions, a skill that can be developed with practice and feedback (Briggs 1984). Whether in research or in practice, we need to learn to elicit elaborations of a response without shaping the answers. Furthermore, rather than assume that a respondent who gives a response that is not readily framed in the line of questioning has not understood the question, we should be open to the possibility that an alternative (though relevant) frame of meaning may be present. Gilligan (1982) discovered in her study of girls' moral development that one of the girls did not respond in terms of the interviewer's conception of the question about moral dilemma that was based on Kohlberg's research on males. When the interviewer failed to consider the girl's way of understanding the question, her responses were rated lower for moral development than those received by children who accepted the question in the interviewer's terms. We are always at risk of imposing our theoretical preconceptions in interpreting interview responses even as the interview is being conducted. Just as we have to overcome the tendency to use familiar observation categories, we need to be aware, during interviewing, of blind spots in our understanding that are a function of our own background (Douglas 1985). The ultimate challenge is to uncover the respondent's personal context and frame of reference while meeting the requirements of the task of inquiry. More will be said in the next chapter about the cognitive and social aspects of information processing in relation to professional judgment. Perceptual bias and errors of inference represent a common issue in all forms of interviewing.

How we conduct an interview and analyze the interview data depends on the assumptions we hold about interviewing as a method of inquiry. Due to the tendency to treat methods as techniques, we often neglect to consider the theory of knowing behind the method. Interviewing as a method used in the research context is particularly in need of an epistemology. Kvale (1983) provided a useful explication of a model of the research interview, as a phenomenological-hermeneutic endeavor. He depicted the interpretive process of the interview as following a part-to-whole logic, with each bit of information gained from questioning and observation being contextualized by the emerging pattern of understanding. Mishler (1986b) further attempted to reformulate general principles for understanding the research interview in terms of social discourse within its proper cultural and linguistic context. He questioned the validity of decontextualized survey interviews that utilize fixed response categories and standardization of interviewer behavior, pointing out that meanings are a function of rules of syntax, semantics, and pragmatics that are culturally determined. We cannot assume that a given set of questions will have the same meaning to all respondents, nor can we assume that the interviewer and interviewee will share a community of meaning. Mishler's thesis is based on sociolinguistic research on discourse and the study of speech acts (Gumperz 1982). This narrative conception of the interview is consistent with social constructionism. Barrell, Aanstoos, Richards, and Arons (1987), using experiential-perceptual and hermeneutical-phenomenological frameworks, described how interview questions are formulated as a function of the research purpose and how the interpretive process reflects the assumptions of each framework. They illustrated the different processes of developing questions and understanding in each framework with the study of a common phenomenon, the experience of anxiety.

In the context of practice, there are more theoretical frameworks available for conceptualizing interviewing, typically in connection with a therapeutic model (Cormier and Cormier 1991; Mahrer 1986; Rogers 1980) or mainly in terms of helping skills (Corsini and Wedding 1989; Egan 1990). To discern general principles of interviewing, largely with the purpose of intervention, one may consider generic models in which particular relationship and communication skills are specified (Ivey and Authier 1978; Ivey 1988; Patterson 1985b). In that a client's response to one's interventions in interviewing provides information for further intervention, most forms of therapeutic interviewing may be considered to be a continuous process of inquiry. In fact, this is probably the most common means by which practitioners test their working hypotheses and evaluate the fit of their schema with the presenting phenomenon. It will be important for us to reflect on this process of knowing as we conduct therapeutic interviews. More systematic effort at describing and understanding this process of inference will enable the profession to document the knowledge of practice (Hoshmand and Polkinghorne 1992).

Models of clinical interviewing conducted with assessment as a goal have been most clearly defined in behavioral interviewing (Morganstern 1988; Masters, Burish, Hollon, and Rimm 1987; Wolpe 1990) and diagnostic interviewing (Hersen and Turner 1985; Morrison 1988; Othmer 1989;

Stangl, Pfohl, Zimmerman, Bowers and Corenthal 1985; Spitzer and Williams 1985). Behavioral interviewing is problem oriented and guided by learning principles for conceptualizing behavior. The questions asked usually have face or content validity. For example, a client presenting with a problem of substance abuse will be asked questions concerned with the frequency and intensity of the target behavior of substance use. Additional questions may be related to the circumstances of use, its effects, and other relevant environmental and personal factors, depending on the practitioner's hypotheses about contributing factors.

In diagnostic interviewing, questions about mental status and the client's presenting complaints are designed to help the practitioner confirm the presence of dysfunction as categorized in the *Diagnostic and Statistical Manual of Mental Disorders* (American Psychiatric Association 1994) and to rule out other possible categories for describing the clinical picture. The logic of diagnostic interviewing has been depicted with decision trees and represented with computerized simulations of interviewing and decision making (Erdman, Klein, and Greist 1985; Hand 1981). The latter practice has raised ethical and validity questions (Rogers, Ryack, and Moeller 1979; Spitzer, Endicott, Cohen, and Fleiss 1974). Much of the research on the reliability and validity of such diagnostic interviews has been intertwined with evaluation of the diagnostic system itself and the interview schedule used (Costello, Edelbrock, and Costello 1985; Matarazzo 1983; Robins, Helzer, Ratcliff, and Seyfried 1982; Rutter and Graham 1968). The implicit model in diagnostic interviewing is one of an expert observer eliciting signs of an individual-centered trait-type pathology or syndrome. Communication is instrumental to the determination of signs of problems, and observer objectivity is emphasized. The reciprocity between interviewer and interviewee is only incidental to the diagnostic process.

A more interactional conception of the interview is found in Sullivan (1954), who provided an especially well-formulated model, in conjunction with detailed inquiry into a client's personal history. The interviewer is regarded as a participant observer who uses his or her own reactions and observations of the interview process to make inferences about the interviewee. Hypotheses are formulated on the basis of observed changes in communication and the experience of reciprocal anxiety and attitude changes. These hypotheses are systematically tested through questioning in areas that appear to be sensitive for the client. Sullivan's model of clinical inquiry provides a useful framework for evaluating contemporary approaches of clinical interviewing and hypothesis testing. Current thinking about the interview is generally based on interpersonal, interactional models informed by social psychology (Maddux, Stoltenberg, and Rosenwein 1987; Strong and Claiborn 1982; Strong, Welsh, Corcoran, and Hoyt 1992) and models of social perception and cognition (Fiske and Taylor 1984; Ingram 1986; Martin 1992; Toukmanian 1992; Wyer and Srull 1984). With the emergence of social constructionism, the contributions of all participants to the interview data are acknowledged in the form of meanings coconstructed through dialogue (Mahoney 1991; McNamee and Gergen 1992; Neimeyer and Neimeyer 1993). The reciprocity of human information exchange is mediated by cognitive, social, and cultural factors.

The implications of dialogical conceptions of the interview are that the narrative data must be interpreted in the interpersonal context in which they are generated by the participants and that the meanings of reported experiences and actions are reflexively linked to our participation in the discourse. Whereas standardized and structured interviews tend to be relationally asymmetrical and hierarchical, with the interviewer having power and control (Mishler 1984), a more egalitarian relationship is entailed in collaborative forms of interviewing (Belenky, Clinchy, Golberger and Tarule 1986; Laslett and Rapoport 1985). This is generally true in research approaches that permit the human subject to have more voice. Qualitative interviews associated with ethnographic and phenomenological paradigms of research and practice are supposed to be empowering of the participants (Kvale 1983; Mishler 1986b). The interviewer assumes a nonjudgmental attitude and allows the interviewee to supply native information and personal meanings. In the process, the embedding context and frames of reference of the participants are given prime consideration. Decontextualized approaches to interviewing, like any other form of decontextualized inquiry, will have problems of ecological validity (Cicourel 1982). This last issue will be further discussed as we complete our overview of methods.

It is important to bear in mind the overall interpretive context and analytical process in qualitative inquiry involving the use of the interview. Giorgi (1975) explained the application of a phenomenological approach to an interview study of learning. The descriptive data were presented in the context of the questions asked by the researcher. The themes derived were reported along with the linguistic units in the transcribed interview responses. Further analytical steps were explained as the researcher inferred situated structures of the learning experience from the thematic patterns, and finally inferred general structures in the manner of generative theorizing. Similarly, Fischer and Wertz (1979) provided an excellent account of their phenomenological study of the experience of being criminally victimized, in which fifty interviews were transcribed and analyzed. Using the original transcript material, they illustrated each level of analysis, from individual case synopses to general case synopses and generalized psychological structure. Further discussions of the methodology and illustrative materials of this study are available in Wertz (1983).

The systematic analysis of narrative data gathered with interviews usually involves either content analysis of specific categories or a more open search for emergent themes and patterns. The procedures and applications of content analysis have been described in a number of sources (Krippendorff 1980; Viney 1983; Weber 1990). O'Dell and Bahmer (1981) used content analysis to study the differences among the interviewing approaches of three therapists of varied theoretical orientations. Viney (1993) gives a case example of its use with narrative data obtained from a client in therapy. Grounded-theory approaches and ethnographic research also involve systematic sorting until the apparent meanings in the text are exhausted (Altheide 1987; Glaser and Strauss 1967; Silverman 1993; Strauss 1987). This may be done in conjunction with the procedure of negative case analysis which provides a check on interpretive errors (Conrad 1978). Rennie (1992) illustrates the use of grounded-theory methods of deriving categories of meaning in studying clients' experience of psychotherapy. Some practitioners have shown a preference for conversation analysis, following the methods used in the area of discourse analysis (e.g., Gail and Newfield 1992). Potter and Wetherell (1987b) described a ten-stage process of analyzing discourse, based on a functional view of talk and writing. This is similar to the hermeneutic approach of treating the interpretive process as a dynamic transaction between the interpreter and the text (Kvale 1987a; Van Maanen 1990). Mishler (1986a) discussed interview analysis from a sociolinguistic point of view, illustrating the contribution of the interviewer's experience and cultural knowledge to the interpretive process. A transcript of an interview-narrative is provided to help the reader understand how the interview data were analyzed.

Interest in the narrative approach has been extended to the use of written documents such as biographies and self-characterization sketches to supplement orally obtained data (Denzin 1989; Epting and Landfield 1985; Epting and Nazario 1987; McAdams and Ochberg 1988; Runyan 1982), following the historical work of Allport (1942) and Kelly (1955). History methods such as Sullivan's (1954) detailed inquiry and Satir's (1983) family life chronology are fruitful ways of gathering information in therapeutic practice with interviewing. Personal narratives generated in group settings (Hoshmand 1993) may serve as data sources in community and organizational studies. With the influence of social constructionism (McNamee and Gergen 1992), further development is expected in the procedures of narrative data analysis for use by professional psychologists. Neimeyer (1993) presents examples of constructivist assessment methods utilizing narrative data mostly generated with interviews. It is helpful to obtain instructional manuals from researchers, if possible, that explain the detailed procedures and process of the narrative analysis. Brown's (1988) guide to reading narratives of conflict and choice in moral development is an example of such a resource.

Increasing interest in qualitative approaches to interview analysis has been accompanied by the development of computer software tools (Blackman 1992; Fielding and Lee 1991; Tesch 1990). Evaluation of these programs for data analysis will require more field testing and wider usage by researchers. Analytic procedures have also been proposed for articulating the relationship between entities, using mathematical models that avoid quantification (Katzner 1983). Whether such procedures will be of value to qualitative researchers remains to be determined.

TESTING AND ASSESSMENT

Testing and assessment methods involving instrumentation and measurement are often identified by the public as the main tools of our profession. This is because of the visibility and social impact of test use. The testing movement has been attributed to the historical influence of the individual-differences tradition in psychology (Dawis 1992) as well as the sociological and institutional circumstances surrounding the rise of our profession (Fass 1980; Leahey 1991). Applied areas of psychology, in particular, have been associated with the development of the field of psychometrics, or psychological measurement. Technological advances in computer scoring and interpretation also promoted testing as an efficient method of gathering information (Butcher 1987). Although test theory and test usage have been the subject of much debate (Anastasi 1985; Buros 1977), the use of testing and methods of psychological assessment has continued to be a major mode of professional inquiry. Psychological tests are routinely used in research to measure constructs because of the emphasis on operationalization and quantification in experimental methodology and most types of survey research. Interest in individual and group differences also supports the use of testing in educational, clinical, and employment settings. Tests are thus categorized by their purpose in intellectual, educational-achievement, neuropsychological, personality, and vocational assessment.

Similar to observation and interviewing methods, testing can be differentiated in terms of the type of relationship between the examiner and the subject or client, the degree of standardization, as well as the relative contribution of quantitative and qualitative interpretations. Standardized testing such as most forms of intellectual assessment, achievement and aptitude testing, and the use of objective personality inventories, tends to be norm referenced. The individual's responses are compared to population norms (which should be compatible with the person's demographic characteristics) for the purpose of selection, educational placement, and diagnostic classification.

Interpretation of responses is based on statistical distribution of measured responses or scores. In contrast to norm-referenced testing, criterion-referenced testing focuses less on how the individual compares with a group, and more on how he or she performs to a set criterion (such as a word list prepared by a teacher for remedial learning). Less standardized forms of testing, such as the use of projective personality tests, tend to involve more qualitative, clinical interpretations, as is true for alternative assessment methods like card sorts (Goldman 1983, 1990). They depend on the level of skill and experience of the examiner, as opposed to reliance on the instrument *per se.* Whereas standard instructions and a formal relationship are used in standardized test-administration, the less common process-dynamic approach (Feuerstein, 1979; Lidz 1983) attempts to ascertain how the individual may perform under optimized testing conditions (Budoff and Hamilton 1976). By attending to the process of how the subject or client responds (such as in terms of strategies and errors), this type of testing could be, like criterion-referenced testing, more relevant to remediation and change-inducing interventions. Furthermore, the dynamics of the relationship between the psychologist and the client are emphasized, as in qualitative forms of clinical testing (Dana and Leech 1974; Fischer 1979; Leventhal Slepian, Gluck, and Rosenblatt 1962).

Computer-assisted testing is a new modality with potential contributions and limitations (Butcher 1985, 1987; Matarazzo 1986; Sampson 1990). Used most often with objective tests such as the MMPI, computer-based test interpretations are made available to practitioners. These interpretations are based on actuarial research data on particular populations and the statistically derived judgments of expert practitioners. Another form of computer-assisted testing is interactive testing such as the SIGI used in vocational self-assessment. While welcomed as time-saving practices, computer-assisted testing in general has caused ethical concerns. They include unqualified users, misuse by uninformed clients, inadequate professional attention, and possible failure to provide the needed services (Sampson 1986).

The various forms of testing and their applications in professional practice reflect different assumptions about how to gain knowledge of the human subject and what the role of the psychologist should be in client assessment. Standardized testing shares the same objectivist assumptions with detached observation and standardized interviewing. Dynamic and process-oriented testing that utilize the relationship context is similar to participant and qualitative modes of observation and interviewing. Computer-assisted testing assumes that the test stimuli are adequate without the human context of interaction and that interpretations are rule governed. Although the psychologist remains the ultimate judge of the information obtained in most cases, the professional's role varies. Some practitioners view themselves as psychometricians and appraisers, relying on the power of the test instrument to yield valid information. Others assume a participant observer's role as the human instrument for evaluation, drawing on the relationship context in which information is obtained. Still others adopt a consultant's role in assembling an array of information of which test data constitute only a part of the basis for recommending the appropriate action.

The type of action that results from testing and assessment may include intervention on an individual, person-environment interaction, or system's level. In terms of the core metaphors discussed in chapter 4, trait assessment and diagnostic testing generally subscribe to a formistic, static view of individual differences. Treatment is targeted accordingly at the individual. Although trait-type information can be used to arrange for a person-environment fit (Chartrand 1991), process-dynamic (and possibly criterion-referenced) testing is more transactionalist in assumption and likely to focus on person-environment interactions (such as match of the student with a learning task or setting). If supplemented by observational data, they may contribute to ecological understanding of a problem. Most psychologists recognize the conceptual and empirical limitations of testing, and would consider any given test mainly in terms of incremental value in adding to the total pool of information contributed by multiple methods of inquiry (Garb 1984). In making testing referrals, administering tests, and communicating test results, the practitioner should consider the impact on the entire client system. The timing of assessment and the rationale given to the client or research subject, as well as how test results are presented, involve therapeutic and ethical-legal considerations (Anastasi 1986).

As with other modes of inquiry, testing needs a theory in use or model of application that defines its place in research and practice. The applied epistemology of test use is distinguished from, but related to, the psychological theories (e.g., Baron 1985; Gardner 1983; and Sternberg 1985a on intelligence) associated with the development of particular test instruments (Crocker 1986). The latter raise questions of an ontological nature as they reflect our constructs and models of reality. Those questions should also be the subject of reflective study. They can have practical significance, such as in the proposal of testing for competence rather than for intelligence (Barrett and Depinet 1991). Linn (1986), in discussing the uses of testing in education, pointed to the need for integrating advances in cognitive psychology with improving test design and the educational applications of testing.

Principles and applications of psychological testing can be found in various sources (Anastasi 1982; Cronbach 1990; Murphy and Davishofer 1988). Available standards and guidelines (American Educational Research Association, American Psychological Association, and National Council on Measurement in Education 1985) help to set general parameters for the profession. Particular guidelines have been developed with respect to computerized testing services (Colorado Psychological Association 1982), computer-based interpretations (American Psychological Association 1986), and how to deal with ethical problems involving computerized assessment (Ohio Psychological Association 1983). The challenge for the professional psychologist is to develop an integrative perspective from which to view test usage and the many issues related to it, and with which to evaluate the contribution of testing as part of a repertoire of inquiry methods.

In any type of testing, the researcher or practitioner follows a procedure designed to elicit the relevant responses with the aid of an instrument or stimulus task. Based on the subject's or client's response to particular aspects of the presented task (or test items), psychological characteristics and dispositions are inferred. Furthermore, predictions and generalizations are made about the person outside of the situation of appraisal. If we were to apply objectivist, dualistic assumptions whereby the observer and subject are independent of each other and the method of inquiry, much of the power of testing would seem to rest with the instrument or assessment procedure itself. The question, therefore, is whether the instrument is well enough designed to really measure what it purports to measure. This is the traditional concept of validity.

Alternatively, if we were to view the testing situation as a social event embedded in motivational and cultural context, the personal frames of reference of the participants and the cultural and motivational factors entering into the situation should become a prime consideration. For example, the interaction context can affect examiner behavior (Masling 1961). Culturally-related learning contexts are known to affect cognitive functioning, casting doubt on the practice of generalizing cognitive performance from standardized tests (Miller-Jones 1989). A number of questions arise that have implications for the validity of the test data. Is it possible for any standardized-test item to have the same meaning to all subjects? Could the procedure of assessment and the mode of desired response be culturally alienating to the subject? Will a tested ability or measured attitude reflect the characteristics of the person under different motivational contexts? A cultural perspective on the meaning of test performance calls for theory and research that would involve ontological assumptions different from objectivist assumptions (Helms 1992). These in turn have philosophical and practical implications for testing as a method of inquiry. It is crucial that we examine the epistemological assumptions behind the use of testing because these underlying assumptions entail different views of the respective contributions of human, contextual factors, relative to the test instrument or assessment procedure. The scientific support for the claims we make with the test data not only must derive from the test itself but must account for these other factors inherent in test usage.

Traditional approaches to test validation have been based on a trinitarian distinction among content, criterion, and construct validity (Guion 1980). Content validity refers to the degree to which sampling of the assessed domain is representative (as, for example, in the sampling of particular academic skills with an achievement test). Criterion validity is concerned with the ability of a test to classify the status of an individual (such as based on a diagnostic criterion) or predict a performance (such as in relation to a job-selection criterion). Soundness and robustness of the criterion is important, and should be determined independently from the test itself. Construct validity is related to the ability of a test to measure the theoretical construct or psychological trait(s) and state(s) in question. It is closely linked to theory testing and the tradition of hypothetico-deductive research. Recent discussions on the issue of validity have, however, favored a departure from this trinitarian distinction and the traditional emphasis on the instrument (Angoff 1988; Ellis and Blustein 1991). In that all test scores and measured observations can be considered to be operational definitions of a theoretical construct, construct validation is proposed as a comprehensive framework that can subsume content and criterion validity. Content and criterion validation involve inferences that are aspects of a broader set of inferences about the construct being instantiated. The quality of such inferences becomes a matter of the framing of the research hypothesis, the research design, and the methods used. In other words, it should be evaluated in the same way as other claims made in our scientific inquiry.

Along with this revised conception of test validity is the focus on the context of testing. Validity is conceived in terms of the context of test use rather than assumed to be a permanent property of an instrument. The user, the process by which the test data are obtained, and the inferences drawn from the test are to be evaluated. Fiske (1991) proposed a strategy of process validation that involves examining the processes that generate the test responses. The processes by which subjects respond to items in tests of personality (Kuncel and Fiske 1974) and mental ability (Sternberg 1983) have been investigated. Such research can shed light on the context (instructional and perceived) in which clients and research subjects respond to being tested. It would appear that process validation needs to be carried further, in a dialogical, coconstructive manner, to uncover the motivational and interpretive context in which the responses are obtained. In this way, inquiry will be reflexive, reflecting back on the user and the process. This type of contextual accounting should become a fundamental dimension of validity.

Additional issues surrounding the use of testing are concerned with the decisions made on the basis of test results and the impact of testing on people's lives. Are we invading privacy, discriminating, and stigmatizing (Ebel

1964)? Do test findings serve our human clientele and society well, in comparison to the deleterious effects they may have (Kleiman and Faley 1985; Messick 1980, 1981)? What should be our profession's stance with respect to the political and economic uses of testing (Messick 1984; Murphy 1986; Reilly and Smither 1985)? These value questions must become part of the applied epistemology of testing. Test use should be informed by a viable conception of the social, psychological processes involved in the context of assessment as well as being guided by ethical considerations. Messick (1988) emphasized the consequential basis of test validity. If a test used for selection purposes shows sex or ethnic differences in score distribution, the relevance of such variability to criterion validity and overall construct validity must be evaluated. The professional judgment involved in evaluating the use of a particular test includes reflexive, theoretical knowledge in the research context as well as ethical considerations in the value context. Validity is multifaceted and requires a comprehensive conceptualization (Messick 1989).

The complexity of issues related to testing is most evident in the testing of handicapped, culturally different, or non-native English speakers. Willingham (1988) presented an excellent discussion of the problems involved in testing the handicapped. As with all groups who may be affected by population invalidity or systematic biasing sources of variance with no intrinsic connection with the construct being measured, testing the handicapped poses an issue of test fairness that is difficult to address scientifically (Cole 1981). Should we develop comparable test items or tasks and/or comparable criteria? Would having extended testing periods and large prints, for instance, be sufficiently fair to the visually handicapped and not be biasing toward those who are not? Should admission criteria be different for disadvantaged groups when there is evidence suggesting, for example, that there is overprediction by 0.39 standard deviation of the performance of students labeled learning disabled (Reynolds 1984)? The problem with testing the learning disabled is further compounded by the confounding between the method by which the group is usually defined in psychoeducational decision making and the method for determining whether test scores for such groups are valid (Reynolds 1984). Traditional emphasis in test validity has been concerned with the utility of the testing to the consumers of test data (such as educational programs and employers). Yet it may be argued that when dealing with minority groups, the validity of inference has as much to do with test bias and fairness to these groups as with utility to programs and institutions.

If we refer to the professional standards on testing (American Educational Research Association, American Psychological Association, and National Council on Measurement in Education 1985, 9), validity is supposed to refer to the appropriateness, meaningfulness, and usefulness of the specific inferences made from test scores. Validation should include several types of evidence (spanning the three traditional categories) to support such inferences. Ultimately, decisions about the relevant evidence are to be made in the light of the intended uses of the test and possible alternatives to testing. It is a matter of professional judgment, as observed by Messick (1988):

> Validity is an overall evaluative judgment, founded on empirical evidence and theoretical rationales of the adequacy and appropriateness of inferences and actions based on test scores. (33)

Professional judgment about the hypotheses regarding the construct involved is made within a theoretical and empirical context of cumulative evidence. This context is intertwined with the value context for evaluating the actions and social consequences that result from the inferences made. Cronbach (1988) compared testing decisions to evaluation research, stating:

> Validity speaks to a diverse and potentially critical audience; therefore the argument must link concepts, evidence, social and personal consequences, and values. (4)

Cronbach's view on test validity is that we cannot sidestep questions of truth and worth by a narrow operationalism or reliance on measured observations, and that constructs in a broad sense are always involved in interpretation.

The reason for the appeal to the construct meaning of tests as an integrative perspective is that constructs allow us to extrapolate or reach beyond the testing situation to new circumstances of prediction and generalization. In addition to providing a rational basis for hypothesizing predictive relationships to criteria, the construct in question may address potential outcomes and anticipate possible biases of application and limitations of a consequential nature (Messick 1988, 1989). As indicated in chapter 4, concepts and constructs are the medium of discourse for a scientific profession. All inquiry hinges on the issue of whether we are dealing with meaningful ideas that can be interpreted within the existing network of ideas shared by the profession. This is one dimension with which to integrate our review of the different modes and methods of inquiry. The other theme is that the practice of professional judgment in both theoretical and value contexts must lead to useful actions that can be justified.

THE CENTRALITY OF MEANING AND VALUE

If we reflect on the problems inherent in each of the modes of inquiry considered in this chapter, it should be apparent that the central issue concerns whether we are able to obtain relevant information and whether the inferences we make about our clients and research subjects constitute meaningful, valuable interpretations of their behaviors and experiences. No method of inquiry is free from the problems of valid interpretation. Observed phenomena are open to interpretation by the observer whose perspective may vary according to the observational stance adopted. An observed event could also have different meanings in different cultures. Narrative data from interviews have to be interpreted in the context of the interview and the frames of reference of the participants. Clients make certain statements to us in part as a function of the particular relationships we have with them. Test responses are also a function of context and are subject to interpretation by the examiner. A given test score can measure different variables in different persons, depending on the style or process of test taking. Whether in research or in practice, there is a long chain of reasoning and inference between the gathering of information and the drawing of conclusions. The practitioner or the researcher has to cast about for plausible hypotheses in interpreting the data. Another commonality is the presence of an interpersonal context of information exchange and interpretation that is further embedded in sociocultural, political, and value contexts. Our data and inferences are coconstituted by these contexts and what we do in inquiry. A practitioner must keep in mind not only the objective of information gathering but process goals such as making certain that the particular form of inquiry conducted with the client will have a therapeutic effect. Similarly, a researcher must consider the effects of the investigative process on the self-esteem and psychological well-being of the subject.

For a given situation of inquiry, the critical question becomes, What is the most appropriate process of verifying a hypothesis and eliminating alternative inferences, within the realm of ethical practice? Testing, for example, represents one of many possible operationalizations of a construct of interest. Multiple operationalism has been proposed in the multitrait-multimethod tradition (Campbell and Fiske 1959), and is still advocated in the hypothesis-testing approach to validity (Cronbach 1990). Having different kinds of data obtained with a broad repertoire of methods is essential to building an adequate picture of what we are trying to describe meaningfully, whether in research or in practice (see, for example, Cole, Howard, and Maxwell 1981). This is evident when we conduct a comprehensive case study, a topic to be discussed in chapter 8. In addition, a more flexible conception of acceptable processes is suggested. For instance, Cronbach (1988) recommended using exploratory factor analysis, case studies of persons with extreme scores, and having subjects free-associate to test items orally as additional ways of improving test interpretation. This is in recognition of the limiting effects of the standard format in which operational hypotheses are tested with measured scores.

Other forms of alternative inquiry have been suggested to probe the boundaries of our assessment data and inferences. Process-dynamic and criterion-referenced testing may be considered an option in situations where traditional standardized testing seems inappropriate. For example, with students who have been repeatedly placed as below norm in standardized testing, the use of process-oriented and criterion-referenced testing is more relevant to the purposes of remediation. Besides, such alternatives may avoid further subjecting these clients to the experience of failure. Goldman (1990) explained how certain qualitative assessment methods allow the client to have an active role in the process and can be adapted to the situations and cultural contents that are appropriate to the particular client. Healy (1990) proposed a collaborative model for career appraisal as an alternative to traditional approaches in which the professional gives expert opinions to the client based on relatively context-free interviewing and testing results. A joint process of test selection, data review, and client self-directed decision making is used instead to contextualize the findings. Constructivist assessment, based on the assumptions of interactive and contextually embedded inquiry, offers additional procedures and processes of establishing our knowledge claims (Neimeyer 1993).

Although we are less likely to confuse operational definitions with the full meanings of a construct in the case of natural forms of narrative data, we are still faced with problems of interpretation. Do clients and research informants mean what they seem to be saying? There have been debates about the accessibility of cognitive events and the veridicality of verbal reports as data (Ericsson and Simon 1980; Nisbett and Wilson 1976, 1977; Smith and Miller 1978; White 1980). Cognitive research has indicated that observations and reports of inner experience are a function of verbal abilities, memory, and other mental processes. Granted that our methods of access have limitations, it is still reasonable to expect some degree of replicability (Ericsson and Simon 1984; Klinger 1978). In clinical practice, cognitive retrieval can be enhanced with the appropriate motivational set and the use of facilitation such as with guided imagery and clues of retrieval (Meichenbaum and Cameron 1981). The extent to which one would insist on applying traditional standards of verifiability depends on the assumptions one holds with respect to verbal data (Meichenbaum and Butler 1980). Veridicality in the objectivist, detached-observer sense might not be as much of an issue to those who simply regard self-reports as valuable in revealing the construals of people. Verbally communicated narrative data are as much a function of the cognitive retrieval of experience as they are the ongoing products of culturally constituted and socially constructed meanings (Williams 1992).

Current approaches to memory research have included social constructionist perspectives (Middleton and Edwards 1990) that conceive of cognitive events as nonprivate and primarily social in origin. Even a realist conception of cognitive processes would require us to consider factors of social significance in the interpretive context (Neisser 1982). In view of the fact that the meaning of the data depends on context in all modes of information gathering, it is appropriate to include context as part of assessment. Scheflen (1966) attempted to outline an approach to context analysis in communication research on psychotherapy. Cicourel (1987), in studying medical encounters, pointed to the need for ethnographic information on context in analyzing discourse data. The use of multiple modes of inquiry to generate layers of embedding information for interpretive purposes is demonstrated in the study of organizational forgetting by Engestrom, Brown, Engestrom, and Koistinen (1990). As mentioned earlier, practitioners in their work as program consultants and therapeutic-change agents also function in a manner similar to participant, ethnographic researchers. In this way, they learn about the relevant contexts in order to have valid understanding of problems and to function effectively in their professional roles. The operationalization of context is not easy to achieve, as witnessed in research on practice (Wampold 1991), and will likely require the use of multiple and alternative methods.

In spite of the growing knowledge in human cognition and language use, and the changing assumptions about the nature of data in human inquiry, we are still left with certain dilemmas in professional practice. What does it mean, for example, when a practitioner claims that a client has recalled a repressed memory of trauma? Does it represent an accurate retrieval of a verifiable memory under facilitative conditions? Or does it represent essentially a therapeutic construction of meanings and experiences consonant with the client's current motivation and existential issues, regardless of verifiability? Given that only some recalled events are verifiable, on what assumptions should the practicing psychologist proceed with inquiry in such areas as prior abuse and incest? This depends on a number of factors, including our beliefs about the prevalence of such trauma, current knowledge about memory and cognition, and epistemic assumptions about the process of inquiry in an interpersonal context. A critical constructionist may treat the client's report as a reconstruction constrained by the context of inquiry, the cognitive and verbal capacity of the participants, and the realistic limits of historical circumstances.

It is important to stress that in constructivist approaches to knowledge, the issue of validity is reframed as one of viability or usefulness to the parties concerned (Neimeyer and Neimeyer 1993). This is the distinction between useful, worthy knowledge and truthful, accurate knowledge. Useful knowledge is functionally valid in the sense of being valued or consequential (Messick 1988). Whether our methods of inquiry would allow us to generate knowledge that results in useful action is a question of value that builds upon the central criterion of meaningfulness. Howard (1982) suggested that the usefulness of a given method can be gauged by research on the relative information yield of different methods. This type of research effort should be extended to evaluating the usefulness of all inquiry methods in professional practice. Goodyear (1990), reviewing research on clients' use of test information and feedback from assessment, concluded that clients seem to prefer individual interpretations and that there are possible interactions between client variables and the assessment process, consistent with the notion of aptitude-treatment interaction (Cronbach and Snow 1977). More research is needed on the utility of our methods of inquiry and the psychological factors influencing receptiveness to and usage of the information they yield. Consistent with the pragmatist orientation in support of methodological pluralism, an informed choice of methods requires that we evaluate their respective value as demonstrated by the experience of application in research and practice. In doing so, our profession must also consider the full spectrum of conceptions of validity in judging the value of each method, such as discussed in the previous chapter.

Perhaps the key to valid inference and useful inquiry is judgment. Cronbach (1982a), drawing from the lessons of program evaluation, emphasized the role of qualitative understanding. One can learn from the scrutiny of observed variations after formal hypothesis testing as well as from reflections on the limits of one's ways of defining a construct. Rice (1992), reflecting on the construction of category systems for psychotherapy research, stressed that researchers should not assume certain behaviors to be conceptually related in a given system of classification and that more than one system should be constructed to reflect the multiple dimensions that may be involved. The experienced knowledge of research practice in this case has enabled the researcher to make such judgments. The type of experienced knowledge of practice discussed by Hoshmand and Polkinghorne (1992), and the personal knowing of experienced researchers described in Hoshmand and Martin (in press) can be examined in terms of their role in guiding professional judgment during the inquiry process. It is to this area of professional judgment and the knowledge of practice that we shall turn in the next chapter. The judgments of researchers and practitioners, while in need of reflexive self-evaluation, are further evaluated by the broad audience of our professional community who will consider the fit of our observations with the existing system of ideas and practices. That is why our inquiry practices must involve some form of demonstration and be open to communal evaluation.

SUGGESTED ADDITIONAL LEARNING

1. Construct an observation code for systematic observation of a videotaped interaction (such as a therapy session), based on a selected problem focus and conceptual scheme or theoretical rationale. This exercise is best carried out with a partner serving as an independent observer or in class with multiple observers. As you apply the observation system to answer your preformulated questions, identify problems of reliability and evaluate the adequacy of your operational definitions of the targeted units and the sampling procedures. After completing the data gathering with the coding system, try to set it aside and see if you can develop other ways of observing the same tape. Reflect on the processes involved in the shifts you experience as you make the second effort as an observer. Evaluate this detached mode of observation overall in terms of merits and limitations and how it fits with your preferred ways of knowing.

2. Conduct a participant observation of a group that is personally and culturally alien to you, in a naturalistic setting. Begin by writing down your preconceptions of the target group, reflecting on the sources of such preconceptions. Keep a journal on the process of your planning, making entry to the setting, and managing your observer role. In addition to keeping notes on observed events in the setting, try to obtain permission for audio-taping conversations with informants. Reflect on the issues that you encounter during the process and what you have learned about yourself as a participant observer. Evaluate the participant mode of observing in contrast with your experience of the detached mode.

3. Using the narrative data obtained from your participant observation, develop a method of analyzing the transcribed information. Select an approach among qualitative models as a basis for starting, and evolve a system that will allow you to identify significant meanings and events or recurrent patterns in the data. Make a written description of the process of analysis so that others can follow the path you have taken. Work with a partner who can independently review the transcripts, following your evolved process of analysis. Discuss your interpretations with the peer reviewer. Additionally, attempt an analysis of the narrative transcript of an interaction in which you were not a participant. (You may exchange data with a partner who has done a similar participant-observation project.) Compare this experience as an uninvolved reviewer with your previous interpretive stance as a participant observer.

4. Read the following study by Giorgi and discuss its use of the interviewing method, the nature of the interpretive process, and the soundness of the conclusions in the data analysis:

Giorgi, A. 1975. An application of phenomenological method in psychology. In *Duquesne studies in phenomenological psychology,* ed. A. Giorgi, C.T. Fischer, and E. Murray, *2:* 82-103. Pittsburgh: Duquesne University Press.

5. Read and discuss the following articles by Willingham and Geisinger in terms of the issues of test validity, fair testing, and the responsibilities of the professional psychologist:

Willingham, W. W. 1988. Testing handicapped people: The validity issue. In *Test validity* ed. H. Wainer and H.I. Braun, 89-103. Hillsdale, NJ: Lawrence Erlbaum.

Geisinger, K. F. 1988. The golden rule in psychological testing: Please, please don't do it unto me. *Theoretical and Philosophical Psychology* 8: 15-23.

7

The Applied Epistemology of the Scientist-Practitioner

In this chapter, we shall take a closer look at ourselves as the human instrument in inquiry and the manner in which we generate and act upon the knowledge we help to create. Specifically, we should try to understand the cognitive skills and processes involved in the inferences and judgments we make as scientist-practitioners. This will begin with considering the nature of conceptual understanding and perceptual inference in the social context. Some of the research on professional expertise and the psychology of the scientist will be reviewed for implications. The discussion will return to the issue of the self in relation to ways of knowing. Implications for the applied epistemology of research and practice in psychology will be considered throughout.

THE NATURE OF CONCEPTUAL DEVELOPMENT

There are a number of sources of ideas on how new knowledge is developed and integrated into our conceptual understanding. Psychology has adopted the information-processing model of cognitive science in much of the experimental research on cognition (Hayes-Roth 1977; Neisser 1967; Mayer 1981) and as a theoretical framework for applied areas such as clinical psychology (Ingram 1986; Turk, Salovey, and Prentice 1988). Recent theories of social cognition that are guided by contextualist, ecological conceptions also assume an active system of perceptual information processing at work in producing meaningful knowledge (Fiske and Taylor 1984; Neisser 1976; Weimer 1977a). The concept of active constructing of meaningful information provides a common bridge between information processing models of cognition and constructionist perspectives on knowledge (Guidano 1984). Both cognitive research and constructionist metaphors have been utilized in developmental theories to understand conceptual knowledge and how it is acquired (Hill 1961; Mahoney 1988b; Piaget 1970). Although different labels may be used to refer to the cognitive organization of meaningful information, the term "schema" is commonly accepted (Anderson 1981; Rumelhart 1981, 1984; Taylor and Crocker 1981). A schema is a modifiable information structure that represents knowledge of the interrelationships between events, objects, and situations that we encounter. It is a prototype of what are frequently experienced, stored in memory.

It is generally believed that information is acted upon by each person as a function of preexisting understanding organized in the form of schemata. Thus, meaningful perception is in the nature of apperception or, in a manner of speaking, filtered through the interpretive structures that have been developed from past experience. The constructing of experience in interaction with existing schemata results in structural changes or new cognitive organization (Craik and Lockhart 1972). The process of knowledge acquisition can be thought of as a successive development of schematic structures that are tested and revised in ways that facilitate learning and thinking. When there is significant schematic change, the quality of learning is supposed to improve (Ausubel, Novak, and Hanesian 1978; Rumelhart 1981; Wittrock 1974). It appears that when we bring different mental operations to bear on new experience, the structure of schemata becomes differentiated and expanded, leading to higher levels of understanding. In other words, cognitive skills are needed in order to bring about conceptual gains or to activate knowledge that is otherwise inert. The mental operations involved in this kind of conceptual development have been referred to as "metalearning and metacognitive strategies" (Brown 1978; Forrest-Pressley, McKinnon, and Waller 1985; Novak 1985). They include reflection and self-monitoring (Glaser 1984). Reflective metalearning and metacognition may be facilitated by the use of Vee heuristics and methods of concept mapping, as well as Socratic questioning and interactive dialogue (Glaser 1984; Gowin 1981, 1990). These demonstrations suggest that reflective means of using mental operations can be facilitated in education and professional training (Pressley and Levin 1983; Schon 1983), a point we shall consider later.

Schemata are conceived to function also in anticipating new information. Besides providing us with interpretive structures with which to frame new experience, they direct our attention selectively. Sometimes, our perceptions are of an automated nature that permits an efficient way of dealing with familiar or redundant information (Bargh 1982; Shiffrin and Schneider 1977). Readily accessible schema enables us to develop highly practiced routines in those contexts that are relevant (Linville and Clark 1989). On the other hand, automated processing or recognition of the familiar does not allow us to engage in active perception and create new knowledge when needed. This is the limitation of automated or scripted responses (Schank and Abelson 1977). Studies of clinical judgment suggested that practitioners sometimes formulate impressions prematurely, based on insufficient information (Kleinmuntz 1984; Oskamp 1965; Sandifer, Hordern, and Green 1970). Thus it is important to ask to what extent our professional inquiry involves automated perceptions and judgments, and whether such automated modes should be minimized in certain situations in order for new understanding to occur.

Developmental theorists, following Piaget (1969), regard some perceptual experiences as involving assimilation of information with no major changes in schematic structure, and others as involving accommodation or transformative construction and schematic changes. The latter kinds of change are essential to higher-level conceptual development, and involve complex, deliberative mental operations as mentioned previously. It will be helpful to understand the conditions under which effective accommodation occurs. For example, when can we expect a person to confront misconceptions of any kind or be open to a change in worldview? Clinical and counseling psychologists often wonder about how clients may modify their personal paradigms of living in the course of therapy. The same question can be asked reflexively of scientist-practitioners with respect to our professional paradigms, knowledge structures, and understanding. It is likely that cognitive processes related to the development of core constructs and belief structures hold the key to human change processes, especially changes in conceptual understanding (Janoff-Bulman 1989; Mahoney 1991).

Two factors that have been proposed as central to concept development are the self as agent and the role of action. In active perception, the observer is an agent engaged in intentional comprehension through symbolic processes (Hamlyn 1983; Werner and Kaplan 1963). Our self-schema is central to changes in conceptual understanding. Research suggests, for example, that one's ability to imagine possible selves can lead to schema change (Markus and Nurius 1986). Motivation is generally required in conceptual change, as mediated by what is experienced as an optimal environment. This certainly is hypothesized to be the case for therapeutic change. People seem more willing to question their core beliefs and assumptions about life when there is a personal incentive and a sense of psychological safety in doing so. Rokeach (1960), in depicting the open and the closed mind, emphasized our self-protective tendencies toward new information. Created schema further serves an action-control function by shaping our response to life situations and our feelings about self and others (Cantor and Kihlstrom 1987). These cognitive structures that make up our personality-in-action are continuously evolved in our doing of life tasks (Cantor 1990).

The mutability of personality has much to do with cognitive adaptability or our ability to modify schemas and problem-solving strategies in the light of experience. Here, too, lies the link between our epistemologies-in-action and our evolving professional knowledge. Our "doing" in research and practice constitutes the experiential base of our knowledge structures. The "doing" aspects of conceptual change are central to the translating of declarative, factual knowledge or "knowing that" to procedural knowledge or "knowing how" (Anderson 1982). From an action standpoint, the applied knowledge of the scientist-practitioner is context bound and modified by experience in dealing with problem tasks (Hoshmand and Polkinghorne 1992). Our intellectual adaptability consists in a flexible transforming of conceptual knowledge into procedural knowledge

Thus, it appears that conceptual development is a function of ego-involved, purposeful, transformative experiences (likely involving action) in particular contexts. Contextualist and ecological orientations emphasize the adaptive transaction of people with the environment (Stewart 1989; Veroff 1983). Social-historical approaches further stress the cultural milieu (Cole 1983; Vygotsky 1962) and the role of social agents as formative forces in individual cognition (Belmont 1989; Rogoff 1990). They improve on the social dimension of cognitive theorizing that in the past has not been sufficiently articulated in developmental theories. They also offer an alternative to individualistic conceptions prevalent in most psychological theorizing. How meanings of self and the world are developed has been formulated in social constructionist terms (Harre 1984; Shotter and Gergen 1989). Such meanings are considered to be constituted in cultural and social practices. Philosophical views of conceptual development as the learning of concept meanings in particular language games (Toulmin 1969; Wittgenstein 1968) similarly regard conceptual understanding as culture dependent. These perspectives suggest that the social context of meaning making and knowledge development is just as important as the intentions and skills of the learner or observer. This has significant implications for professional development which we will consider in the last section of this chapter and more fully in chapter 9. In examining the processes of knowledge acquisition and knowledge construction by psychologists in research and practice, we must take into account the nature of the epistemic processes we apply in the social context as well as the social nature of our knowing.

In summary, conceptual development can be understood in terms of the network of knowledge schemata developed with experience and the level of skills one has acquired for constructing and transforming knowledge. Our capacity for learning to learn is just as important as the knowledge we have acquired. The self of the knower serves as an active agent, carrying out purposeful actions in interaction with the social environment. The processes and context of knowing are largely social in nature. We will consider next how these processes may operate in the social settings of our professional inquiry.

PERCEPTUAL INFERENCE AND JUDGMENT IN SOCIAL CONTEXT

There is a body of research on social-information processing, some of which is directly related to the judgments and cognitive strategies used by scientist-practitioners. As was apparent in the discussions of the previous chapter, a central issue in professional practice concerns the quality and validity of the judgments and inferences we make. What kind of model can we use to describe how psychologists make inferences in situations of practice? Are scientists more rational in their cognitive processes than nonscientists? Do clinicians make sound judgments? How may we improve upon our judgments and inferences? These are some of the questions that have been raised.

We can begin with the conceptions of the cognitive processes involved which have guided research and evaluation in this area. The influence of cognitive science is reflected in attempts to develop models of perceptual inference and judgment processes such as expert systems (Churchman 1971; Pople 1982). It became apparent in such modeling efforts that the real situations of practice often involve ill-structured problems that are too fuzzy to describe precisely (Cantor, Mischel, and Schwartz 1982; Wood 1983). Those who regard psychological practice as an art rather than an exact science would tend to support such a conclusion (Matarazzo 1971). Others have tried to apply decision theory to describe the criteria used in judgments and predictions and to evaluate the optimality of judgments and predictions (Einhorn and Hogarth 1981; Treisman and Williams 1984). This line of research is consistent with studies of the heuristics used to infer from an observed sample to a population (Stevenson 1972; Tversky and Kahneman 1974). They examine how close one comes to matching the criterion in probabilistic terms. The relative reliance on qualitative judgment and statistical judgment was captured in Meehl's (1954) characterization of professional judgments in psychological practice as either clinical or statistical in nature.

According to Meehl's conception, professional judgment in the context of practice would seem to include an inductive process of data gathering, holding general assumptions or laws about human behavior, deriving hypotheses about the particular case in question, assessing the fit of the hypothesis with the case, and making predictions based on the best fit. How these various processes contribute to a final judgment, however, has been debated (Einhorn 1988; Holt 1958, 1988). Although some research on clinicians' diagnostic judgments suggested the use of inductive processes to build a meaningful formulation or prototype to which to fit a case in question (Kleinmuntz 1963, 1968, Koester 1954), others pointed to the initial use of more holistic impressions from which to deduce hypotheses or make diagnostic decisions (Gauron and Dickinson, 1969; Phelan 1964). Additional descriptive research is needed on the processes by which professionals develop their inferential base or formulate their hypotheses in problem solving.

Meanwhile, the dichotomy between clinical and statistical modes of prediction (Dawes, Faust, and Meehl 1988; Meehl 1960) has continued to permeate discussions about professional decision making in clinical practice. For example, in the area of behavioral interventions, there are some who emphasize the flexible clinical thinking needed in making the moment-to-moment decisions (Evans 1985; Kanfer 1985), in contrast to the use of decision theory and statistical or actuarial models of prediction (Mash 1985). The former entails self-correcting and -questioning, and the latter, a methodic application of decision rules. If we regard these two contrasting modes as different but complementary ways of knowing, we may be able to have a more complete understanding of the applied epistemology of practice.

On the question of whether scientists treat information in a more rational manner than nonscientists, there is evidence suggesting that scientists are just as likely to make errors of inference. Tversky and Kahneman (1971) found that both scientists and nonscientists assumed that random selection guarantees representativeness of samples, and were insensitive to sample-size differences. In investigating the use of sample representativeness as a heuristic, these researchers found additional evidence of misuse of this heuristic in predictive judgments (Kahneman and Tversky 1973; Tversky and Kahneman 1974). What is of note is that even when errors of inference occur, people are not inclined to adjust their judgments. Hamill, Wilson, and Nisbett (1980) found that subjects continued to use the representativeness heuristic even when presented with evidence of sample bias or nonrepresentativeness. When initial impressions based on incorrect use of heuristics continue to cause bias in subsequent judgments and predictions, it is referred to as an "anchoring effect."

The persistence of error and bias becomes a critical problem in what we do as scientist-practitioners, given our reliance on working theories or hypotheses in guiding our inquiry and professional actions. Chapman and Chapman (1969) found that trained psychologists, when making theory-based judgments, perceived a relationship between clinical symptoms and signs on Rorschach responses where none actually existed. Wason (1960) and Wason and Johnson-Laird (1968, 1972) documented a pervasive confirmatory bias in human problem solving. Subjects persisted in using an incorrect hypothesis and largely refused to disconfirm it. Mahoney and DeMonbreun (1977) demonstrated that physical scientists and psychologists were just as likely as nonscientists to show problem-solving bias. Although the implications of their study were subject to alternative interpretations (Bowers 1977; Weimer 1977b), it is interesting to note that the nonscientists (ministers) in this case took more time before speculation with their hypotheses and experimented more in problem solving than did the scientists. The propensity for theory-based interpretations of information opens us to the potential for error. Theory-based judgments, as compared to judgments where no theoretical information was provided, have been shown to overestimate and distort the objective relationships among variables (Kahneman, Slovic, and Tversky 1982).

The sources of errors of judgment appear to be our perceptual processes. Studies of attitude change revealed biased assimilation of information (Lord, Ross, and Lepper 1979). Actor-observer differences have also been found with respect to the perceived cause of behaviors (Jones and Nisbett 1971; Nisbett, Caputo, Legant, and Maracek 1973). There is a tendency to underestimate the importance of environmental forces and overestimate the role of personal disposition when we judge the behavior of others (Bem, 1967; Kelly 1973). This tendency seems to be a function of whether one likes the person in question; negative actions are attributed to situational forces if we like the person and to personal disposition in those we dislike (Regan, Straus, and Fazio 1974). Initial bias can lead to biased assimilation and use of information, compounding judgment problems at every stage (Hogarth 1981). Furthermore, through self-fulfilling behavior, social perceptions become linked to social causation (Snyder 1976). The labeling of clients by professionals reflects biased assumptions and attributions (Batson 1975; Batson, Jones, and Cochran 1979; Langer and Abelson 1974; Plous and Zimbardo 1986). Gender-related biases in the perceptions of mental health profession-also represent one such example (Franks and Rothblum 1983; Kaplan 1983). Considering the sociocultural and political contexts of psychological inquiry and practice, and the fact that self-fulfilling prophecies are especially likely in situations of unequal power such as between professional and client (Snyder and Thomsen 1988), the potential for perceptual bias seems great.

We should include our self-schema as a factor when evaluating our perceptual inferences. Self-concept has been found to be involved in the perception of others (Markus, Smith, and Moreland 1985). Research from the perspective of personal construct theory has shown constancies in people's self-judgment and judgment of others (Adams-Webber, 1990; Frey and Adams-Webber 1992; Lefebvre, Lefebvre, and Adams-Webber 1986). Positive evaluation of others appears to be at a constant ratio to positive evaluation of self. The probability of positively evaluating others on a dimension in which the self is evaluated negatively is constrained. In other words, positivity bias in social cognition usually occurs with constructs relevant to oneself, and does not apply to constructs on which the self is evaluated negatively. Personal construct studies on therapists (Soldz 1989, 1992) indicated that these professionals used distinct construct systems for construing clients, personal acquaintances, and self. Clients in general were construed more negatively than personal acquaintances and judged to be less like oneself, irrespective of expected improvement in therapy.

Research further suggests that confirmatory bias and theory perseverance are due to social factors (Anderson, Lepper, and Ross 1980; Mackie and Cooper 1984) and emotional commitment to one's own biases (Nisbett and Ross, 1980). In the area of clinical information processing, the risk of confirmatory bias has been linked to the professional's preconceptions and dispositional assumptions about the case (Eells and Guppy 1963; Houts and Galante 1985; Meehl 1960). There is a strong pathology orientation among mental health professionals in their dispositional assumptions about clients, which enters into assessment, diagnosis, and treatment (McReynolds 1989; Wills 1978). Furthermore, bias in conceptualization and treatment planning has been found to be a function of psychologists' theoretical orientations (Kopta, Newman, McGovern, and Sandrock 1986). These biasing factors seem to be moderated to some extent by interpersonal attraction and the nature of interaction between the professional and the client (Wills 1982). Behavioral confirmation and the presence of judgment errors in clinical practice have been amply documented (Sarbin, Taft, and Bailey 1960; Snyder and Thomsen 1988; Turk and Salovey 1988). It is therefore critical for us to give reflexive attention to our perceptual processes and to scrutinize our interpersonal motivation, use of judgment heuristics, reliance on preconceived ideas, and tendency for confirmation.

The idea that human perception and cognition are social in nature has implications for how we can find countermeasures for biased inferences and unsound judgments. From a social constructionist perspective, the data in psychological research and practice are coconstructed by the professional and the human subject. This should, in principle, narrow the gap between actor-observer differences in attributions and interpretations of behavior. Clinical practice that is based on the social constructionist perspective now includes the active involvement of the client in the formulation of problems (e.g., Andersen 1991). The context in which professional judgment errors may occur is modified by dialogical modes of problem assessment and treating the client as the expert on his or her own experiences and meanings (Anderson and Goolishian 1992). How these attempts at social negotiation and sharing of responsibility will influence professional judgment in the long run deserves to be systematically investigated.

RESEARCH ON PROFESSIONAL EXPERTISE

Another line of research that is relevant here has been concerned with the knowledge processes of experts or competent professionals in various fields. What can we learn from those who are experienced in their domain of knowledge? How is it that those who are skilled can solve problems more effectively? Certain general postulates have been used to depict the processes of knowledge acquisition and utilization in human problem solving. In terms of the distinction between declarative and procedural knowledge, it appears that we need to acquire both a factual knowledge base and the procedures and means of using the given knowledge base (Anderson 1982). For example, it is just as important for a clinical practitioner to learn about the various theories of psychopathology and the signs associated with a certain psychological problem as it is to know how to apply these signs in diagnosis. In making inferences of any sort, we utilize cues, try to isolate invariances that fit a conceptual category in our knowledge structure, develop tentative hypotheses, and search for confirming cues (Bruner 1957; de Groot 1969). Heuristics, such as means-ends relationship and representativeness of an observation sample, may be employed (Newell and Simon 1972; Nisbett, Krantz, Jepson, and Kunda 1983). This ability to use heuristics appears to be just as important as having the required knowledge base in problem solving. Another way to describe problem solving is that we engage in pattern recognition (Uhr 1966; Uhr and Vossler 1963) in evaluating new information and searching for familiar cues. Particular patterns are represented in conceptual schema that serves as a working model or prototype against which we can compare our observations (Glaser 1984). New structures developed from experience must be interrogated, instantiated, or revised to develop increasingly useful conceptual structures. The ability to recognize problem structures and to evolve useful patterns of understanding is essential to problem solving.

In the case of experts compared to novices, research has shown that they have better conceptual as well as procedural knowledge (Glaser 1984). The availability of a strong conceptual knowledge base enhances cognitive functioning. Those with more conceptual knowledge did better in memory and encoding of information than those with less knowledge (Chase and Simon 1973). Individuals with low knowledge were found to encode information at surface level rather than at levels of generalizable concepts, thus limiting their inferential ability (Pellegrino and Glaser 1982). For the purpose of problem solving, conceptual knowledge of problem structures or how problem information is represented schematically, will make a practical difference. Research suggests that the quality of problem representation is different between experts and novices (Chi, Glaser, and Rees 1982; Lesgold, Feltovich, Glaser, and Wang 1981). The experts seemed to have well-connected schemata, representing prototypes that subsume information not apparent in a problem situation but derived from previous experience (Horowitz, Post, French, Wallis, and Siegelman 1981; Horowitz, Wright, Lowenstein, and Parad 1981). Novices, on the other hand, appeared to organize information in terms of the literal objects given in a problem statement. They were unable to invoke meaningful principles for pattern recognition, which the experts seemed able to do tacitly (Polanyi 1962). This may explain why students and new professionals in clinical training often wonder about how their instructors and supervisors are able to "see" a particular relationship in a case that is not immediately apparent to them. Sometimes, they wish for a clear set of rules to guide them. The difference between mechanical rule following and the ability to resort to an adaptive mental model for inference (Johnson-Laird 1983) is another way of describing novice-expert differences.

Perhaps because of the quality of schematic representation available to experts, they can readily decide which types of information are relevant for a given type of problem. Thus, familiarity with problem types gives one an advantage in continuing inquiry and problem solving. Inexperienced researchers and practitioners also find themselves wondering about what types of questions are most productive to pursue in research and clinical inquiry and how those with experience come to choose the particular methods and approaches they use. Whereas some descriptive work has been done on the epistemic skills of practitioners, little is known about the epistemologies-in-action of researchers in applied areas of psychology. Research on the decision making of experienced researchers over extended periods of their programmatic research may provide us with methodological insights and examples of creative or productive inquiry (Hoshmand and Martin, in press).

Superior pattern recognition among experienced social and physical scientists has been reported in Bransford and Vye (1989), just as the thought processes of experienced teachers have been the focus of Berliner (1986). Research on the nature of expertise in decision making and diagnostic judgments in a variety of domains has been documented by Chi, Glaser, and Farr (1988). An additional dimension of difference between experts and novices consists in the ability to monitor one's own thinking and problem solving (Brown 1978; Markman 1979). Due to experience, experts can more accurately judge the difficulty of problems and plan their time in problem solving more effectively. They can evaluate their own progress and predict their outcomes more accurately (Chi, Glaser, and Rees 1982; Chi, Bassok, Lewis, Reimann, and Glaser 1988). These findings confirm again the importance of metacognition and self-monitoring (Gavelek and Raphael 1985; Pressley and Levin 1983).

The implications of the above for the novice are that one must acquire the appropriate knowledge base in the specific domains of interest and obtain as much practical experience as possible in the application of such domain-specific knowledge (Glaser 1984). Case studies, the topic of chapter 8, are excellent vehicles for learning how to derive working prototypes of problems and for practicing pattern recognition (Collins and Stevens 1982). During the process of conceptualization and problem solving, we must engage in self-monitoring (Palinscar and Brown 1984). Reflection on practice enables us to revise patterns of understanding and to monitor our own thought processes and assumptions. For example, in reviewing a therapy session that we have conducted, we can reflect on the communication context in which our working assumptions were tested and evaluate the fit of our pattern of understanding under alternative assumptions. The ability to reflect and to adopt a reflective attitude, which have been a thematic concern in this volume, are recommended as an essential quality of the effective scientist-practitioner (Baron 1981; Hoshmand and Polkinghorne 1992; Schon 1983). Chapter 9 will offer specific suggestions on the cultivation of reflective habits. One of the benefits of reflection is in discovering our preferred ways of knowing and our own contributions to the knowing process.

WAYS OF KNOWING AND THE SELF

Although it is instructive to consider cognitive factors and conceptual structures as the basis of individual differences with respect to knowledge, it may be useful to broadly conceive of personal ways of knowing and being as relevant to our applied epistemology. The previously mentioned theory and research on personality and cognition, as well as the literature on epistemic styles, support the notion that approaches to knowing are constitutive of higher-order personality factors and the self-in-action. Particular ways of knowing seem to be related to one's commitment to particular worldviews, and thus influence one's entire way of relating to the world. To understand ourselves as knowers is more than a cognitive issue. The implications for how we function professionally are far-reaching.

A typology that is a theory of personality as well as a theory of knowledge by implication is Jung's (1923) psychological types. Jung conceived of four mental functions—thinking, feeling, sensation, and intuition—that are present to different degrees in all persons at different stages in life. He further postulated three levels of consciousness (personal conscious, personal unconscious, and collective unconscious) and two attitudinal orientations (introversion and extraversion) in interaction with these mental functions. His theory has been developed into temperament-based personality types (Keirsey and Bates 1978; Myers 1962). Temperament theory does not presume unmodifiable constitutional differences. Rather, individual propensities are expected to be nurtured by the environment. Furthermore, one can develop aspects of personality that are less dominant, to achieve a mature balance. For example, a person strong in thinking can develop the capacity for feeling as a perceptual response mode. In other words, we can potentiate ways of knowing that are not as prominent in our repertoire.

Using the modified Jungian typology of Keirsey and Bates (1978), Golay (1982) derived a description of four types of learners; the actual (sensory) -routine, the actual (sensory) -spontaneous, the conceptual (intuitive)-specific, and the conceptual (intuitive) -global. The actual-routine learner requires structure and rules, and is adept at learning factual information through concrete examples. The actual-spontaneous learner needs sensory experience and learns by action and doing. The conceptual-specific learner is analytical and adept at working with abstract principles. The conceptual-global learner is holistic in his or her approach to knowledge, requiring personal relations and integration in learning. Golay demonstrated in consultative practice in school settings that these different types of learners have different ways of knowing that can be matched with the appropriate learning environment. The implication is that being aware of one's learning style may enable one to optimize one's learning.

Another classification by Royce and his colleagues (Diamond and Royce 1980; Mos, Wardell, and Royce 1974; Royce 1964, 1975) distinguishes among three epistemic styles: empiricism, rationalism, and metaphorism. The empiricist style of knowing depends on sensory data gathered in an inductive fashion. The rationalist style relies on conceptual and logical analysis of a deductive nature. The metaphoric style focuses on the construction and symbolization of meanings, using analogical and holistic interpretation. (One may speculate in terms of Jungian typology that the empiricist style will favor sensation, whereas the rationalist and the metaphoric will favor thinking and intuition respectively.) Research indicated that these three different styles of knowing involve the use of different epistemological criteria, and can be measured with the Psycho-Epistemological Profile (Diamond and Royce 1980). The empiricist style has been used to characterize those who are committed to empiricism and behaviorism (Lyddon 1989a). The other two styles have been linked to rationalist and constructivist orientations, respectively (Mahoney 1991). In his research, Lyddon (1989a) was able to show that personal epistemology, as measured by the Psycho-Epistemological Profile, is related to clients' preference for counseling approaches representing behavioral, rationalist, and constructivist orientations.

It is likely that psychologists would also favor theoretical and therapeutic orientations that are consistent with their worldview and preferred ways of knowing (Krasner and Houts 1984; Martin 1988; O'Donohue 1989). Coan (1979) studied the personal and theoretical pathways of a sample of psychologists. McGovern, Newman, and Kopta (1986) explored the relationship between clinicians' attributions of patients' problem causality and responsibility for treatment outcome, and their metatheoretical assumptions and therapeutic orientation. Metatheoretical assumptions, as explained in chapter 4, are underlying core beliefs constituting one's philosophical commitments. Although there have been writings on the psychology of science and the scientist (Eiduson 1962; Maslow 1966; Roe 1952; Mahoney 1979), there has been surprisingly little work on how psychologists as scientist-practitioners produce psychological knowledge.

How scientists may be classified by their preferred ways of knowing has been researched outside of the psychology profession. Mitroff and Kilmann (1978) applied Jungian ideas to creating a typology of scientists. The dimension of sensing-intuition was translated into a continuum of the particular, the analytic, and the conceptual; and the dimension of thinking-feeling was used to characterize theoreticism and humanism. The resulting types, analytic-theorist, conceptual-theorist, particular-humanist, and conceptual-humanist, are conceived to have respective preferred modes of inquiry, evaluative norms, and orientations to knowledge, as well as differing interests. An important point made by Mitroff and Kilmann (1978) is that no one type of knowing is ascendant or should be regarded as the only model for scientific inquiry. The elevation of a particular orientation to knowledge is a value judgment that does not need to be absolute.

An example of how a particular way of knowing is valued differently in different times and cultures is intuition. Westcott (1968) defined intuition as the reaching of a conclusion on the basis of less explicit information than is ordinarily required to reach such a conclusion. His research on intuition was based on an assumption about the quantity and explicitness of information in situations of problem solving. It did not consider the quality of information or situations and subjects of knowing that are not cast in a problem-solving mode. Nonetheless, the place of intuition has been evaluated in clinical problem solving. Sarbin, Taft, and Bailey (1960) adopted an anti-intuition position in their study of clinical inference. Levy (1963) applied a logical empiricist approach to clinical interpretation, asserting that it should follow objective, nonintuitive principles. Bunge (1962), in addressing intuition in science, considered it to be just special cases of rapid inference. When placed in historical perspective, the anti-intuition position is consistent with the positivistic rejection of the classical view of intuitive knowing represented in the rationalist ideas of Plato (and later revived by Kant). The contention is with the fallibility of intuitive judgment. Contemporary views are divided on whether intuition should be evaluated by the quality of insight as opposed to correctness as validated against the criteria of logic (Royce, Coward, Egan, Kessel, and Mos 1978). It is agreed, however, that intuitions are based upon prior knowledge and experience and that intuitive leaps can be either good or bad depending on what results.

The tendency here to place more trust on analytical thinking than on intuition may be cultural. In contrast with Western concepts of rationality, intuition has a special place in Eastern philosophies of the mind. In Buddhism and Hinduism, intuition is an apprehension of the truth in existence. The intuitive way of knowing requires self-discipline and concentrated perception devoid of the distractions of the material world and self-centered desires. It is regarded as superior to other ways of knowing, and may be facilitated by psychological forms of practice such as yoga (Sinha 1958). Ways of knowing are not separate from ways of being in Eastern conceptions of consciousness. Jung was influenced by Eastern philosophy in conceiving of the collective unconscious, a type of knowing that represents the wisdom of generations about the recurrent problems of mankind (archetypes). Viewed from a cultural perspective, different ways of knowing can be better appreciated. Bruner (1957) argued for an equal recognition of both analytical and intuitive thinking as complementary processes. He pointed out that the lack of recognition of intuition may pose problems for society by depriving it of the perspectives and contributions of certain types of knowers. Research on creativity in both the arts and the sciences supports the role of intuition and imagination (e.g., Getzels and Csikszentmihalyi 1967). Consideration of women's ways of knowing has been more recently voiced (Belenky, Clinchy, Goldberger, and Tarule 1986), which underscores the importance of a cultural acceptance of different ways of knowing.

In psychology, the intuitive approach has been championed by some. Allport (1961) was in favor of holistic, intuitive comprehension or patterned perception in personality study. Recent studies of lives with histories and biographies are consistent with this holistic approach (McAdams and Ochberg 1988; Rabin, Aronoff, Barclay, and Zucker 1981). Bruner (1986) referred to the holistic, pattern type of thinking as the narrative mode of knowing, in contrast with propositional, logico-scientific reasoning. Narrative knowing that has been prevalent in the humanities is being adopted in the psychological study of human conduct and endorsed in constructionist approaches to knowledge (Polkinghorne 1988; Sarbin 1986a). Tolerance for pluralistic ways of knowing comes with not viewing different modes as adversarial. In his conception of intuition, Jung (1923) allowed for the intuitive function to be shaped by the other mental functions. Intuitive and metaphoric ways of knowing represent important complementary ways of knowing to the propositional knowing so characteristic of hypothetico-deductive reasoning in psychological research and practice. The fact remains that empiricist and rationalist styles of knowing by sensory data and analytical thinking are emphasized in academic and scientific settings. This means that the training of psychologists as scientist-practitioners may not potentiate all modes of knowing or support knowers of a different orientation until alternatives to the dominant ways of knowing are legitimated. Hoshmand and Polkinghorne (1992) suggested, for instance, that experienced practitioners who utilize patterned types of inference exemplify a type of knowing that the profession should formally recognize. Attention to our applied epistemology or ways of knowing must begin during professional development, a point to consider again in the final chapter of this book.

DEVELOPING REFLECTIVE QUALITIES OF MIND AND WAYS OF BEING

In consulting the developmental literature, we can find a number of hypotheses and descriptions of how we develop those qualities of mind and ways of being and knowing that we have considered above. These frameworks and the related research may be helpful in understanding and guiding graduate education and professional development. One area of research has been focused on conceptual-level functioning and the possibility of matching learners to educational approaches by their conceptual level (Hunt 1966, 1970). Holloway and Wolleat (1980) studied counselors' hypothesis formation as a function of conceptual level. It is believed that the level of cognitive and conceptual development has implications for professional development and practice (Berg and Stone 1980; Germain 1984). Although conceptual-level functioning has considerable theoretical appeal, difficulties with its measurement (Van Hesteren, Sawatzky, and Zingle 1982) have probably contributed to the lack of programmatic research involving professionals in training that is the population of interest here. The present discussion will therefore be focused on other models that seem to be more currently in use.

A model by Perry (1970) was derived from longitudinal research of intellectual and ethical development in college students. It suggested that young adults move through a number of positions of thinking about knowledge, self, and the world, as a function of their educational and life experiences. In the early stages, a dualistic distinction between the self and the world is maintained. The person thinks of himself or herself as a receiver of truth in an absolute sense. Learning depends on authoritative sources, and involves reducing different points of view to true-false or right-wrong positions. There is not much room for ambiguity until the person moves into a middle stage of tolerating multiplicity. From exposure to pluralistic points of view, and under the experience of conflict, the self becomes an arbiter that rejects authority. This relativistic position, which in some cases elevates subjectivity in order to accommodate conflicting personal paradigms, does not facilitate intellectual or social commitment sufficiently. Perry conceived of the resulting frustrations as requiring movement into a mature stage of contextual relativism. It represents an increased awareness of the importance of contexts and the need for knowledge to come from interacting with the world in a reasoned, committed fashion. (For a discussion of the implications of Perry's scheme for developmental counseling practice, see Widick 1977.)

Perry's model suggests changes in epistemological positions with development. It also implies that individuals will have different receptivity to unfamiliar worldviews depending on where they are developmentally and will respond accordingly to learning environments that involve teaching from authority versus challenging absolute beliefs. We may use this framework to consider when a young professional in our field will be ready to challenge authoritative sources of ideas and what kinds of learning experiences will facilitate someone in moving from the confusing experience of total relativism to some form of reasoned commitment that is made with an awareness of personal, cultural, and value contexts. Cooper and Lewis (1983) outlined specific ways of helping students who are in the various stages to cope with the epistemological crisis each stage of development brings. It should be pointed out that Perry's cognitive-developmental model makes use of system concepts of nonreducible levels of organization. The developmental changes described are not linear or simply additive, in the sense that more mature levels are conceived to be subsuming earlier levels of development that have been transformed into greater complexity.

Another model that addresses both cognitive processes and epistemic development is Kitchener's three-level model (Kitchener 1983). In this model, the first level refers to basic perceptual and cognitive processing, the second to metacognition, and the third, epistemic cognition. The third level of organization is referred to as "epistemic cognition," as it represents the processes a person employs to monitor the epistemic nature of problems and the truth value of alternative solutions. According to Kitchener, epistemic cognition involves evaluating our basic cognitive and metacognitive competencies. In other words, it is a highly developed form of reflective judgment that questions the very assumptions by which we justify the processes used to attain knowledge. These assumptions include one's assumptions about what can be known and what cannot, and how certain one can be in knowing. Similar to Perry's model, each form of knowing is viewed in this model as entailing an understanding of how beliefs can be justified in the light of the type of knowing process involved.

Kitchener and her colleagues conducted research on reflective judgment in epistemic cognition, using the Reflective Judgment Interview (King 1978, 1983; King, Kitchener, Davison, Parker, and Wood 1983). This research was extended to undergraduate and graduate students in college (Brabeck 1983; Strange and King 1981; Welfel 1982). Gains in reflective judgment were found over long periods of time and not in short time spans. There is support for the sequential development of reflective judgment, suggesting that epistemic assumptions evolve in a structured manner over qualitatively different stages. Compared with the stage of formal operations described by Inhelder and Piaget (1958), epistemic cognition seems to be distinctly different and may be regarded as a post-formal development (Kitchener 1978). In other words, analytical thought and the understanding of formal logic are likely prerequisites for epistemic reflection. Epistemic cognition enables individuals to utilize frameworks with which to monitor the nature of problems and the way in which solutions are knowable, as well as to identify appropriate criteria of justification for ill-structured problems (Kitchener 1986). It is therefore of particular relevance to the epistemic development of reflective professionals who have to function in a complex societal context and deal with problems that are difficult to define precisely.

There are other areas of cognitive-developmental theorizing and research that may be relevant here. In reviewing the work on formal reasoning in adults in Piagetian-based theory, research, and educational practice, King (1986) concluded that the ability to use formal logic does not account sufficiently for mature thinking and problem solving. Formal reasoning seems to function as a necessary, but not sufficient, condition for higher-order reasoning. Knowledge of formal logic and rules of reasoning is not sufficient in dealing with ambiguity and uncertainty. Studies of moral development also point to a relativity of thought that can be characterized as postformal thinking (Commons, Richards, and Armon 1984; Murphy and Gilligan 1980). Moral judgments involve both cognitive and affective processes (Rest 1986), a conclusion that supports the holistic nature of human judgment. In the area of creativity, the discovery orientation has been studied in the form of problem finding (Getzels and Csikszentmihalyi 1976). The ability to formulate productive questions and to construct new problems seems to be related to how information is organized within a problem space and what kinds of frames are applied (Schon 1963; Sternberg and Davidson 1983). Again, postformal thinking is invoked to account for such cognitive flexibility and the ability to free oneself from the constraints of particular frames.

Finally, dialectical thinking as a cognitive organization that appears in young-adult years is found to be crucial to moral, epistemological, and metaphysical reasoning (Basseches 1986). Dialectics means movement through forms via constitutive and interactive relationships. Dialectical worldviews (such as found in certain Eastern cultures) emphasize ongoing processes of change in reality and the coherence of parts in the whole of existence. Dialectical epistemologies emphasize both individual and collective forms of knowledge and the interrelationship of ideas and the lives of knowers in determining meanings. Dialectical analysis, in contrast to formal operational thinking, aims to describe dynamic relationships and changes rather than immutable laws and fixed realities. The capacity for dialectical thinking makes it possible to see the limits of the context in which we apply formal analysis, and enables us to embrace the contradictions between our own reasoning and that of other people. It is thus a form of cognitive flexibility, and may have adaptive value when a person is confronted with complex problems and conflicting points of view. Dialectical thought is considered to be a way of personal being associated with a reflexive consciousness (Harre

1984), necessary in the judgment of worth (such as of one's actions). It is held to be central to the higher-order self-reflection constitutive of human agency (Rychlak 1988; Taylor 1985).

The converging picture from these various developmental models and research programs is that reflective and reasoned approaches to knowledge require interactive and dialectical forms of knowing that do not look for truth either in the world or in the self alone. The contextual relativism of Perry's model is relevant to mature cognitive functioning such as found in experienced problem solvers. It is probably fair to expect the same in psychologists as skilled scientist-practitioners. We also learn that scientific creativity may be facilitated by the cognitive capacity for problem finding through working flexibly with information and playing with possible frames. Cognitive flexibility enables us to evaluate different frames of ideas and to derive value from them without being overly constrained. Above all, tolerance for diverse orientations to knowledge is more likely under dialectical ways of thought. The kinds of epistemic issues discussed in the present volume, and the reflective questioning promoted throughout, probably involve epistemic cognition as defined by Kitchener, as well as other processes that constitute postformal thought.

The practical question is how we can use these ideas to benefit the epistemic development of students and young professionals. All the models point to a developmental progression in the source, form, and content of knowledge. One can see some parallels in the development of professional knowledge as depicted by Dreyfus and Dreyfus (1986). In the novice stage, the source of knowledge is external to the practitioner, and practice consists of applying the rules and procedures learned in academic training. In the expert stage, the source of knowledge is the practitioner's experience, and practice involves accommodating previous understanding to the uniqueness of a particular problem context. Expert knowledge differs from a compilation of independent facts or sets of rules. It is a dynamic and contextualized understanding that is the result of the interaction with the environment, resulting in the transforming of schemata. We have learned that metacognitive and evaluative processes are involved in this transformation of experience into useful knowledge.

One of the keys to the development of mature ways of knowing is reflection. Reflective thought, according to Dewey (1933), always involves searching and has an end action in view. The attitude of open quest keeps one from the premature cessation of search in favor of certainty. Reflective thought includes scanning the situation, sorting and conceptualizing the problem, looking for inner coherence to the various aspects of the solution, testing it in action, and looping back to earlier steps when necessary. Flexibility is a major requirement of the process, as are checks and balances.

Dewey viewed creative problem solving as involving a mix of inductive reason and intuitive insight. Schon (1983) described practitioners' use of reflection on their professional action, such as evaluating the adequacy of one's frame of thought. Past experience and knowledge of problem prototypes provide the practitioner with a repertoire of working patterns or frames to interpret new problems and test their fit with the situation. As far as how one can develop such a repertoire, Schon (1987) is in favor of practicum experience and learning with case examples. Kohlberg (1984) had similarly utilized specific moral dilemmas to facilitate advancement to a higher stage of moral development. Kuhn, Amsel, and O'Laughlin (1988) also support the practice of reflective thinking in concrete instances rather than learning abstract principles of reasoning. In the next chapter, case study is recommended as a training ground.

Reflection should be directed not only at one's cognitive processes and problem solving but also at the contribution of one's personal ways of being to the inquiry process. As stated previously, accounting for oneself as a participant-observer embedded in all activities of knowing is one of the distinguishing features of qualitative or clinical methods of research. Berg and Smith (1988) provided a number of examples of researchers' reflections on their personal contribution to the research process. Steier (1991c) illustrated how researchers engage in reflection about their own approaches to knowledge, suggesting that research in the human realm must involve reflexive methodology. Similarly, Tomm (1986) had suggested the inclusion of the therapist in a theory of therapeutic action. These recommendations are predicated on a reflexive orientation to knowledge that grants the self a central role. Additionally, Hoshmand (1989, 1991) mentioned a number of ways of facilitating epistemic development, some of which will be considered in chapter 9.

In order to facilitate the development of the self as knower, it will be helpful to have a theory of how self-knowledge develops. The previously cited work of Cantor and her colleagues on the nature of schema in social cognition and personality development, and the personal construct research on affective evaluation of self and others, would seem to support such a conclusion. Weinstein and his colleagues have proposed a developmental theory of self-knowledge education (Weinstein 1981; Weinstein and Alschuler 1985; Weinstein, Hardin, and Weinstein 1976). They identified four stages of self-knowledge—elemental, situational, pattern, and transformational—which correspond more or less with the stages of cognitive development (from the preoperational to the postformal). They suggested that reflexive questioning can promote self-knowledge. Based on their experience with self-knowledge education classes, they recommended that stage change is difficult to bring about and less important to achieve than stage elaboration that extends a person's existing patterns of self-knowledge to new areas of experience. (This recommendation seems consistent with the schema research by Cantor and others). Weinstein and Alschuler (1985) provided detailed examples of the objectives of self-knowledge education and the types of reflexive questioning that can be used to promote self-knowledge.

Another critical dimension to epistemic development is the learning environment. The models reviewed above point to the importance of interaction between the self and the world and the role of education and life experience in a person's progression to mature ways of knowing. A movement that is gathering force in higher education is collaborative learning. It is based on current developmental models and constructionist perspectives on knowledge (Bruffee 1986, 1987; Tarule 1989; Whipple 1987). The collaborative approach to teaching and learning is consistent with the research on conceptual development, social cognition, and cultural contributions to individual differences in orientation to knowledge. Its emphases include the construction of knowledge communities, learning through dialogue, and connected knowing that accounts for context. Their implications will be discussed in chapter 9 as we consider specific ways of enhancing the development of reflective scientist-practitioners.

SUGGESTED ADDITIONAL LEARNING

1. Compare and contrast the assumptions about the epistemic processes and criteria used by psychological practitioners in the following articles by Meehl and Anderson and Goolishian. What do you see as their respective implications?

Meehl, P.E. 1960. The cognitive activity of the clinician. *American Psychologist* 15: 19-27.

Anderson, H., and Goolishian, H. 1992. The client is the expert: A not-know ing approach to therapy. In *Therapy as social construction* ed. S. McNamee and K.J. Gergen, 25-39. Newbury Park, CA: Sage.

2. As a self-study, write about the type of learning environment that you consider personally to be most optimal for your professional growth, the methods of knowing you prefer, and the sources and criteria of validation that you trust. Reflect on your own learning style and the type of knower you may be. Ask a peer who knows you well to review what you have written, and discuss your self-observations and -reflections.

3. Referring to the following article by Weinstein and Alschuler, apply the procedures for conducting the Unforgettable Experience Recall with yourself, and use the reflexive questions provided to analyze your response patterns.

Weinstein, G., and Alschuler, A. S. 1985. Educating and counseling for self-knowledge development. *Journal of Counseling and Development* 64: 19-25.

Consider what you learn about yourself from this exercise in the light of the previous assignment (2).

4. Interview an experienced researcher in your field of interest. Ask for personal reflections on what has been learned from the experience of doing research or program evaluation, in terms of the choice of research questions, theoretical frameworks, and methodological approaches. Find out about how this person has made decisions during inquiry and what kinds of contextual and personal factors have shaped his or her orientation to research.

5. Interview an experienced practitioner in your area of training. Ask for personal reflections on what has been learned from the experience of doing therapy, consultation, or other activities of practice. Try first to get a description of how the knowledge of practice has evolved for this person, then find out about his or her views on the knowledge of practice and the criteria of justification to be used in evaluating the knowledge processes of practitioners.

6. Miller (1985) described the Counselor Assessment Questionnaire (CAQ) developed by Holloway and Wolleat (1980), and suggested that the six tasks covered by it can be used to analyze a professional's questioning strategies and hypothesis formation when working with clients. By referring to the CAQ tasks listed in Miller, apply the six criteria to taped samples of your intake or assessment interview with clients, and evaluate your hypothesis formation and hypothesis testing in these sessions.

Miller, M. J. 1985. Counselor as hypothesis tester: Some implications of research. *Journal of Counseling and Development* 63: 276-78.

7. Based on practitioners' apparent preference for eclecticism and a similar eclectic trend in the professional literature, Brabeck and Welfel (1985a) examined students' view of eclecticism from a developmental perspective, particularly in terms of reflective judgment. Read the following articles by these authors and Patterson and Rychlak, respectively, for views on eclectic theories and beliefs in the field of psychological practice and how they may be related to one's cognitive development and the ability to question particular kinds of beliefs.

Brabeck, M. M., and Welfel, E. R. 1985a. Counseling theory: Understanding the trend toward eclecticism from a developmental perspective. *Journal of Counseling and Development* 63: 343-48.

Brabeck, M. M., and Welfel, E. R. 1985b. Truth in counseling theory: A rejoinder to Patterson and Rychlak. *Journal of Counseling and Development* 63: 354-55.

Patterson, C. H. 1985a. New light for counseling theory. *Journal of Counseling and Development* 63: 349-50.

Rychlak, J. F. 1985. Eclecticism in psychological theorizing: Good and bad. *Journal of Counseling and Development* 63: 351353.

8

The Case Study as Training Ground

Professional inquiry involves an ability to assess the requirements of a problem context, to judiciously select models and methods to generate information, and to integrate the findings from diverse sources into a pattern of understanding that will lead to useful action. As indicated by the research reviewed in the previous chapter, this requires the development of well-connected and generalizable knowledge structures in specific domains. It is not sufficient to learn isolated components of knowledge and skills or to engage in solitary practice of their application (Brehmer 1980). One needs to have the opportunity to apply them in meaningful problem solving with supervision and feedback. For the student who is learning about the various conceptual models in our field and the diverse methods of inquiry and their possible applications, an integrative learning experience can be found in case studies. For this reason, the present chapter is focused on case study.

THE CASE STUDY AS AN EPISTEMIC DEVICE

The case study, according to Yin (1989), is "an empirical inquiry that investigates a phenomenon within its real-life context, when the boundaries between phenomenon and context are not clearly evident, and in which multiple sources of evidence are used" (23). It is often occasioned by a problem in need of investigation, to be followed by professional actions that have personal and social consequences. Information has to be gathered for purposes that may require a range of methods of inquiry. The case study gives us an opportunity not only to learn to discern patterns of relationships but to formulate and test hypotheses. It also provides training in discrimination among representations of different logical types and in applying rules of interpretation and logical inference. In the previous chapter, it was suggested that the knowledge of professional practice and the maturing of professional judgments come about in the form of schematic or gestalt-like changes. The discerning of patterns and relationships in case study and the progression from knowledge of the particular case to the general, prototype case may be an illustration of such developmental shifts. The fact that case study can be reflexive in nature, as we reflect on our own interpretation and inference, makes it a significant vehicle for epistemic development.

"Case study" as a general term refers to the description and analysis of a person, group, event, condition, or process. In the social sciences, case study has been used as a method for the psychological study of personality and life history, the sociological study of group behavior, and the anthropological study of social structures, classes, and processes. Thus, it is not restricted to the study of an individual person. In recent years, its use in psychological inquiry has been influenced by the medical profession and by psychiatry in particular. Many case studies are primarily for clinical purposes (Bolgar 1965). Additionally, case study methodology can be used in research. Yin (1989) explained the use of single- and multiple-case study as a naturalistic research strategy. He pointed out that there have been misunderstandings of the uses of case study and that it is more than a strategy for exploratory research. Bromley (1986) attributed the under-utilization of case study in psychology to the rise of psychometrics, survey methods, and statistical analysis. Despite earlier writings on case research (Davidson and Costello 1969; Shapiro 1961, 1966), it was not until the availability of quasi-experimental procedures and designs for controlled investigation of the single subject that case study has become more widely adopted in systematic inquiry (Cook and Campbell 1979; Hersen and Barlow 1976; Kazdin 1982; Kratochwill 1978). Interest in the statistical treatment of single-case time-series data has continued (Huitema 1986; Morley and Adams 1989; Wallace and Elder 1980), along with the discussion of methods of analyzing serial order and sequence structure (Valsiner 1986).

The lack of appreciation for case study as a method of knowledge has continued to the extent that its scientific status has not been entirely defined. This is perhaps because the rationale and epistemic criteria for its use are varied. In the use of case study for functional behavior analysis, such as exemplified by Hersen and Barlow (1976) and Kazdin (1982), a linear statistical logic is implied. Psychological variables are defined in terms of discrete, measurable behaviors observed over a time series. Discrete interventions are systematically introduced in order to confirm effects that we hope to attribute to the isolated stimulus event. This linear, reductive rationale is in contrast to the configural approach to case study (Dailey 1971; Sarbin 1940). Personological case studies such as in the tradition of Murray (Shneidman 1981), or life histories as influenced by psychodynamic theory, cultural anthropology, and sociology (Abramson 1992; Denzin 1970, 1989; Linde 1983; Runyan 1982, 1983), examine comprehensive personal information and life stories in full context. Cases are considered to exist in a context of naturally occurring circumstances. The two types of logic involved in these contrasting approaches to case study reflect Bruner's (1986) distinction between the paradigmatic and the narrative mode of understanding, respectively, that was discussed in chapter 7. It was also mentioned in chapter 6 that behavioral assessment has become more contextualist in approach, which may eventually narrow the gap between reductive forms of propositional reasoning and holistic types of narrative interpretation.

From a contextual view of cases, by drawing attention to different contextual and temporal factors, one can interpret a case in terms of more than a single pattern of relationships. In other words, one can think of a case as existing in the minds of different parties who construct the meaningful whole from particular perspectives (as would opposing lawyers in a court case). This second characterization is more in line with the narrative, social constructionist orientation to knowledge. The logic of interpretation is closer to practical reasoning or the implicit grammar of narrative understanding (Polkinghorne 1988); it is not a statistical or formal logic. Rather than being arrived at by means of statistical calculation, the basis of belief in the interpretations and predictions of a case study rests on the cogency of argumentation of a psychological nature. The argumentative statements are anchored in particular actions, circumstances, and relationships described in natural language. For these reasons, Bromley (1986) proposed a quasi-judicial model for case study as a scientific method. It is characterized by a particular mode of reasoning suited for use with arguments that consist of a mixture of common sense and psychological explanation (Antaki 1981). Noting that the argumentation in a psychological case study is not as stylized as in the physical sciences or jurisprudence, Bromley suggested that in order for such inquiry to be granted scientific status, it has to be better than common sense and open to critique like other methods of knowledge. Abramson (1992), following Popper's ideas of falsifiability (Popper 1972, 1983), argued for the inclusion of case study in scientific inquiry on the basis that we can apply rational criticism to it. It is good practice to provide an audit trail or a chain of evidence that others can follow in reviewing a case study.

For the most part, case study evidence is accumulated for the purpose of inductive inference. Citing the work of Carnap (1950), Abramson further pointed out that inductive probability includes beliefs and credibility that are more consistent with the everyday inferences we make beyond our personal experience. The case study data simply extend the scope of available information within boundaries of credibility. There is always an element of persuasion, as with cases presented in court. Unlike in judicial practice, however, psychological case studies have not been systematically applied to generate case laws. (Behavioristic time series studies simply follow principles of learning theory). Recent constructionist interpretations of everyday understanding as socially based cognition and discursive construction (Semin and Gergen 1990a) provide a general context in which to place the case study. It is possible that the generalized structure of meanings and experiences from holistic case studies would follow what is held to be native structures and plots in narrative knowing (Polkinghorne 1988). As Runyan (1982) had argued, among the advantages of the case study is its ability to illuminate the meanings of relevant events and experiences within the social and historical world of the person—and, we may add, the person(s) who construct the case.

The fact that at least two types of logic have been associated with case study suggests the use of differing styles of knowing. Case study approaches that follow a linear logic, and involve a hypothesis-testing approach based on a particular theoretical paradigm, may be preferred by those who utilize propositional or paradigmatic logico-scientific reasoning. Given its emphasis in professional training, it is not surprising that this type of reasoning is depended on particularly by trainees and novice practitioners. Narrative case study approaches, in which holistic interpretations and a pattern-type logic are used, may be preferred by those who are willing to draw upon their life experience and native understanding of narrative plots in this latter kind of knowing. Although there may be a tendency to prefer either approach, the two modes of reasoning can be applied in a complementary fashion to a case study or other situations of problem solving in practice. The paradigmatic hypothesis-testing approach enables us to formulate the presenting information and to match hypotheses with particular evidence. The narrative mode of understanding enables us to integrate different pieces of information into a whole pattern or story that can serve as the interpretive context for prioritizing the various questions and distinguishing among hypotheses about the case or problem situation. The capacity to integrate case information in a holistic fashion is evident in experienced practice, as supported by the research on expertise discussed in the last chapter.

As an epistemic device, case study offers many opportunities for training the enquiring mind. As will be explained below, the construction of a case study involves data-gathering skills and the ability to pose questions relevant to the context. A variety of methods may be used along with the idiographic goals of a case study, such as explained by Runyan (1983). Once the information is assembled, often in the form of natural language data, we have to be able to discriminate between the various statements on a case by whether they represent descriptive information, qualifiers, interpretive rules, tentative conclusions, or warranted claims. Just as a student of history has to evaluate secondary sources against primary sources, as well as to discriminate between facts, opinions, and reasoned conclusions, we need to apply critical thinking to case study information. The task of discrimination is complex, because a given piece of information may assume different logical functions (rhetorical, inferential, etc.), depending on the perspective applied and how the information relates to different elements in a line of reasoning. The basic principle is not to muddle conclusions and claims with relatively descriptive information and presumptions.

The epistemic status of single-case study has been examined from a measurement point of view and contrasted with the logic of group experiments (Mace and Kratochwill 1986). Single-subject designs (Barlow and

Hersen 1984; Kazdin 1982; Valsiner 1986), even in complex forms of combined time-series or multiple-baselines, are held to be only approximations to the standards of scientific methodology. It is often questioned as to whether an individual level of analysis can contribute to a science of behavior. The methodologist Campbell had criticized the case study for its lack of a true comparison to a "control" condition against which to evaluate the threats to validity (Campbell 1957; Campbell and Stanley 1963). In later writings (Campbell 1975), he conceded that in a single case, each additional piece of information provides another instance with which to probe one's hypothesis and therefore functions like another "degree of freedom" (as in studies aggregating information from a number of independent cases to perform a statistical analysis of variance). Nonetheless, like many, he continued to view the case study as relatively fallible and vulnerable to researcher error. This skepticism is qualified by the acknowledgment that qualitative ethnographic case studies can have epistemic value as one of several sources of knowledge by providing theory-probing opportunities. It may be argued (Rosenblatt 1981) that the use of case study is disciplined and rigorous to the extent that the enquirer is open to evidence of error and able to think through alternative interpretations and their implications. A self-critical approach to inquiry, as advocated here, allows us to use the available "degrees of freedom" in assessing our conclusions and to capitalize on the merits of the case study as an epistemic device.

A REFLECTIVE ORIENTATION TO CASE ANALYSIS

In conducting or reviewing a case study, it is essential that we distinguish the data base from the assumptive base to the extent that it is possible. When reading a case report, one should try to discern the difference between descriptive statements of behavioral events and circumstances and conjectural statements. Opinions, hypotheses, and theoretical constructs should be treated as a different level of information from relatively factual description of dates of occurrence and verifiable frequencies of a problem. Professional reports of case studies are unfortunately overloaded with diagnostic jargon and theoretical or hypothetical statements. It is always a helpful practice to identify clearly the latter for what they are and to state the perspective from which one's conclusions are derived. In other words, clarity of meanings requires an accurately identified context. We should be aware of the misuse of language and the problems with buzz words and cliché statements (Hayakawa 1978). Such care in language use is essential to a reflective approach to case analysis. Discrimination of logical types represented in language is especially helpful in making judgments about information presented at case conferences.

The distinction between description and conjecture is a practical measure for discourse and analytic purposes. It is not intended to convey the impression that we can philosophically separate "facts" from how they are framed when facts are theory-laden. Professional communication about "facts" may be made from diverse perspectives, ranging from assumptions of total objectivity to the view that all we have is reality as constructed by those making the description. In attempting to distinguish between description and conjecture, we make a conscious effort to uncover the assumptive base of descriptive statements. For example, a statement in a report that reads "The client *denies* any illicit drug use" may suggest that the writer of the report speculated that there might be such drug use, even though the client reported otherwise. This example may represent a habit of professional communication that is intended to protect the professional from the prospect that a conjecture may turn out to be correct, the effects on the reader's perception of the client not withstanding. (It was noted in the previous chapter that practitioners tend to hold negative construals of clients.) As another example, one gets different impressions from the statement "The patient reports no auditory hallucinations" and the statement "The patient *denies* auditory hallucinations." Thus, we should try to consider the apparent assumptive base of those who have a role in constructing the case data, as well as constantly question our own preconceptions and interpretive frames when conducting a case study.

Research as reviewed in the previous chapter has indicated that when presented with minimal data, even novice clinicians are quick to arrive at diagnostic impressions and theoretical conjectures about a case (Oskamp 1965; Sandifer, Hordern, and Green 1970). It behooves us to postpone our commitment to a firm conclusion and to continue searching for more data. If, in fact, we do proceed by gradual constructions of interpretive patterns or schemata, as suggested previously, each tentative pattern of understanding will need to be revised in the light of new information. This new information can be available only if we consciously look for evidence while remaining open to the possibility of a lack of fit between the evidence and our particular interpretations. We will subsequently return to the notion of data guidance in professional judgment, which is important to both research and practice.

PROBLEM SPACE AND ALTERNATIVE CONCEPTUAL TOOLS

Approaches to case study vary for the reason that there are different definitions and conceptions of a given problem. In chapter 4, we considered the various conceptual models in the field. These models translate into different ways of conceptualizing problems. A reductionistic approach often results in a more focused definition of the problem, as in the case of identifying the immediate antecedents and consequences of a child's disruptive behavior in class. These antecedents and consequences are sought within the immediate environment of the classroom and the temporal events surrounding the discrete disruptive behavior. On the other hand, a more systemic conception of the problem would lead to searching for the relational and motivational aspects of the school and home environment that may have contributed to the disruptive act. The problem space is expanded beyond the focus on immediate circumstances to the broader ecology in which the child's presenting problem is manifested.

As explained in chapter 6, behavioral assessment has shown a shift from reductionistic to more contextualist conceptions of problems. This has come about with the realization that the targets selected for intervention must be representative of, or relevant to, the presenting problem. Reconceptualizations that expand the problem space are needed to make it more commensurate with what experience has shown to be sound clinical practice. The same holds true for organizational practice and the practice of health, educational, and school psychology. The professional psychologist has to work with conceptions of the problem that will lead to useful action. The practitioner evaluates alternative problem formulations heuristically, just as a researcher should evaluate alternative theories in investigating a problem.

Case study provides us with the opportunity to practice applying different conceptual tools for understanding a problem. Provided that one has a broad repertoire of conceptual tools, it is possible to apply alternative problem conceptions that in turn lead to the search for different kinds of data. Having available a multitude of conceptual lenses allows us to seek information not considered otherwise. In this way, theory serves to provide sensitizing concepts. Our theoretical frameworks direct us to certain sets of information and the relationship between them. For example, the case of a client who has suffered recent injury that resulted in impaired functioning may be formulated at both a personological and sociological level. Psychological reactions to loss and issues of self-esteem are just as pertinent as the interpersonal dynamics and social-systems consequences of impairment. These problem formulations are useful to the extent that they illuminate the experience of the client and his or her problems of living in a manner that can move us toward problem solving. The interventions in this case could be targeted at both the client and the social systems involved, and may include individual psychotherapy, family counseling, and vocational rehabilitation, as well as environmental engineering to accommodate the impairment. These varied approaches that constitute a comprehensive rehabilitation plan would not have been possible without a broadly differentiated conception of the problem.

Obviously, problem conceptions ultimately affect the solutions proposed for case-problems. Many practitioners use solutions that have been routinely applied to a type of problem. This happens, for instance, with psychoeducational case studies where the recommended actions typically fall into a limited set of standard solutions such as various types of program placements. As pointed out in the previous chapter, automatic perceptions lead to routinized reactions. There is a tendency to try to match a familiar problem with known and available solutions. Creative problem solving, however, requires us to consider alternative problem conceptions and their potential solutions. Brainstorming, free associating, inverting ideas and relationships, and so forth, can help us think creatively about a case. Switching back and forth between highly focused reductionistic lenses for specific problems to more global lenses for whole problem areas, we can loosen the problem space and eventually develop a broad repertoire of problem types to guide our thinking in problem solving. The repertoire building that has been recommended by research on expert practice also involves testing problem formulations in order to derive useful prototypes. Formulation of the problem is the starting point of professional inquiry, as is true for case study.

INITIAL FORMULATIONS AND HYPOTHESES

After scanning the presenting information on a case, we usually arrive at some tentative formulations. These are to be treated as working hypotheses. As mentioned previously, one needs to examine the basis of one's initial formulations and to acknowledge the particular perspective (including biases) brought to the problem situation. It is helpful to differentiate between strong hypotheses and vague conjectures. The former would appear to be supported by either a greater amount of data points or a contextually significant piece of information. In principle, we follow the strong hypotheses until they lead us into blind alleys or prove to be less useful than an alternative formulation. However, confirmatory tendencies, especially in clinical practice, may work against proper hypothesis revision, in that we may continue to seek "evidence" to prove our hypothesis while ignoring contrary information.

It is not always easy to know if one is following a useful hypothesis or if one is working under bias. Certain theoretical formulations seem elegant or intuitively appealing. Others may become habitual by reinforcement from one's professional models and peers. In general, the novice practitioner would likely refer to abstract principles and standard examples learned in academic training for diagnostic purposes, whereas an experienced practitioner uses prototypes refined by experience. As indicated previously, practitioners are vulnerable to errors and biases that occur often at the stage of initial formulations. Keeping alive multiple hypotheses and interpretive patterns could have pragmatic value in understanding a problem situation, as in the rehabilitation case example given in the previous section of this chapter. The ultimate criterion for evaluating working hypotheses in practice is whether they result in useful, constructive action such as fruitful inquiry, interventions, or remediation.

When conducting a case study, initial working hypotheses can help us organize the existing data as well as pose questions about gaps in the data. Typically, one goes through several rounds of formulation—posing questions, gathering information, and discarding weak hypotheses—in order to narrow down possible formulations to strong, useful hypotheses. It is helpful to use diagrams to chart logical sequences and relationships. Diagrams, like textual statements, can represent information to us at different levels of abstraction and generality as we make sense of the case data. By helping us track our own thinking, they serve as tools for metalearning and metacognitive processes. In reflecting on our own interpretive frames and problem-solving heuristics, we can evaluate them and select what seems appropriate. As the practitioner conducts a frame experiment in reflection, patterns are revised in the light of new information arising from the experience of practice. For instance, the experience of interviewing a client's family may give a new understanding of the client's problem that was not available previously, modifying the picture that was originally constructed to fit the story given by the client in individual contacts with the psychologist. Thus, formulation of hypotheses and interpretive patterns constitute an ongoing process that goes hand in hand with the posing of questions for inquiry, and the gathering of data.

POSING QUESTIONS FOR INQUIRY

We frame questions not only about the missing information from the data picture but also about the available information. These questions help us set goals for assessment and investigation. If, for instance, a client from a minority culture was tested with standardized instruments that are not culture sensitive, one would question the validity of the test data. A new question will be, How may the client perform on a more culture-sensitive test or culture-fair functional assessment? Questions are heuristics for setting the direction of inquiry. When several questions are posed, we have to decide on priorities. With a clinical case, the professional psychologist has to consider the state of the client and the therapeutic process. Referring a client for diagnostic testing immediately at intake may not be an appropriate action if the client is questioning his or her own sanity and is unsure of how he or she is viewed by the therapist; it will be more appropriate for the therapist to broach the subject of testing when sufficient trust is established. Similarly, vocational assessment may need to be postponed for a client who is not optimally motivated. As explained in chapter 3, all professional inquiry has to be carefully considered in context. Certain formats of data gathering may not be appropriate at certain times if they disrupt the professional-client relationship or are nonfacilitative of the client system. In other words, we do not push for answers only to satisfy our curiosity. In cases such as suspected child abuse or potential for harm, we are ethically and legally bound to proceed with investigation. In these situations, additional effort should be made to maintain the therapeutic viability of the professional relationship with the client and the client's family system.

Another skill essential to the problem formulation and investigative stages is the ability to identify viable targets of inquiry. This requires posing questions that can be answered. Sometimes, for theoretical reasons, we use hypothetical constructs that are hard to operationalize in terms of observable behaviors and events; or a question may be practically unfeasible to answer because the data simply cannot be retrieved. These types of questions are probably not as useful as questions that will allow us to attain particular goals of assessment and investigation. Again, the questions we pose to a case do not have to be only theory driven in the sense of paradigm-based hypothetico-deductive reasoning. Narrative modes of configuring the whole picture or story given by clients can suggest questions that are related to a theme or plot. For example, a client who has reported various incidents of abuse and victimization by others may have a story that is missing any report of grieving about one's own suffering or coping with the infringements. One would then ask questions about how the client has reacted to such experiences and what meanings they have in the client's life.

FACTORS IN THE CHOICE OF PROCEDURES

Once we have a set of goals and a direction for inquiry, we need to select the best possible procedures. Should we speak to the client's significant others in conjoint meetings? Do we seek permission to review past records of schooling and employment? Would standardized testing or alternative procedures be more appropriate? These are additional decisions to make in the course of a case study. Again, there are therapeutic as well as strategic considerations. One may ask a parent to make systematic observations of a child's behaviors at home, not only to generate information about the child's problem behavior, but to educate and empower the parent who is feeling helpless about the problem. The approach to data gathering in this case serves an information purpose as well as a therapeutic one. In studying an organization, collecting organization stories from all members conveys an interest on the part of the professional in the perspectives and experiences of the informants. It helps to build trust as well as a balanced base of understanding for the unit under study.

Approaches for data gathering and hypothesis testing about a case are further guided by the criterion of match with client characteristics. As stated in chapter 6, the client's cognitive style and native mode of responding are practical considerations in the choice of inquiry methods. A client who uses frequent visual images in conversation may be a better candidate for a cognitive-assessment approach that involves the use of imagery than one who is not. Complex inquiry that overtaxes a client's abilities to respond will only be counterproductive. This is not to suggest that clients cannot be "trained" to access data that are essential. Cognitive assessment often involves teaching clients to search for retrieval clues or using relaxation techniques to facilitate work with imagery. When training and motivational facilitation do not bring about the information needed, the best possible alternative may then be considered. For example, a problem may require collective information from all parts of an organizational system. If data are not forthcoming from the system as a unit, separate accounts from different departments would have to be used. Again, a versatile repertoire allows the practitioner to match the approach to the needs of the clients and the contexts involved. Knowledge of the potentials and limitations of a method must be linked to its actual usage in a particular context. One builds a repertoire of inquiry methods, refined by the experience of application in context.

DATA GUIDANCE AND SYSTEMATIC INFERENCE

The importance of ongoing attention to data was mentioned earlier. A prime example of data guidance is the use of time-series data in single-subject study to monitor departures from baseline (pretreatment) levels when stimulus events and interventions are introduced. Although everyday professional practice may not be as systematically monitored, the concept of data guidance is useful to therapeutic practitioners and those involved in program development and evaluation. Data guidance can include using new data to perform a reflective frame experiment on a heuristic pattern of understanding, to evaluate its fit with the problem. It can also involve the use of ethnographic observation and participant reports from front-line workers to assess the quality of a program that is being implemented. We rely on ongoing data to help us make inferences. All case studies require data guidance on an extended basis. Einhorn and Hogarth (1986), in reviewing research on the judgment of probable cause, for example, recommend that we should be less theory driven and more data driven, as a way of avoiding overconfidence in our judgments.

The most basic form of data tracking over time is found in chronologies. In chronological studies, events are analyzed along a time line as a sequence. It is assumed (1) that certain events must occur before other events, (2) that some events must be followed contingently by other events, (3) that the passage of time is a requisite for the sequence to occur, and (4) that particular time periods or stages can be identified by a certain class of events and their indicators. Examples are the chronological study of such processes as grieving over loss and adaptation to a new cultural environment. In the case of grieving, it is theorized that certain reactions such as denial and anger will predictably follow a loss and that the passage of time is necessary for acceptance of the loss to come about. A chronology of events helps place the individual in the postulated sequence. In the case of adaptation to a different cultural environment, certain classes of coping responses may be identified in relation to the hypothetical stage in which a new immigrant is chronologically placed. In chronological as well as other time-series studies, an initial causal inference is made when a predictable sequence of events is verified (as opposed to a rival or anomalous sequence), especially if replicated across multiple cases.

The inferences made in the case of a single-subject time-series study are based on temporal logic of a linear nature. To infer a meaningful change from a previous trend, however, one needs to embed the observation in the context of the slope during baseline. If the slope of a desired behavior is already upward before treatment, for instance, observed upward trend after intervention cannot really be attributed to the intervention. In this respect, it does not differ entirely from inferences that involve the logic of parts to a whole. The piece of information constituting the part in question is interpreted in the context of a whole, just as a change in trend is defined by the preexisting baseline. When a new pattern is discerned, this new context can give new meanings to each of the parts previously interpreted, as the meaning of a figure would change with background changes. Thus, an iterative and recursive cycle of interpretation takes place, whereby new evidence is contextually reinterpreted in the light of an emerging total context. Systematic inference requires a continuous interplay between the evidence at hand and the interpretive context. The latter tends to be dynamically changing in most situations of practice. We need to reflect on and revise inferences with the benefit of data in-context.

Whether it involves sequential or holistic pattern building, pattern matching, or a measured time-series strategy, the common logic in case studies is a replication logic. The same pattern may be replicated across time or across multiple cases. An empirically derived pattern can be matched or compared with an existing theory. When conducting case study, it is important to be clear about the analytic strategy we are using. It is also helpful to first learn to conduct a simple case study, in which one particular strategy is used, before proceeding to more complex case studies. Within the common logic of alternative strategies, it is possible to gain additional insight into a case by incorporating a second strategy. For example, a participant-observation study can be analyzed in terms of a time-series design, even though the interpretive process follows a holistic part-to-whole logic at any given point. In a study reported by Becker (1963), the experience of marijuana users was studied with a participant-observation mode. The postanalysis by Kidder (1981) differentiated a time series of an initial smoking phase, an effects phase, and an enjoyment phase. It was concluded that regular marijuana users are only those who experienced all three phases, whereas others did not. Thus, additional insight was gained by incorporating the linear logic of a time series after the participant field research that produced holistic, descriptive data.

OTHER INQUIRY HABITS REQUIRED IN CASE STUDY

My experience in the supervision of both clinical and research case studies suggests that students can learn habits of disciplined inquiry and standards of critical evaluation from case studies (Hoshmand 1994). The role of the human instrument features prominently in gathering and evaluating case study information. One of the surprises experienced by students comes from the realization of the need for thoroughness in a case study. Due to the contextualized nature of case study and the fact that the boundaries between the phenomenon of interest and the relevant data are not always clear, we have to search diligently for a large scope of information. Once we have amassed a satisfying array of data, we are confronted with the complex task of analysis. The only way to avoid being overwhelmed is to be clear about the analytic strategy or strategies to adopt, as well as the type of logic we are following. Reflection on our working hypotheses or existing theoretical suppositions are helpful as we ponder the fit between interpretive frames and data.

To guard against errors of interpretation and inference, we need to constantly critique our ongoing ways of processing information. Habitual asking of "what-if" questions, and looking for alternative interpretations, can prevent us from premature cessation of information search and analysis. In ethnographic and grounded theory research, such as described in chapter 5, the researcher has to conduct negative case analysis as a potential challenge to an emerging conclusion. The same occurs at the micro level in the construction of patterns in a case study, with subsets of data being examined for their challenge to the emergent picture. In addition, we have to prepare the case study for external review and audit. In practice, this means keeping accurate verbatim records and other documents, labeling and indexing clearly to help differentiate among different types of information, and making explicit the perspectives from which various sets of data are constructed.

Writing a case study report provides an opportunity for us to sharpen our skills of accounting for our inquiry and the basis of our claims to knowledge. Writing the case interpretation constitutes additional opportunities for refining our analysis or rejecting a line of interpretation. (Recall that in hermeneutic inquiry, another cycle of interpretive process occurs in the constructing of a written account.) Doing several drafts enables us to review the evidence with rigor and consistency. When pieces do not fit well together after careful documentation and assemblage, we may consider additional information gathering or retrace our process of inference to detect prior error and omission. It is not uncommon to discover only after writing a case report that we do not find the conclusions sufficiently convincing. Preparing a case report for peer review by leaving a good audit trail means describing and marking one's interpretive and analytic journey so well that others could identify the evidential base for inferences and thus follow our logic and argument. The researcher or practitioner should be able to see from the eyes of a reader of the report how warranted are the interpretations claimed.

A comment about case records and report writing in professional practice is in order here. Much of professional communication relies on written documentation. Deficiencies and biases in such documentation can be a disservice to the client. Tallent (1988) provides useful guidelines on psychological report writing as well as examples of pitfalls in professional reports. The latter not only perpetuate muddled thinking but also undermine our professional credibility, such as in courtroom testimony (Tallent 1988; Ziskin 1981). To learn about case construction and presentation, one may review available case studies.

TYPES AND EXAMPLES OF CASE STUDY

There are several kinds of case study in the professional practice of psychology. Clinical, counseling, school, and educational psychologists conduct case studies that may include general psychological investigation, psychoeducational assessment, and some aspects of vocational and neuropsychological evaluation. In the practice of health and rehabilitation psychology, the case study will likely include more medical and neuropsychological investigation in addition to psychological inquiry and vocational assessment. The range of methods reviewed in chapter 6 are generally employed in these case studies. In organizational practice, instead of a focus on the individual client, the case study is directed at the organizational unit or subunits. The methods of inquiry may include field interviews, on-site ethnographic observations, and survey methods.

The main dimension of difference across these various types of case study consists in their purpose and the kinds of recommendations and actions that are supposed to result from the study. The clinical or psychoeducational case study is intended to produce diagnostic judgment and recommendations for psychological or psychoeducational interventions. The rehabilitation case study, though largely similar, is intended to provide further information for the planning of an overall rehabilitation process that includes coordination with medical, social, and vocational services. The organizational case study is expected to yield information and recommendations that may have implications for the management of the organizational unit and factors that impact on the culture and climate of the organization that in turn affect the functioning of individual members.

In the use of case study for research, either a single case or multiple cases may be involved. A single case can be selected on the basis of uniqueness and not so much for generalization purposes. Alternatively, it may be argued that the particular experience or phenomenon represented is of a universal nature, such as psychological reactions to loss, for it involves certain basic human emotions. The information gleaned from the single or limited number of cases may still be considered to have general interest for this reason. In multiple-case study, individual cases can be selected as theoretically representative of different aspects of a phenomenon. In other words, theoretical or purposive sampling, as opposed to statistical sampling, is used (Patton 1980; Yin 1989). A common framework may be used to describe and analyze the individual cases as members of a set. At the same time, the individual cases in a set may be used to ascertain the same or different facets of the phenomenon under examination. For example, persons at different points of the life span who share a similar experience (such as relocation to a culturally different environment) may be studied if it is assumed that they will manifest both common features (because of the relocation experience) and, at the same time, different reactions due to age, maturity, and the developmental task at hand. The multiple cases are used here to construct a differentiated pattern, with individual cases representing developmental prototypes, and common themes related to the generalized experience (of relocation). It is important to recognize that case study, especially when involving multiple cases, can be conducted to explore an unknown pattern, to match a hypothesized pattern, or to refute a theorized pattern. Thus, case study can serve not only descriptive and exploratory purposes but theory-building and theory-probing purposes (Yin 1989).

A case-formulation approach to psychotherapy outcome research has been proposed (Persons 1991). It is argued that, being individualized and more similar to actual clinical practice where assessment and formulation interact in guiding intervention, the case-formulation approach will improve the ecological validity of psychotherapy research. Although critics have indicated that this approach has its own logistical problems and may not necessarily be better than existing strategies of therapy-outcome research (Garfield

1991; Herbert and Mueser 1991; Messer 1991; Schacht 1991), it seems to be a good starting point for thinking about research on professional interventions. A case-formulation approach requires us to use intensive local observation and to document reliably the decision rules used by a practitioner. It will enable us to track the effects of working hypotheses throughout the intervention process to a measurable outcome that represents an independent criterion of effective problem solving.

There are a growing number of sources in the literature that provide actual examples of case studies or part of the case data. Descriptive clinical data are presented in a number of casebooks in abnormal psychology and clinical interviewing (Hersen and Turner 1985; Oltmans, Neale, and Davison 1991; Weinberg and Hire 1962). Treatment cases are found in the psychotherapy and counseling literature (Bernstein 1984; Corey 1982; Hollis and Woods 1981; McCullough 1984; Mirkin and Koman 1985; Persons 1989; Scott, Williams, and Beck 1989; Walsh 1991; Wedding and Corsini 1989). Case histories can be found in the psychoanalytic literature (Erikson 1958; Greenwald 1959). Case studies on behavioral treatment represent another category (Bistline and Frieden 1984; Eysenck 1976; Turkat 1985; Ullman and Krasner 1965). Psychoeducational case studies can be found in connection with testing and assessment approaches (Drummond 1988). Constructivist assessment approaches have been presented in the form of casebook illustrations (Neimeyer 1993). The case study method has been used in family research involving ethnic minorities (Handel 1991) and in the study of family violence (Ammerman 1991). The journal *Psychotherapy* carries reports with brief case illustrations on a regular basis. Case vignettes are commonly used in textbooks on counseling the culturally different client (McGoldrick, Pearce, and Giordano 1982; Sue and Sue 1990). For examples of organizational case studies, one can consult the literature on action research and program evaluation research (Argyris, Putnam, and Smith 1985; Beer 1982; Cronbach et al. 1980; Levine and Levine 1977; Patton 1978; Van Maanen 1983). With continuing search effort, we can develop a collection of case studies that may include recent examples from the practice of rehabilitation and health psychology, as well as policy research.

Obviously, not all case studies are of quality or are defensible in their claims. In trying to identify exemplary case studies in both research and practice, I have chosen a few cases that illustrate not only some of the varied purposes described but also the different types of rationale and logic of case study mentioned here. The reader is referred to the original sources for the complete documentation of the case material.

A good example of a time-series single case study that illustrates clinical assessment and intervention is found in Barlow, Reynolds, and Agras (1973). This is a case study of a transsexual client that involves extensive data monitoring, obtaining multiple baselines on observational, self-report, and physiological measures, as well as the systematic introduction of treatment interventions and evaluation. The authors applied an inductive reasoning style in conjunction with paradigmatic hypothesis testing based on learning theory. As you read the journal article in which the case study is presented, you will appreciate the precision of observation and measurement, and the fact that clinical inferences about what turned out to be an appropriate treatment priority were made possible only because of continuous data guidance. The methodology in this case is largely behavioristic and reductionistic. The data analysis follows a linear logic. Although some information was given on the overall functioning of the client and the personal implications of treatment, contextual information such as the client's relationship with treatment agents, his personal meanings, and the larger social milieu involved were not fully described. It would be instructive to consider how a more holistic approach utilizing additional qualitative methods of inquiry can enrich the understanding of this case. The analysis of narrative data from the client and significant others, for instance, may illuminate the phenomenology and personal issues associated with the presenting problem. This case is interesting for discussion purposes also because it involves ethical issues. The client had considered a sex-change operation at one point. There were concerns about depression and suicidal tendencies. Aversive reconditioning was included as part of the treatment intervention. A number of professional issues are present.

An example of case study in which a narrative-hermeneutic style of reasoning is used can be found in Fischer and Wertz (1979). (This study was previously mentioned in chapter 6 in connection with the process of interpreting narrative data.) The authors describe a phenomenological study of the experience of being criminally victimized. The results are presented at several levels, from individual case synopses and illustrated narratives to general condensation and exemplar case synopses, with eventual theorizing about general psychological structure. This report is of interest because of the rich narrative excerpts included for illustration and the demonstrated use of case study in generative theorizing.

The use of a case study approach to psychotherapy process and outcome research has been advocated as an alternative to controlled group studies. Hill, Carter, and O'Farrell (1983) used their case study to argue for descriptive and discovery-oriented research strategies. Although their study utilized multiple process and outcome measures, it was subject to certain criticisms (Lambert 1983). A further collection of research case studies in brief psychotherapy is provided by Hill (1989). For a comparison of approach, we can consider Elliott and Shapiro (1992), who described the analysis of significant events in therapy by client and therapist in a case, focusing on discrepancies between perspectives. In reading these cases, we can appreciate the fine-grained probing of practice issues and how the case study approach complements the literature generated with group experimentation that follows the standard paradigms.

Skrtic (1985) provides an example of an organizational case study, with a clear illustration of the process. In this multiple-site study of the impact of educational service agencies on rural school district implementation of the Education Act for All Handicapped Children (PL 94-142), the reader is guided through the emergent design, the use of purposive sampling, field interviewing, the delineation of roles for all participants, and the definition of issues that help focus the data analysis. Skrtic explained the detailed indexing and cross-referencing in writing the case study report, as well as the higher level of data analysis that was based on synthesis of the written case interpretations. Information from different sites were used to construct a pattern of understanding, following a part-to-whole logic. This case study is also distinguished by its use of external audit, and the reflective accounting of areas of uncertainty from the ongoing case study that require further investigation as the investigator proceeded with study of an additional site.

Ultimately, the best way to learn about case studies is to actually conduct one. In the process, one can review the repertoire of methods at one's disposal, assess their utility in the context, and take note of the types of reasoning and logic applied.

SUGGESTED ADDITIONAL LEARNING

Group Activity A

As a class exercise I have asked students to react to the following case information as it unfolds in stages and to answer the questions given at each point:

Case Information:

You are presented with a thirty-six-year-old Caucasian male client at a community counseling agency. He is referred by a social worker who investigated him for suspicion of child neglect. The worker believes that there are "mental problems." The client has been estranged from his wife for eight months, and is living with their seven-year-old-son. He was reported by school authorities for evidently neglecting the daily care of his son.

In your first meeting with the client, he appears guarded and agitated. When assured that you are interested in his welfare, he becomes more calm. He shows little affect when questioned about his son. He states that he is a "good family man" and never misses a day of work; he holds a job as a butcher. When asked about his marriage, he declares that his wife would not have left him if he had been able to find a "respectable job." He sees himself as a "well-educated man." Then he mumbles something which you could not understand for a couple of minutes. When asked to explain what he was saying, the client looks down and shakes his head and remains practically unresponsive for the remainder of the session. As the time for his session is over, he nods vaguely when you ask if he is willing to return for another meeting.

Based on the above case information, please answer the following questions:

1. What are your initial hypotheses about this case? State the basis of your hypotheses.
2. What assumptions do you have about this client? What do you suppose is the source of these assumptions?
3. What types of questions and issues do you see as relevant?
4. How would you approach this case?

Additional information leading to separate scenarios:

Suppose that this client is from an ethnic and cultural minority background (consider various alternative identities).

1. How would this information change your understanding?
2. What types of resources do you have in reconfiguring the case?

Suppose you find out that the client has a serious drinking problem.

1. How would this information change your conception of the case?
2. Would you approach the client differently?

Suppose you find out that the client's wife left him because of physical abuse.

1. How would this information influence your view of the client?
2. Would it alter your approach to the case?

Suppose you find out that the client was incarcerated two years ago for stealing funds from the company in which he worked.

1. How would this information change your view of the client?
2. Would you approach the case differently?

Suppose you find out that the client was in an auto accident last year in which he suffered head injury and was subsequently hospitalized for six weeks.

1. How would this information change your formulation of the case?
2. What would you do differently?

Reflect on the shifts in your own pattern of thinking, your present knowledge base, and the additional knowledge you feel you need in order to deal with the increasing complexity of the case.

Group Activity B

Most supervisors usually encourage students to formulate hypotheses about cases in clinical and consultative practice. Prior to students presenting their hypotheses that are drawn from psychological theories, it is important to encourage the verbalization of preconceptions and folk theories of any sort. Furthermore, as a student applies separate conceptual frameworks to certain aspects of the case, it is helpful to ask which formulation(s) appears to have stronger support. Finally, the student should be encouraged to look at the entire case holistically as a story and apply narrative logic to integrate the various types of case data available. This usually helps to integrate the picture that may not be clear from separate formulations. The same dual strategy of paradigmatic-analytic thinking and holistic-narrative thinking can be applied to the review of one's work with a client. Separate counseling and therapy sessions and process issues can be reinterpreted within the total context of a series of professional contacts with the client.

Cases for Discussion

It can be instructive to study the classic cases in the literature and to learn to critique them. For example, the following references on Freud and Wolpe and Rachman may be used:

Freud, S. 1955. Analysis of a phobia in a five-year-old boy. In *The standard edition of the complete works of Sigmund Freud*, ed. J. Strachey, 20: 5-149. London: Hogarth.

Wolpe, J., and Rachman, S. 1960. Psychoanalytic evidence: A critique based on Freud's case of little Hans. *Journal of Nervous and Mental Disease* 130: 135-48.

How would you evaluate the reasoning style and logic used in the above examples? Compare and contrast them with the mode of reasoning and the logic found in the following articles by Barlow, Reynolds, and Agras and by Fischer and Wertz:

Barlow, D. H.; Reynolds, J.; and Agras, S. 1973. Gender identity change in a transsexual. *Archives of General Psychiatry* 28: 569-76.

Fischer, C. T., and Wertz, F. J. 1979. Empirical phenomenological analyses of being criminally victimized. In *Duquesne studies in phenomenologi cal psychology* ed. A. Giorgi, R. Knowles, and D.L. Smith, 3: 135-58. Pittsburgh: Duquesne University Press.

Conducting a Case Study

The best way of learning the skills of case study is by conducting a live case study in clinical practicum or supervised practice in consultation and writing a case report for presentation. This can be supplemented by field notes, transcripts, test data, figures, and examples of other information generated in the process of the case study. Oral presentations can include video-taped or audio-taped interview data that can be used for ongoing supervision. As preparation for the presenter and others who will participate in the case discussion, it is instructive to read the provocative article "Why I do not attend case conferences" from Meehl's (1973) edited book on psychodiagnosis.

The following guidelines summarize the considerations discussed in this chapter as well as a general format for a clinical case presentation. (They may be adapted for use in consultation and modified accordingly for the case study of larger units such as organizations.)

Case Study Data Base

referral problem and context of referral

client's socioeconomic background and identifying information, includ ing cultural and linguistic characteristics
history: developmental, medical-psychiatric, family, social, educational, vocational, and immigration history if recent
results of prior assessment and diagnostic procedures used
observational and interviewing data

Conceptual Framework and Process

separating the descriptive data from the assumptive base
identifying initial hypotheses and their conceptual and empirical basis
defining the problem: evaluate and integrate perspectives of the client and other client systems
formulating questions for setting the goals and direction of inquiry
considering therapeutic issues in the choice of inquiry approach
developing the working data base, as modified by continuous investigation
prioritizing inquiry and testing strong hypotheses
formulating treatment plans at the personal and ecological levels
evaluating the overall therapeutic/consulting process

Areas of Emphasis in a Clinical Case Report

context of referral and perspectives on the referral problem
pertinent client information and initial data base
questions and working hypotheses
your goals of inquiry and observations
evaluation of the therapeutic/consulting relationship
intervention priorities and rationale for choice of approach
evaluation of the therapeutic/consulting process; use taped interviews and other samples of client's interaction for presentation and analysis
questions and goals for the future
Your reflections on the case and remaining issues

Conducting Case Study Research

Finally, to bridge research and practice, the student can undergo the experience of developing a research plan around a case from practicum. The tasks should include, but are not limited to, the following:

1. description of client characteristics, presenting problem(s), therapist characteristics, and other contextual factors
2. operationalization of assessment approach and methods, using standardized or replicable methods, as well as alternative approaches as needed

3. report of findings on preintervention measures selected for their match with the nature of the case
4. report of ongoing process data obtained with the assessment methods
5. documentation of the case formulation(s) and diagnosis, if any
6. description of intervention approach or treatment protocol in terms of replicable or verifiable procedures
7. documentation of client's contributions to the formulation and development of the treatment plan, such as with video-taped samples, interview transcripts, and process recall stimulated by viewing video tape
8. evaluation of outcome: immediate, intermediate, and final, using multiple, replicable indicators congruent with the problem formulation and intervention approach
9. designing independent reliability checks by a peer on items 5, 6, 7, and 8

The types of research questions that can be posed may include:

1. Did the ongoing assessment data inform the formulation of intervention plans and the course of intervention?
2. Is there reliability in case formulation, process measures, documentation of client's contributions, and the pre-post outcome measures?
3. Does the case formulation lead to useful interventions?

Further discussion and brainstorming can also be done regarding research beyond this single case, such as:

1. How can multiple cases be used to evaluate the utility of one formulation compared to another as manifested in the intervention results?
2. Would different practitioners derive different or similar intervention plans based on the same case formulation? What may be the reasons?
3. What is the role of the client's contribution to problem formulation and problem solving in a case? Does the process fit with a coconstructive model in the social constructionist sense?
4. How do case formulations influence the practitioner, the client, and the relationship?

9

Development of the Reflective Scientist-Practitioner

How do we facilitate the development of reflective scientist-practitioners? This is a question asked by educators and all who are concerned about professional development. Some ideas would have crystalized, one hopes, from the preceding chapters. In this final chapter, I will comment on a selected number of areas, beginning with goals.

SETTING GOALS FOR PROFESSIONAL DEVELOPMENT

For students and those newly entering into the profession, professional development can have rather broad meanings that need to be clarified. Setting goals for oneself is usually based on individual needs, aspirations, and current levels of achievement. Goal setting may also be viewed as a form of person-environment interaction in the sense that goal selection is embedded and must take into account the relevant context. As discussed in previous chapters, the context of our professional functioning includes social, cultural, political, and ideological dimensions. This larger context interacts with personal worldviews and values in shaping one's orientation and development. Consideration of context may clarify why certain goals are chosen and perceived as particularly important, how one's image of an ideal professional role comes about, what the nature of one's commitment should be, and what kinds of professional satisfaction and frustration may be anticipated. Goal setting is a dynamic process that continues throughout one's professional life, and should in principle respond to changing needs and contexts.

The discussion about goals in professional training is taken up with varying degrees of openness and enthusiasm in different academic settings. Cohesive faculties usually manifest a well-articulated educational or training philosophy. In such cases, program philosophy is shared with students who may have opportunities to give input on educational goals and training objectives. The setting of individualized goals of professional development, however, is usually a less formalized process. Outside of the evaluation of academic performance, monitoring of personal goal attainment is also less systematic. Thus, much depends on the individual's initiative and the interest of advisors and mentors in making this happen. It is helpful to set explicit goals and to have periodic review of one's own goals of professional development and attainment with the counsel of others.

There are various types of goals for professional development. Typically, people are interested in identifying content areas of knowledge and competencies to be targeted for attainment. It is desirable to acquire domain-specific knowledge by learning multiple theoretical models and a broad range of inquiry methods. While competency goals are certainly important, it is also essential to include process goals and holistic developmental goals. Process goals are concerned with such emphases as one's intellectual habits and approach to inquiry, the means by which learning and development can be accomplished, and the environment in which one becomes socialized into the profession. For example, we can set as a process goal the development of reflective thinking, maintaining relationships with mentors, or creating supportive environments for our epistemic development. Holistic developmental goals refer to matters of personhood and the integration of learning experiences. Part of it involves finding out who we are and how we see ourselves developing. Part of it is concerned with finding our niche in the profession and articulating our place in the world.

Behavioral psychology as well as the psychology of human agency that addresses intentional action suggest that goal setting is important for change and the occurrence of desired outcomes. Whether we regard professional development as behavioral attainment, role scripting, or the constructing of a future self, having goals may be the first step toward such development. There is an element of conscious choice, in addition to what others have prescribed for us as appropriate educational and training objectives. Obviously, these goals cannot be actualized in a vacuum. Hence, it is important to consider the learning environment in which we acquire professional skills and the cultural and relational contexts in which we evolve our professional identities. Every member of the profession reflects, to some extent, his or her academic culture of origin and its particular values and practices. Many of us can identify significant others who have served as role models. There are also times when personal goals seem mismatched with the educational and training goals available to us. Academic and professional training in different programs may give differential attention to competency goals, process goals, and holistic developmental goals. A lack of match can be frustrating for both students and trainees and their teachers and supervisors.

Goal setting and the continuous evaluation of goal attainment are intertwined with self-motivation. Gambrill (1990) identified factors that contribute to our resistance to the development of critical thinking and reflective habits of mind. Nickerson, Perkins, and Smith (1985) stressed that cognitive development is a function of the existing repertoire of cognitive skills as well as adequate goals and a capacity for metacognitive self-monitoring. Some degree of self reflection on our own motivation and sources of resistance may be necessary as we begin to set goals for epistemic development.

Personal beliefs about learning, thinking, and knowledge should be examined. For those who are inspired by the image of psychologists as scientists, the idea of a self-experiment (Neuringer 1981) may help in designing approaches to developing one's cognitive resources and inquiry habits as well as evaluating one's gains. Others may follow a plan of self-directed change (Watson and Tharp 1993), which can be adapted to one's personal orientation and be as holistic as desired.

Critical reflection should be part of the process of goal setting. Some may find it necessary to follow professional directions quite different from those of their teachers and peers. The ability to self-consciously question our own goals of professional development and those prescribed for us probably comes with maturity. Educational and training environments also vary in their tolerance for the questioning of fundamental training assumptions and in their ability to accommodate differences. In making the above statements, I am suggesting that we should be open to a constant review of our goals for professional training and development. We need to create environments in which students and trainees can self-consciously articulate their goals and question the rationale and values underlying the objectives we have set for their development. This is one way in which we can model a reflective orientation, an orientation that I believe may facilitate a healthy development of our profession.

CULTIVATING REFLECTIVE HABITS

It is my hope that the reader will come to see that reflective habits are essential to all inquiry, whether in research or in practice. Reflection, as discussed throughout this book, is the tool for critical, reflexive thought. In choosing the development of reflective habits as a goal, we have to set aside time for reflection. This is because personal lifestyles and the demands of work settings for immediate action usually mitigate against taking time for reflection. Schon (1983) noted that it is nearly impossible to expect reflection-in-action; it is more likely for us to engage in reflection on our actions after they have occurred. Supervision hours may be a time for reflection, which must be supplemented by personal time for reflection. Personal time in self-reflection becomes increasingly important for independent professionals. It is perhaps the single most important tool for self-monitoring and consolidating the lessons of experience.

Having set this as a goal, one should find the means of developing reflective habits. Writing assignments may serve to clarify and refine thinking, as the recursive process of writing involves reviewing prior understanding, the basis of one's ideas, and transforming the framework of thought (Bracewell, Frederickson and Frederickson 1982; Flowers and Hayes 1981).

Another useful tool for individual reflection is journaling (Hettich 1990). Instructors can encourage students to keep course journals in which they can write about their preconceptions, questions, and reactions. Interactive journaling between teacher and learner can further stimulate reflection through dialogue. A journal is also useful during training in professional practice. Issues and dilemmas can be recorded and reflected upon. Frame experiments have also been used as a conscious way of evaluating one's frame of analysis or hypothesis in relation to a problem context (Schon 1983). Trying on alternative frames and modifying assumptions may free one from a particular way of thinking about a problem.

Reflection can be facilitated in supervision by allowing the supervisee to think aloud and pose his or her own questions. For example, in reviewing a taped session of therapeutic practice, the supervisee can be encouraged to identify critical choice points when decisions on action alternatives were in question. By reflecting on one's own rationale for the chosen action, evaluating its fit with the needs of the context and its impact on the interaction, and considering possible alternatives with the benefit of hindsight, one can use the process to build a repertoire of contextualized thought and action sequences. Reflective self-questioning can also help us to critique implicit assumptions and identify reasoning biases in practice (Arnoult and Anderson 1988). Reflection seems most effective when it is self-directed, activating the person's own resources. Process notes that track one's thought process and action sequence or interaction sequences can be an adjunct device. In group supervision, the availability of multiple process tracking can stimulate reflective thought. Hillerbrand (1989) described how students can observe and articulate their own thought processes in supervision that emphasizes the self-reflective process.

In a reflexive orientation to knowledge, reflection serves as a form of self-observation and self-monitoring. It is an important part of a personalized approach to knowledge that includes the self in understanding (Hamacek 1985). Thus, the development of reflective habits of mind goes hand in hand with holistic teaching and learning that focus on the total person. Use of self by teachers and supervisors and the modeling of reflexive questioning can facilitate similar reflective habits in students and trainees. Levine, Gallimore, Weisner, and Turner (1980) described how instructor reflexivity can help facilitate the development of student reflexivity in the teaching of participant observation and field research methods. Suspension of judgment and a willingness to consider what appear to be opposing possibilities or a breadth of meanings are intellectual habits and dialectical ways of thought that can be modeled.

Much has been written about critical thinking and how it can be nurtured in education (Ennis 1985, 1987; Halpern 1989; Paul 1984, 1990). The recommendations from researchers and educators in the field of critical thinking are generally applicable to the development of reflective thought that is promoted here. Paul (1984) defines critical thinking as involving a set of macrological skills (beyond discrete microreasoning skills) that is integrated with insight into one's own cognitive and affective processes. Thus, critical thinking, like reflective thought, entails a holistic understanding of self as knower. Our ability to think critically and reflectively in situations of conflict or of differing opinions requires open-mindedness and dialectical thought. Paul advocates the development of dialectical reasoning through appropriate teaching and dialogue. In comparing cognitive psychology with what philosophy offers to the field of critical thinking, he further argued that a philosophy-based approach enables critical thinking across subject matters and domains (Paul 1990). This is consistent with the frameworks discussed in chapter 7, which emphasize the development of epistemic reflection.

Reflective thinking is considered central to the articulation of the knowledge of practice (Schon 1983). Professionals who engage in reflective thought and reflective dialogue can improve upon their working schemas and personal theories of action in practice. That this is also true for the practice of research is suggested by a number of accounts (Bamberger and Schon 1991; Gergen and Gergen 1991; Steier 1991a). Reflexive methodologies require reflective thinking about one's own inquiry process. It is often upon reflection that new questions surface in our consciousness, about the substantive problem as well as our approach to it. From the standpoint of the integration of research and practice, reflective habits may constitute the essential elements of scientist-practitioner functioning.

FRAMING QUESTIONS OF PRACTICE FOR THEORY AND RESEARCH

Recent discussions of the role of scientist-practitioners have emphasized the potential contributions of practice to developing the knowledge base of professional psychology (Hoshmand and Polkingborne 1992; Phillips 1989). Heppner, Carter, Claiborn and associates (1992) made a number of specific recommendations on how the profession can improve the integration of science and practice. Among their recommendations is the idea that practice should be a wellspring for research. This may be interpreted as having the following implications. One is that exposure to situations of practice will provide the scientist-practitioner with opportunities for practical reasoning and problem solving. These opportunities may lead to problem finding that is otherwise not suggested by theoretical interests alone. Another is that inquiry in the context of practice involves domain-specific questioning and learning. These context-bound applications of our epistemic skills can produce findings and feedback on our inquiry approaches that are essential to our professional knowledge.

Research into the applied aspects of intelligence and practical reasoning (Sternberg 1985b; Sternberg and Kagan 1986; Sternberg and Wagner 1986) has pointed to the importance of learning from realistic problem solving. Professional knowledge and the type of intelligence we develop from academic training will remain inert knowledge unless we have the opportunity to translate them into procedural knowledge and practical reasoning in real-life situations. Much of what a practitioner does is observation and discovery of problems. Problem finding in the context of practice may become creative inquiry if it is followed by systematic investigation, probing the boundaries of current understanding, and reconceptualization. This cycle enables thought and action, or theory and practice, to be reciprocally informative.

From the standpoint of the professional's epistemic development, inquiry in the context of practice offers domain-specific learning. To the extent that thinking as a skill is context bound (Nickerson, Perkins, and Smith 1985; Perkins and Salomon 1989), this type of immersion and learning is critical to our cognitive development and professional functioning. Within this context, problem solving, decision-making, communicating, and understanding become connected. These connections represent a form of connected knowing (Mirman and Tishman 1988). The lessons we learn from experiencing such connections can help to shape our inquiry skills and perspectives on the relative contributions of our theoretical knowledge and practical knowledge, transforming them into professional knowledge that is relevant to the context of practice.

It has been my observation that questions arising from practice are seldom framed as research questions during the supervision of practice. This is partly due to the mindset that we have in clinical supervision and the boundaries maintained between the realms of research and practice. On the other hand, when students are encouraged to bring forth their practice-related interests and to utilize modes of inquiry that are used in the context of practice for research purposes (Hoshmand 1994), problems of practice can be fruitfully investigated as research problems. Many examples come to mind from student research projects that I have supervised. Rather than the details of design and methodology, I will present them by purpose and rationale as well as in terms of possible implications.

One type of problem encountered by professional psychologists in the practice setting is *when an intervention based on a particular theoretical rationale does not work.* For example, punishment and the use of time-out procedures (applications of learning principles in behavior modification) for discipline purposes were found to be ineffective in reducing disruptive behavior in the classroom at a junior high school. The researcher in this case wanted to find out why the intervention was not effective and what may be alternative solutions. She decided to conduct ongoing observation in the classroom as well as the time-out setting in the school where students with disruptive behaviors were sent. In addition, she conducted in-depth interviews with the students and staff involved on their perceptions of the intervention and their perspectives on the problem. Academic records and case histories of the students were also reviewed. The data suggested a number of explanations for the ineffectiveness of the intervention. They included the perception by the students of a lack of understanding on the part of the teachers and disciplinary staff, as well as adult irrationality in continuing a procedure that only increased resentment and made them more agitated. Many of the students reported intentionally escalating their conflict with teachers whom they regard as uncaring and punitive, even though they dislike being in the time-out setting. The school staff confirmed the lack of effectiveness and increased antagonism, but revealed an increased desire to control and suppress what they perceive to be hostile attitudes. There were self-reports of home-related issues that contributed to the emotional state of the students when they came to school. The records indicated a history of poor or marginal academic performance that seemed to support low academic self-esteem as expressed in the interviews. Observations further pointed to less than optimal interactions between the teachers and the students involved, and an authoritarian atmosphere contributed by the staff in charge of the time-out setting.

The researcher was able to obtain more suggestions for alternative solutions from the students than from the staff in this case. They included changing the disciplinary action from a punitive to a helping context, encouraging students to inform the teachers when they feel upset at the beginning of the school day, and using time-out as an alternative to escalation of conflict. The proposed solutions seemed to be possible ways of regaining the credibility of school personnel in the light of what students had experienced as adult irrationality in continuing to use a procedure that is ineffective. In addition, the data pointed to the need for improving the school climate in general and providing counseling services for students with academic and family problems. While the research was systematically conducted in this case, the inquiry engaged in by the researcher is similar to the activities of a consulting psychologist. Whereas the same observations may have been made by a psychologist providing behavioral consultation, there may not have been as much self-report data gathered from the students. This particular study suggests a broader person-environment conception of the problem that takes into account the interaction of personal perceptions, intentions, and behaviors with the social environment. Follow-up research may verify if the proposed solutions are effective and would support a revised conception of the problem in our theory of intervention.

A second type of problem in the practice setting is *when we are faced with an unfamiliar phenomenon and do not know how best to proceed.* For example, a number of my students were interested in learning about counseling incest victims and decided to conduct research on the process of working with these clients' memories of the abuse. This is an area that is lacking in both theory and research as well as tools for assessment (Loftus 1993). Psychotherapy process research has not been extended to this type of clients and presenting problem. By conducting in-depth interviews with the clients and therapists involved, as well as participant observation as practitioners who work with this problem, the researchers were able to derive a rich description of the memory-construction process (both in and outside of therapy sessions) and the therapeutic contexts that were regarded as facilitative or nonfacilitative by both therapists and clients. Each project was designed as a multiple-case study, using a separate type of rationale that included dynamic theories of abreaction, cognitive theories of memory, and social constructionist perspectives. The commonality was in the purpose of seeking full descriptions of the subjects' phenomenology and behaviors and their experience of the therapeutic process of memory construction. The findings were strikingly similar across projects. One of the clearest implications is that professionals are insufficiently informed about this problem and that clients can inform us as to how to work with them in ways that are facilitative and not harmful. Again, like the first problem we have considered, this kind of phenomenon calls for a similar type of inquiry by researchers and practitioners alike.

A third type of situation is *when we have a familiar phenomenon for which we do not have a complete understanding or strong theory of intervention.* In other words, we are still asking "why" and "how to intervene" questions. For example, some of my students were interested in the phenomenon of gang affiliation among youths and how to work with clients who are at risk of joining gangs as well as those who have gang membership. Perspectives on gang phenomenon range from sociological explanations to hypotheses about low self-esteem. There is also a cultural dimension, as most youth gangs seem to be homogeneous in ethnic membership. The research projects in this case followed a grounded-theory approach in conjunction with a selected set of tentative hypotheses derived from the literature. Group and individual interviews combined with ethnographic observations helped to generate themes that are suggestive of why gang membership is important to the youth concerned. Rather than follow, for instance, a hypothesis that these youths have an amotivation syndrome, which does not indicate exactly how we may intervene, the findings suggest that they are differently motivated and are adapting to their environment in ways that make sense to them. It follows that our interventions must be relevant to their environment and take into account their frame of reference. The inquiry by the researchers was different from what a practitioner working with this problem may do, only in terms of systematic documentation and more attention to reliability and validity. There is no reason to assume that a scientist-practitioner cannot work towards evolving new or revised theories by integrating the field observations and grounded knowledge from practice-related inquiry with existing theories and research. Many problems of practice fall into this category of familiar phenomena with no definitive theory of action.

The context of practice can remind us to *conduct needs assessment on special populations as well as examine a neglected area that seems important to certain clients.* Some professionals are of the opinion that this is going to be an age of specialization in practice. In addition to the sociopolitical and economic forces that can shape the identification of special services and client populations, our inquiry in the form of thorough needs assessment may ensure that critical needs will be served. Some of my students have targeted their needs-assessment research at groups whom they consider to be underserved by mental health professionals, such as the physically handicapped, grandparents and single fathers with custody of the children, and clients with HIV infection. Others have identified areas that have not had sufficient theoretical and research attention, such as religiosity, spirituality, intimacy issues among males, adult development of midlife females, and the long-term impact of parental loss/absence in clients with different levels of functioning. These topics were all derived from the researchers' exposure to the practice setting and their clinical fieldwork.

Another kind of research question that comes from the world of practice concerns *whether a popular concept or technique formulated by practitioners has utility.* Does the concept of "toxic parents" predict anger and low self- esteem in adult clients? Will genogram discussions with clients and their families lead to enhanced communication? Can "circular questioning" during therapy sessions result in insight into problems? Research on these kinds of questions can help clarify whether certain observations and claims by practitioners are valid in the sense of demonstrating pragmatic value. When combined with the analysis of related theories in the professional literature, the researcher may find ways of bridging these middle-level concepts and techniques with existing conceptual systems that are familiar to the larger professional community. Theories and concepts of intervention used by practitioners can also be verified with procedures that are acceptable to the profession. For example, Eisler, Dare, and Szmukler (1988) recommended that family therapy research be conducted to provide empirical demonstration of clinical observations of family interactions as well as clinical thinking (in terms of how therapists attempt to answer the questions they pose during therapy) in developing an understanding of the family system. This is in order to make systemic theories of practice publicly accessible and verifiable.

Finally, there are also situations *when a new form of intervention is attempted that is not suggested by present theory and research.* For example, one of my students who has had some training in dreamwork within a Jungian orientation wanted to find out how it may work in the context of couple counseling. This is contrary to the individual emphasis in all the available theories on the therapeutic use of dreams. By video-taping and transcription of both sessions with dream discussion and those without dream discussion in case studies of couple counseling, the researcher began to determine empirically whether there were differences in interaction and thematic content between the two types of sessions. In addition to a number of tentative observations of interaction differences, the researcher found that an alternative conceptual framework (such as a social constructionist view of therapeutic conversations) may be needed to account for the apparent impact of this experimental intervention. This type of exploratory research may pave the way to new formulations and innovations while grounding the practitioner's experimentation of practice in careful description and documentation.

Obviously, the above examples do not exhaust the full range of problems of practice that can be framed as research questions. In previous chapters, the importance of assessing the value of our inquiry methods and assessment findings was emphasized. Research on the treatment utility of assessment (Hayes, Nelson, and Jarrett 1987) and the practical uses of test results (Goodyear 1990) has been recommended. Morrow-Bradley and Elliott (1986) found that practitioners are interested in descriptive research on particular populations and treatment models, and suggested a focus on process-outcome links, significant change events, and the therapeutic alliance in future research.

Other questions important to practice concern *how useful a given intervention is with a particular type of clients and presented problems, and whether one form of intervention is more efficacious than another in a given context.* Previous researchers have framed these questions in terms of aptitude-treatment interaction (Dance and Neufeld 1988; Snow 1991) or a matrix of client, therapist, treatment, problem, and setting interactions (Stiles, Shapiro, and Elliott 1986). They have also differentiated between immediate and distal outcomes (Greenberg and Pinsof 1986), and suggested studying aptitude-outcome interactions (Shoham-Salomon and Hannah 1991). Similar questions can also be asked about treatment programs in entirety as well as the program components. It is important to bear in mind that the methodological approach will vary as a function of the type of question asked. Tharp and Gallimore (1982) explained how different types of research methods and strategies are applicable to different aspects of program evaluation.

Many of the problem situations and questions mentioned here may be brought under the umbrella of action research, which I wish to reemphasize.

ACTION RESEARCH AS A MODEL OF PROFESSIONAL INQUIRY

In chapter 5, action research was mentioned as a highly appropriate guiding metaphor in professional inquiry. Like practitioners who find middle-level concepts more useful than high-level constructs or global theories in their practice, action researchers are interested in the microtheories that guide action. Argyris (1985) referred to the researcher's construction of the actor's view of strategic variables that determine the essential formulation of a problem solution as maps of action. When applied to both psychologists and other professionals (such as members of an organization under study), maps of action reveal the kinds of knowledge structures people use while acting. Schon (1983) called our attention to the theories of method, media, language, and repertoires that practitioners use in problem solving. When these maps or microtheories in use are found to be inadequate, they need to be altered. Upon reflexive evaluation, we may modify our own maps of action. We can also provide consultative input to others in changing their maps of action toward more effective problem solving. Examples are given in Argyis (1985, 1993) of such applications in organization consulting. Through a cyclical process, problem diagnosis may lead to planning and implementing action, followed by evaluating a particular learning, and the realization that further assessment is indicated.

It is important to recognize that maps of action, like working hypotheses, are never complete. Middle-level concepts must be supplemented by multi-level analysis. Argyris (1985) included supraindividual and social system variables as units of analysis. A holistic construction can also be made of how individual actors fit into the larger story of a system (be it a family, school, or other social unit). The interdependency of factors must be understood. Stories of action, once created by individuals, become self-maintaining and difficult to change. Hence, the use of systemic and transactional frameworks may help the change agent design new environments for members of a system to understand the factors maintaining maladaptive theories of action and to learn to derive more functional theories of action.

Increasingly, professional psychologists will have to conduct problem assessment and problem solving involving embedding contexts and systems. Thus, we can learn a great deal from the application of the action mode of inquiry in organizations. There are several aspects of such applications that are relevant to all professional inquiry. Action research is intended to have dual relevance—to theory and to practice. With a contextualist emphasis and a pragmatic focus, relevant problem finding and problem solving are enhanced. Problem solutions (such as modified maps of action) can be used to refine theory. Seashore (1985) suggested that case studies of such application in particular sites, with intensive historical data and longitudinal design, can contribute to building theories that have ecological validity. Pettigrew (1985) suggested that the same can be true for long-term study of change processes. This type of research requires us to be open to the unexpected. The action researcher must allow the untidiness of history and social processes to reveal itself. Sometimes, what we find in practice may seem even counterintuitive. A flexible mindset is essential to this type of inquiry.

Another important feature of the action mode of inquiry is its collaborative nature. It involves partnership with the clientele or subjects concerned (Cummings, Mohrman, Mohrman, and Ledford, 1985; Hackman 1985). The relational aspects of the inquiry determine how successful the professional will be in facilitating sense making, exposure to new realities, and envisioning new courses of action. This is not to convey the impression that action research and related consulting are easily accomplished. Goodman (1985) pointed out various difficulties, including institutional structures that are not supportive of such an approach, lack of access to all stakeholders, and limited ability or interest of organization members to be in a research partnership. Although the learning afforded by engaging in action modes of research is tremendous, the challenges presented require a broad repertoire of skills, some of which may be developed in program evaluation, another prototype of action research.

In my judgment, the implementation of program evaluation and action research into organizations calls for professional skills of the highest degree of development. It is also my belief that learning about these two forms of action research will enhance the epistemic development of the professional psychologist. The area of program evaluation has a growing literature, informed by different methodological perspectives. There are quantitative as well as qualitative approaches to program evaluation (Cook and Reichardt 1979; Patton 1980; Stake 1978). Shadish, Cook, and Leviton (1991) provide an excellent resource for understanding the history of program evaluation, evaluation models, and related issues. What is of interest here is what we may learn from program evaluation as a professional activity and purposeful inquiry.

A guiding metaphor associated with program evaluation is that of the experimenting society. Campbell (1969) envisioned a rational society that makes decisions based on data generated by socially relevant research. He held his idealism in reserve for twenty years (Campbell 1988), having witnessed many obstacles to reforms as social experiments. Nonetheless, it is an inspiring call to professional psychology. Scriven (1980, 1986b) argued that we need to have a science of valuing. (Recall the issue of worth and value in our evaluation of inquiry methods in chapter 6). Scriven is of the view that we must be open to all kinds of data in program evaluation and discover all relevant needs, goals, and values in the process of conducting a metaevaluation. What it means is that we do not limit ourselves to the interests of those who have the power to employ professional psychologists as evaluators (recall also the discussion in chapter 3). Rather, all stakeholders should have input in program evaluation. In practice, the professional must become immersed in the setting, invite a diverse group of informants to share perspectives, develop trust by maintaining a balanced perspective and role relationships, and so forth. Many of the skills of participant observation and reflexive self-monitoring are essential here.

Stake (1986) proposed that responsive evaluation is a service in itself. By granting local control to stakeholders, clients, and program staff, the program evaluator tries to preserve the local relevance of the findings, empowering the concerned parties in the process. This is very similar to the approach of action researchers in the organizational area. Utilization is a main goal of evaluation researchers (Leviton and Hughes 1981; Patton 1978). Cronbach (1975) had long emphasized the importance of intensive local observations. His model of aptitude-treatment interaction (Cronbach and Snow 1977) is based on relevance to educational practice. Professional psychologists would do well to be guided by the pragmatic concern of generating proximal knowledge to shape local practices. Case study research that provides knowledge about local cultures (such as schools and organizations) and demonstrates local outcomes (of success and failure) represents a type of research that can inform practice and program changes over time. Cronbach's work (1982a) points to the causal complexity of program performance, the need to identify multiple variables that determine program quality, and the importance of understanding the political context of policy analysis and evaluation. When viewed in these terms, there is no perfect method of inquiry or simple answers. Program evaluation provides a context in which to revisit the complex issues of validity (Cronbach 1989; Messick 1989).

In that program evaluation and organizational studies in an action mode may provide us with integrative learning experiences, students and new professionals should seek the opportunity of doing an apprenticeship in these areas. One can learn a great deal from working with experienced researchers and consultants who can serve as role models.

THE IMPORTANCE OF MENTORING

Professional development can be generally enhanced by mentoring. There have been many writings on mentoring in the academic setting (Blackburn,

Chapman, and Cameron 1981; Cameron and Blackburn 1981; Collins, Barrett, and Citrin 1985; DeCoster and Brown 1982; Erkut and Mokros 1984), including mentoring in psychology programs (Bogat and Redner 1985; Sumprer and Walfish 1988). Although there could be power-dependency issues and other negative effects associated with mentoring (Auster 1984; Carden 1990), its positive effects on the development of young adults have been verified (Levinson, Darrow, Klein, Levinson, and McKee 1978).

In terms of the development of inquiry skills and a reflective orientation to knowledge, mentoring could play a significant role. Mentors who are experienced researchers and practitioners can share their experiences and model effective inquiry. For those in training, working with an experienced field researcher provides the equivalent of a research practicum, which has been recommended as one of the future means of professional training (Heppner, Carter, Claiborn, et al. 1992). New professionals also require the benefits of mentoring in both research and practice, in addition to learning to get along in the profession. Mentoring is supposed to strengthen professional identity particularly for groups lacking in role models (Hall and Sandler 1983). It is important for students and young professionals to have mentors who model different inquiry styles and epistemic orientations and who also represent a variety of professional interests. Stereotypes of professional models are counter to encouraging diversity in orientation to knowledge, and will only discourage certain types of knowers who find it difficult to identify with available role models.

In seeking a mentoring relationship, we are looking for what is not otherwise available in classroom interactions and normal supervision. A mentor may disclose thought processes and self-questioning when sharing stories of research successes and failures. Personal journeys in building theories and models of practice may be described with greater comfort and authenticity. By definition, mentoring means greater investment in the learner, in terms of both time and the sharing of oneself. In addition to mentoring that usually involves a one-to-one relationship, the larger learning environment is essential to professional development. Different situations and conditions are more or less conducive to learning and thinking (Greeno 1989). In chapter 7, I mentioned collaborative learning in relation to cognitive development; environments that support collaborative learning can be intentionally created.

CREATING COLLABORATIVE LEARNING COMMUNITIES

During my years as a student, I had experienced different learning environments, ranging from the traditional didactic lecture mode, where the instructor represents the authority on a subject matter, to relatively open classrooms with considerable discussion among students. It was not until I became an instructor myself that I began to appreciate the wonders and potentials of collaborative learning (Bruffee 1987; Kagan 1989/1990; Whipple 1987). One of my struggles as a teacher has always been trying to effectively bring about integrated understanding, or what is referred to as "connected knowing" in collaborative learning practices (Tarule 1989). As mentioned previously, social approaches to cognition support the notion that knowledge is relational and occurs with active interaction and meaningful dialogue (Vygotsky 1978; Siegel 1984). Following a social constructionist metaphor, knowledge is conceived to arise from the meanings coconstructed by the participants as they accommodate their own understanding to the ideas shared by others in response to their own. When we set up a learning environment that encourages egalitarian forms of participation, individuals may be more likely to present their personal beliefs and ideas. Connected knowing may derive from such dialogue and accommodative changes, especially when combined with activities of self-reflection such as recommended in this book.

The path to this desired interactional model of learning and knowing, however, is rather complex. Personal and social beliefs about knowledge, thinking, and learning differ in their support for the type of cognitive development that is proposed here. Differences in epistemic values and learning styles, such as discussed in chapter 7, imply that not everyone will welcome a collaborative mode of learning. Belenky, Clinchy, Goldberger, and Tarule (1986) observed that some women (and others with similar socialization) present themselves as passively receptive knowers who defer to authority. Furthermore, developmental models such as Perry's (1970) point to a stage of subjective knowing that is not yet open to the accommodation of alternative viewpoints. Only when knowledge is viewed procedurally as a social-intellectual process would a person be receptive to collaborative learning. Trust and the building of a supportive atmosphere are essential to risk taking in the form of participation.

I have observed from experience and verified with other instructors that collaborative learning, as an alternative to traditional formats of learning, can be uncomfortable for teachers and students alike. For the teacher, this is similar to a therapist's letting go of the expert role in the relationship with clients. There are control issues one must be aware of. One is more likely to be challenged and to be faced with diverse and possibly conflicting perspectives. There may be a temptation to use Socratic questioning to promote a particular view or steer the discourse in favor of one's own beliefs (see Trimbur 1989 for a discussion of the politics of consensus and difference in collaborative learning). Students may resist the invitation to take responsibility for their own learning or refuse to accept their peers as agents in their own development. A positive interpersonal climate and a holistic approach that takes into account different types of knowers and developmental and motivational factors are needed (Sadler and Whimbey 1985). It takes time, effort, and system support to make it possible for a community to enjoy the collaborative learning experience.

There is another way in which collaborative learning can be helpful in professional development, namely, in preparing us for professional interactions with colleagues and clients. Collaborative learning teaches us to listen to other points of view as well as to articulate our own while being critical and reflective on all. For example, in case conferencing, the professional psychologist has to work with the perspectives of other professionals and not compromise his or her own integrity. Gambrill (1990) pointed out the importance of self-confidence in enabling us to apply critical thinking and present unpopular views. Additionally, knowledge of group process is helpful in sustaining collegial relationships. These capacities can be developed in a collaborative learning environment. As noted in chapter 5, dialogical forms of knowing are central to collaborative modes of research associated with interpretive research paradigms and action research. Narrative and social constructionist approaches to clinical inquiry and professional consultation also require that we engage in egalitarian forms of communication with our clients and the communities that we serve.

The academic setting can be the first home for a collaborative learning experience. If faculty and program cultures could support the collaborative learning mode, students will have the opportunity to develop themselves as active, social learners and to find their own voice as well as respect the voices of others. The same is true for internship sites where group supervision and staff conferences can become opportunities for collaborative learning. Collaborative learning is congruent with reflective approaches to knowing. Collaborative learning communities are intended to be reflexive and self-questioning. They can be a major vehicle for facilitating the development of reflective professionals.

If the concept of a collaborative learning community can be further applied to the profession at large, we may be able to benefit from constructive dialogue and critical reflection on different types of knowledge and perspectives. Researchers and practitioners can listen to one another and learn from the experience of both the research and the practice enterprise. Psychologists as professionals can enter into collaborative relationships with the communities that we serve. The voices of different stakeholders and the local knowledge of communities can become part of collective problem finding and problem solving. Interdisciplinary efforts can also thrive in collaborative learning communities that include other disciplines and professions. The pluralistic approach to knowledge that is advocated in this book may be grounded in the collective wisdom of learning communities, with checks and balances afforded by self-questioning, collaborative minds.

SUGGESTED ADDITIONAL LEARNING

1. Arrange a meeting with individuals who have different theoretical orientations and scientific worldviews to discuss professional education and training in your program. Conduct an open discussion of goals, assumptions, and processes, and explore the implications of the identified differences in perspectives for the epistemic development and professional growth of students and trainees. Furthermore, discuss how the group could possibly be a collaborative community working with the articulated differences.

2. Take a policy issue that requires the input of psychologists, and hold a brainstorming session with researchers and practitioners in the area of concern. Observe the frames of reference and problem-solving approaches of both groups. Reflect on how problems and solutions are constructed by each group and what the common themes may be. Construct an integrative perspective or dialectical summary and discuss the action implications one may derive from it.

3. Read and discuss the following articles by Campbell and Cronbach:

Campbell, D. T. 1969. Reforms as experiments. *American Psychologist* 24; 409-29.

Cronbach, L. J. 1975. Beyond the two disciplines of scientific psychology. *American Psychologist* 30;116-27.

What do you see as the societal role and contributions of professional psychologists as scientist-practitioners?

4. Read the following articles by Shontz and Rosenak and Strupp on how research may be relevant to practice. Do you agree with the authors' views? What may be additional ways of integrating research and practice?

Shontz, F. C., and Rosenak, C. M. 1985. Models for clinically relevant research. *Professional Psychology: Research and Practice,* 16: 296-304.

Strupp, H. H. 1989. Psychotherapy: Can the practitioner learn from the researcher? *American Psychologist* 44: 717-24.

References

Abramson, P. 1992. *A case for case studies.* Newbury Park, CA: Sage.

Ackerman, R. J., and Pickering, S. E. 1989. *Abused no more: Recovery for women from abusive or co-dependent relationships.* Blue Ridge Summit, PA: Tab Books.

Adair, J.G. 1988. Research on research ethics. *American Psychologist* 43: 825-26.

Adair, J. G.; Dushenko, T. W.; and Lindsay, R. C. L. 1985. Ethical regulations and their impact on research practice. *American Psychologist* 40: 59-72.

Adams-Webber, J. 1990. A model of reflexion from the perspective of personal construct theory. In *The structure of human reflexion, ed. H. Wheeler,* 93-112. New York: Peter Lang.

Albee, G. W. 1981. Politics, power, prevention, and social change. In *Prevention through political action and social change* ed. J.M. Jaffee and G.W. Albee, 3-24. Hanover, NH: University Press of New England.

———. 1986. Toward a just society: Lessons from observations on the primary prevention of psychopathology. *American Psychologist* 41: 891-98.

Allport, G. W. 1942. *The use of personal documents in psychological science.* New York: Social Science Research Council.

———. 1958. What units shall we employ? In *The assessment of human motives,* ed. G. Lindsey, 239-60. New York: Rinehart & Winston.

———. 1961. *Patterns of growth in personality.* New York: Holt, Rinehart & Winston.

Altheide, D. L. 1987. Ethnographic content analysis. *Qualitative Sociology* 10: 65-77.

Altman, I., and Rogoff, B. 1987. World views in psychology: Trait, interactional, organismic, and transactional perspectives. In *Handbook of environmental psychology,* ed. D. Stokols and I. Altman, 1-40. New York: Wiley.

American Educational Research Association, American Psychological Association, and National Council on Measurement in Education. 1985. *Standards for educational and psychological testing.* Washington, DC: American Psychological Association.

American Psychiatric Association. 1994. *Diagnostic and statistical manual of mental disorders.* 4th ed. Washington, DC: American Psychiatric Association.

American Psychological Association. 1979. Principles concerning the counseling and therapy of women. *The Counseling Psychologist* 8: 21.

———. 1982. *Principles in the conduct of research with human participants.* Washington, DC: American Psychological Association

———. 1986. *Guidelines for computer-based tests and interpretations.* Washington, DC: American Psychological Association.

———. 1987. *Casebook on ethical principles of psychologists.* Washington, DC: American Psychological Association.

———. 1992. Ethical principles of psychologists and code of conduct. *American Psychologist* 47: 1597-1611.

Ammerman, R. T., ed. 1991. *Case studies in family violence.* New York: Plenum.

Anastasi, A. 1982. *Psychological testing.* 5th ed. New York: Macmillan.

———. 1985. Some emerging trends in psychological measurement: A fifty-year perspective. *Applied Psychological Measurement* 9: 121-38.

———. 1986. Evolving concepts of test validation. *Annual Review of Psychology* 37: 1-15.

Andersen, T., ed. 1991. *The reflecting team: Dialogues and dialogues about the dialogues.* New York: Norton.

Anderson, C. A.; Lepper, M. R.; & Ross, L. 1980. Perseverance of social theories: The role of explanation in the persistence of discredited information. *Journal of Personality and Social Psychology* 39: 1037-49.

Anderson, H., and Goolishian, H. 1992. The client is the expert: A not-knowing approach to therapy. In *Therapy as social construction*, ed. S. McNamee and K.J. Gergen, 25-39. Newbury Park, CA: Sage.

Anderson, J. R. 1981. Concepts, propositions, and schemata: What are the cognitive units? *Nebraska Symposium on Motivation,* vol. 28, 121-62. Lincoln, NE: University of Nebraska Press.

———. 1982. Acquisition of cognitive skill. *Psychological Review* 38: 369-406.

Angoff, W. H. 1988. Validity: An evolving concept. In *Test validity*, ed. H. Wainer and H.I. Braun, 19-32. Hillsdale, NJ: Lawrence Erlbaum.

Angus, L. E. 1992. Metaphor and communication interaction in psychotherapy: A multimethodological approach. In *Psychotherapy research: Narrative and paradigmatic approaches*, ed. S.G. Toukmanian and D.L. Rennie, 187-210. Newbury Park, CA: Sage.

Angus, L. E., and Rennie, D. L. 1989. Envisioning the representational world: The client's experience of metaphoric expressiveness in therapy. *Psychotherapy* 26: 372-77.

Antaki, C., ed. 1981. *The psychology of ordinary explanations of social behavior*. London: Academic Press.

Apfelbaum, E. 1986. Prolegomena for a history of social psychology: Some hypotheses concerning its emergence in the twentieth century and its raison d'etre. In *Dialectics and ideology*, ed. K.S. Larsen, 1-13. Norwood, NJ: Ablex.

Argyris, C. 1980. *Inner contradictions of rigorous research.* New York: Academic Press.

———. 1982. *Reasoning, learning, and action: Individual and organizational.* San Francisco: Jossey-Bass.

———. 1985. Making knowledge more relevant to practice: Maps for action. In *Doing research that is useful for theory and practice,* ed. E.E. Lawler, A.M.Mohrman, G.E. Ledford, T.G. Cummings, and Associates, 79-125. San Francisco: Jossey-Bass.

———. 1993. *Knowledge for action: A guide to overcoming barriers to organizational change.* San Francisco: Jossey-Bass.

Argyris, C.; Putnam, R.; and Smith, D. M. 1985. *Action science: Concepts, methods, and skills for research and intervention.* San Francisco: Jossey-Bass.

Argyris, C., and Schon, D. 1978. *Organizational learning: A theory of action perspective.* Reading, MA: Addison-Wesley.

———. 1989. Participatory action research and action science. *American Behavioral Scientist* 32 (5): 612-23.

Arnoult, L. H., and Anderson, C. A. 1988. Identifying and reducing causal reasoning biases in clinical practice. In *Reasoning, inference, and judgment in clinical psychology,* ed. D. C. Turk and P. Salovey, 209-32. New York: Free Press.

Ary, D. 1984. Mathematical explanation of error in duration recording using partial interval, whole interval, and momentary time sampling. *Behavioral Assessment* 6: 221-28.

Ash, M. G., and Woodward, W. R., eds. 1987. *Psychology in twentieth-century thought and society.* Cambridge: Cambridge University Press.

Atkinson, B. J.; Heath, A. W.; and Chenail, R. 1991. Qualitative research and the legitimization of knowledge. *Journal of Marital and Family Therapy* 17: 161-66.

Atkinson, D. R. 1993. Who speaks for cross-cultural research? *The Counseling Psychologist* 21: 218-24.

Atkinson, D. R.; and Hackett, C. 1988. *Counseling non-ethnic American minorities.* Springfield, IL: C. C. Thomas.

Atkinson, D. R.; Morten, G.; and Sue, D. W. 1983. *Counseling American minorities: A cross-cultural perspective.* Dubuque, IA: Wm. C. Brown.

Atkinson, D. R.; Thompson, C. E.; and Grant, S. K. 1993. A three-dimensional model for counseling racial/ethnic minorities. *The Counseling Psychologist* 21: 257-77.

Atkinson, J. M., and Heritage, J., eds. 1984. *Structure of social action: Studies in conversation analysis.* Cambridge, MA: Cambridge University Press.

Auster, D. 1984. Mentors and proteges: Power-dependent dyads. *Sociological Inquiry* 54: 142-53.

Austin, K. M.; Moline, M. E.; and Williams, G. T. 1990. *Confronting malpractice: Legal and ethical dilemmas in psychotherapy.* Newbury Park, CA: Sage.

Ausubel, D. P.; Novak., J. D., and Hanesian, H. 1978. *Educational psychology: A cognitive view.* 2d ed. New York: Holt, Rinehart & Winston.

Avis, J. M. 1985. The politics of functional family therapy: A feminist critique. *Journal of Marital and Family Therapy* 11: 127-38.

Ayer, A. J., ed. 1966. *Logical positivism.* Rev. ed. New York: Macmillan / Free Press.

Bakeman, R., and Dabbs, J. M. Jr. 1976. Social interaction observed: Some approaches to the analysis of behavior streams. *Personality and Social Psychology Bulletin* 2, 335-45.

Baldwin, M., and Satir, V. 1987. *The use of self in therapy.* New York: Haworth Press.

Bamberger, J., and Schon, D. A. 1991. Learning as reflective conversation with materials. In *Research and reflexivity,* ed F. Steier, 186-209. Newbury Park, CA: Sage.

Bandura, A. 1978. The self system in reciprocal determinism. *American Psychologist* 33: 344-58.

———. 1989. Human agency in social cognitive theory. *American Psychologist* 44: 1175-84.

Bangert-Drowns, R. L. 1986. Review of developments in meta-analytic method. *Psychological Bulletin* 99: 388-99.

Barath, A., and Cannell, C. F. 1976. Effects of interviewer's voice intonation. *Public Opinion Quarterly* 40: 370-73.

Bargh, J. A. 1982. Attention and automacity in the processing of self-relevant information. *Journal of Personality and Social Psychology* 43: 425-36.

Barker, R. G. 1968. *Ecological psychology: Concepts and methods for studying the environment of human behavior*. Stanford, CA: Stanford University Press.

Barlow, D. H., and Hersen, M. 1984. *Single case experimental design: Strategies for behavior change*. New York: Pergamon.

Barlow, D. H.; Reynolds, J.; and Agras, S. 1973. Gender identity change in a transsexual. *Archives of General Psychiatry* 28: 569-76.

Barnes, B. 1981. On the conventional character of knowledge and cognition. *Philosophy of Social Sciences* 11: 303-33.

Baron, J. 1981. Reflective thinking as a goal of education. *Intelligence* 5: 291-309.

———. 1985. *Rationality and intelligence*. New York: Cambridge University Press.

Barrell, J. J.; Aanstoos, C.; Richards, A.; and Arons, M. 1987. Human science research methods. *Journal of Humanistic Psychology* 27: 424-57.

Barrett, G V., and Depinet, R. L. 1991. A reconsideration of testing for competence rather than for intelligence. *American Psychologist* 46: 1012-24.

Barrios, B. A. 1988. On the changing nature of behavioral assessment. In *Behavioral assessment*, ed. A. S. Bellack and M. Hersen, 3-41. New York: Pergamon.

Barrios, B. A., and Hartmann, D. P. 1988. Recent developments in single-subject methodology: Methods for analyzing generalization, maintenance, and multicomponent treatments. In *Progress in behavior modification*, ed. M. Hersen, R. M. Eisler, and P. M. Miller, 20: 11-47. Newbury Park, CA: Sage.

Basseches, M. 1986. Dialectical thinking and young adult cognitive development. In *Adult cognitive development: Methods and models,* ed. R. A. Mines and K. S. Kitchener, 33-56. New York: Praeger.

Bateson, G. 1979. *Mind and nature: A necessary unity.* New York: E. P. Dutton.

Batson, C. D. 1975. Attribution as a mediator of bias in helping. *Journal of Personality and Social Psychology* 72: 455-66.

Batson, C. D.; Jones, C. H.; and Cochran, P. J. 1979. Attributional bias in counselor's diagnosis: The effects of resources on perception of need. *Journal of Applied Social Psychology* 9: 377-93.

Baum, C. G.; Forehand, R.; and Zegeob, L. E. 1979. A review of observer reactivity in adult-child interactions. *Journal of Behavioral Assessment* 1: 167-78.

Becker, H. S. 1963. Becoming a marijuana user. In *The outsiders,* 41-58. New York: Free Press.

Beer, M. 1982. Research and implementation: A case study; and Teaching note for the Comp Graf case. In *Making it happen: Designing research with implementation in mind,* ed. M. D. Hakel, M. Sorcher, M. Beer, and J. L. Moses, 61-95; 129-48. Beverly Hills, CA: Sage.

Belenky, M. J.; Clinchy, B. M.; Goldberger, N. R.; and Tarule, J. M. 1986. *Women's ways of knowing*. New York: Basic Books.

Bellack, A. S., and Hersen, M., 1988. *Behavioral assessment.* New York: Pergamon.

Bellah, R. N.; Madsen, R.; Sullivan, W. M.; Swidler, A.; and Tipton, S. M. 1985. *Habits of the heart: Individualism and commitment in American life*. Berkeley: University of California Press.

———. 1991. *The good society.* New York: Alfred A. Knopf.

Belle, D. 1982. *Lives in stress: Women and depression.* San Diego: Sage.

Belmont, J. M. 1989. Cognitive strategies and strategic learning: The social-instructional approach. *American Psychologist* 44: 142-48.

Belson, W. A. 1968. Respondent understanding of survey questions. *Polls* 3: 1-13.

Bem, D. J. 1967. Self-perception: An alternative interpretation of cognitive dissonance phenomena. *Psychological Review* 74: 183-200.

Berg, D. N., and Smith, K. K. 1988. *The self in social inquiry.* 2d ed. Newbury Park, CA: Sage.

Berg, K. S., and Stone, G. 1980. Effects of conceptual level and supervision structure on counselor skill development. *Journal of Counseling Psychology* 27: 500-9.

Berger, L., and Luckmann, T. 1966. *The social construction of reality.* New York: Doubleday Anchor.

Berliner, D. C. 1986. In pursuit of the expert pedagogue. *Educational Researcher* 15: 5-13.

Bernstein, R. 1986. *Philosophical profiles: Essays in a pragmatic mode.* Philadelphia: University of Pennsylvania Press.

Bernstein, S. 1984. A case history demonstrating the complementary use of psychodynamic and behavioral techniques in psychotherapy. *Psychotherapy: Theory, Research, and Practice* 21: 402-7.

Bertalanffy, L. von 1968. *General systems theory: Foundations, development, applications.* New York: Braziller.

Bertaux, D., ed. 1981. *Biography and society: The life history approach in the social sciences.* Beverly Hills, CA: Sage.

Bevan, W. 1986. The journey is everything. In *One hundred years of psychological research in America: G. Stanley Hall and the Johns Hopkins tradition*, ed. S. Hulse and B. F. Green, 365-97. Baltimore: Johns Hopkins University Press.

Beza, A. 1984. Review essay: Experiments within surveys. *Contemporary Sociology* 13: 35-37.

Bhaskar, R. 1979. *The possibility of naturalism: A philosophical critique of the contemporary human sciences.* Brighton, UK: Harvester Press.

———. 1989. *Reclaiming reality: A critical introduction to contemporary philosophy* . London: Verso.

Bijou, S. W.; Peterson R. F.; Harris, F. R.; Allen, K. E.; and Johnson, M. S. 1969. Methodology for experimental studies of young children in natural settings. *The Psychological Record* 19: 177-210.

Bistline, J. L., and Frieden, F. P. 1984. Anger control: A case study of a stress inoculation treatment for a chronic aggressive patient. *Cognitive Therapy and Research* 81: 551-56.

Blackburn, R.; Chapman, D.; and Cameron, S. 1981. Cloning in academe: Mentorship and academic careers. *Research in Higher Education* 15: 315-27.

Blackman, B. I. 1992. *Qualpro text database and productivity tools* (computer program). Tallahassee, FL: Impulse Development.

Blair, E. 1977. More on the effects of interviewer's voice intonation. *Public Opinion Quarterly* 41: 544-48.

Bloor, D. 1983. *Wittgenstein: A social theory of knowledge.* New York: Columbia University Press.

Blum, A., and McHugh, P. 1984. *Self-reflection in the arts and sciences.* Atlantic Highlands, NJ: Humanities Press.

Blumer, H. 1969. *Symbolic interactionism.* Englewood Cliffs, NJ: Prentice-Hall.

Board of Professional Affairs, Committee on Professional Standards. 1987. *General guidelines for providers of psychological services.* Washington, DC: American Psychological Association.

Bogat, G., and Redner, R. 1985. How mentoring affects the professional development of women in psychology. *Professional Psychology:*

Research and Practice 16: 851-59.

Bogdan, R. 1972. *Participant observation in organizational settings.* Syracuse, NY: Syracuse University Press.

Bogdan, R. C., and Biklen, S. K. 1982. *Qualitative research for education: An introduction to theory and methods.* Boston: Allyn and Bacon.

Bogdan, R., and Taylor, S. J. 1975. *Introduction to qualitative research methods.* New York: Wiley.

Boice, R. 1983. Observational skills. *Psychological Bulletin* 93: 3-29.

Bolgar, H. 1965. The case study method. In *The handbook of clinical psychology,* ed. B. B. Wolman, 28-38. New York: McGraw-Hill.

Borgen, F. 1992. Expanding scientific paradigms in counseling psychology. In *Handbook of counseling psychology,* ed. S. D. Brown & R. W. Lent, chapter 4. 2d ed. New York: Wiley.

Boring, E. G. 1950. *History of experimental psychology.* Rev. ed. New York: Century.

Bowers, K. S. 1977. Science and the limits of logic: A response to the Mahoney-DeMonbreun paper. *Cognitive Therapy and Research* 1: 239-46.

Brabeck, M. 1983. Critical thinking skills and reflective judgment development: Redefining the aims of higher education. *Journal of Applied Developmental Psychology* 4: 23-24.

Brabeck, M. M., and Welfel, E. R. 1985a. Counseling theory: Understanding the trend toward eclecticism from a developmental perspective. *ournal of Counseling and Development* 63: 343-48.

———. 1985b. Truth in counseling theory: A rejoinder to Patterson and Rychlak*Journal of Counseling and Development* 63: 354-55.

Bracewell, R.; Frederickson, C.; and Frederickson, J. D. 1982. Cognitive processes in composing and comprehending discourse. *Educational Psychologist* 17: 146-64.

Bransford, J. D., and Vye, N. J. 1989. A perspective on cognitive research and its implications for instruction. In *Toward the thinking curriculum: Current cognitive research,* ed. L. B. Resnick and L. E. Klopfer, 173-205. 1989 Yearbook of the Association for Supervision and Curriculum Development. Alexandria, VA: Association for Supervision and Curriculum Development.

Brehmer, B. 1980. In one word: Not from experience. *Acta Psychologia* 45: 223-41.

Brenner, M.; Brown, J.; and Canter, D., eds. 1985. *The research interview: Uses and approaches.* London: Academic Press.

Brewer, J., and Hunter, A. 1989. *Multimethod approach: A synthesis of styles.* Newbury Park, CA: Sage.

Brewer, M. B., and Collins, B. E. 1981. *Scientific inquiry and the social sciences.* San Francisco: Jossey-Bass.

Brewer, W. F., and Nakamura, G. V. 1984. The nature and functions of schemas. In *Handbook of social cognition,* ed. R. S. Wyer and T. K. Scrull, 1: 119-60. Hillsdale, NJ: Lawrence Erlbaum.

Briggs, C. L. 1984. Learning how to ask: Native metacommunicative competence and the incompetence of fieldwork. *Language in Society* 13: 1-28.

Brinberg, D., and McGrath, J. E. 1985. *Validity and the research process.* Newbury Park, CA: Sage.

Brody, G. F. H., and Sigel, I. E. 1990. *Methods of family research: Biographies of research reports. Vol. 2: Clinical populations.* Hillsdale, NJ: Lawrence Erlbaum.

Bromley, D. B. 1986. *The case-study method in psychology and related disciplines.* New York: Wiley.

Bronfenbrenner, U. 1979. *The ecology of human development.* Cambridge: Harvard University Press.

Bronfenbrenner, U.; Kessel, F.; Kessen, W.; and White, S. 1986. Toward a critical social history of developmental psychology. *American*

Psychologist 41: 1218-30.

Broughton, J. M., ed. 1987. *Critical theories of psychological development.* New York: Plenum.

Brown, A. L. 1978. Knowing when, where, and how to remember: A problem of metacognition. In Advances in instructional psychology, ed. R. Glaser, 1: 77-165. Hillsdale, NJ: Lawrence Erlbaum.

Brown, L. M., ed. 1988. *A guide to reading narratives of conflict and_choice for self and moral voice.* Harvard University Graduate School of Education, monograph no. 1.

Brown, L. M.; Tappan, M. B.; Gilligan, C.; Miller, B. A.; and Argyris, D. E. 1989. Reading for self and moral voice: A method for interpreting narratives of real-life moral conflict and choice. In *Entering the circle: Hermeneutic investigation in psychology,* ed. M. J. Packer and R. B. Addison, 141-64. Albany, NY: State University of New York Press.

Brown, L. S. 1989. New voices, new visions: Towards a lesbian/gay paradigm for psychology. *Psychology of Women Quarterly* 13: 445-58.

Bruffee, K. A. 1986. Social construction, language, and the authority of knowledge: A bibliographical essay. *College English* 48: 773-90.

———. 1987. The art of collaborative learning. *Change* March/April: 42-47.

Bruner, J. S. 1957. On perceptual readiness. *Psychological Review* 64: 123-152.

———. 1986. *Actual minds, possible worlds.* Cambridge: Harvard University Press.

———. 1990. *Acts of meaning.* Cambridge: Harvard University Press.

Budoff, M., and Hamilton, J. L. 1976. Optimizing test performance of moderately and severely mentally retarded adolescents and adults. *American Journal of Mental Deficiency* 81: 49-57.

Bunge, M. 1962. *Intuition and science.* Englewood Cliffs, NJ: Prentice-Hall.

———. 1990. What kind of discipline is psychology: Autonomous or dependent, humanistic or scientific, biological or sociological? *New Ideas in Psychology* 8: 121-37.

Burman, E. 1991. Power, gender, and developmental psychology. *Feminism and Psychology* 1: 141-54.

Buros, O. K. 1977. Fifty years in testing: Some reminiscences, criticisms, and suggestions. *Educational Researcher* 6: 9-15.

Buss, A. R. 1975. The emerging field of the sociology of psychological knowledge. *American Psychologist* 30: 988-1002.

Buss, A. R., ed. 1979. *Psychology in social context.* Chicago: University of Chicago Press.

Butcher, J. N. 1985. Perspectives on computerized psychological assessment. *Journal of Consulting and Clinical Psychology* 53: 745-838.

Butcher, J. N., ed. 1987. *Computerized psychological assessment.* New York: Basic Books.

Cameron, S., and Blackburn, R. 1981. Sponsorship and academic career success. *Journal of Higher Education* 52: 369-377.

Campbell, B. A. 1981. Race-of-interviewer effects among Southern adolescents. *Public Opinion Quarterly* 45: 231-44.

Campbell, D. T. 1957. Factors relevant to the validity of experiments in social settings. *Psychological Bulletin* 54: 297-312.

———. 1969. Reforms as experiments. *American Psychologist* 24: 409-29.

———. 1975. 'Degrees of freedom' and the case study. *Comparative Political Studies* 8: 178-93.

———. 1988. *Methodology and epistemology for social science: Selected papers.* Chicago: University of Chicago Press.

Campbell, D. T., and Fiske, D. W. 1959. Convergent and discriminant validation by the multitrait-multimethod matrix. *Psychological Bulletin* 56: 81-105.

Campbell, D. T., and Stanley, J. C. 1963. *Experimental and quasi-experimental designs for research.* Chicago: Rand McNally.

Campbell, S. K. 1974. *Flaws and fallacies in statistical thinking.* Englewood Cliffs, NJ: Prentice-Hall.

Cannell, C. F.; Fowler, F. J.; and Marquis, K. H. 1968. *The influence of interviewer and respondent psychological and behavioral variables on the reporting in household interviews.* Vital and Health Statistics, series 2, no. 26. Washington, DC: U.S. Government Printing Office.

Cannell, C. F.; Oksenberg, L.; and Converse, J. M. 1979. *Experiments in interviewing techniques: Field experiments in health reporting, 1971-1977.* Ann Arbor: University of Michigan.

Cantor, N. 1990. From thought to behavior: "Having" and "doing" in the study of personality and cognition. *American Psychologist* 45: 735-50.

Cantor, N., and Kihlstrom, J., eds. 1981. *Personality, cognition, and social interaction.* Hillsdale, NJ: Lawrence Erlbaum.

Cantor, N., and Kihlstrom, J. 1987. *Personality and social intelligence.* Englewood Cliffs, NJ: Prentice-Hall.

Cantor, N.; Mischel, W.; and Schwartz, J. 1982. A prototype analysis of psychological situations. *Cognitive Psychology* 14: 45-77.

Caplan, N., and Nelson, S. D. 1973. On being useful: The nature and consequences of psychological research on social problems. *American Psychologist* 28: 199-211.

Carden, A. D. 1990. Mentoring and adult career development: The evolution of a theory. *The Counseling Psychologist* 18: 275-99.

Carnap, R. 1950. *Logical foundations of probability.* Chicago: University of Chicago Press.

Carter, J. W., ed. 1968. *Research contributions from psychology to community mental health.* New York: Behavioral Publications.

Carver, C. S., and Scheier, M. F. 1981. *Attention and self-regulation: A control-theory approach to human behavior.* New York: Springer-Verlag.

———. 1982. Control theory: A useful conceptual framework for personality—Social, clinical, and health psychology. *Psychological Bulletin* 92:111-35.

Casas, J. M. 1984. Policy, training, and research in counseling psychology: The racial/ethnic minority perspective. In *Handbook of counseling psychology*, ed. S. D. Brown and R. W. Lent, 785-831, New York: Wiley.

Ceci, S. J.; Peters, D.; and Plotkin, J. 1985. Human subjects review, personal values, and the regulation of social science research. *American Psychologist* 40: 994-1002.

Chaiklin, S., and Lave, J., eds. 1992. *Understanding practice: Perspectives on activity and context.* New York: Cambridge University Press.

Chaplin, J. 1988. *Feminist counseling in action.* London: Sage.

Chapman, L. J., and Chapman, J. P. 1969. Illusory correlation as an obstacle to the use of valid psychodiagnostic signs. *Journal of Abnormal Psychology* 74: 271-80.

Chartrand, J. M. 1991. The evolution of trait-and-factor career counseling: A person x environment fit approach. *Journal of Counseling and Development* 69: 518-24.

Chase, W. G., and Simon, H. A. 1973. The mind's eye in chess. In *Visual information processing,* ed. W. G. Chase, 215-81. New York: Academic Press.

Chen, H. T., and Rossi, P. H. 1981. The multi-goal, theory-driven approach to evaluation: A model linking basic and applied social science. *Evaluation Studies Review Annual* 6, 38-54. Beverly Hill, CA: Sage.

Chi, M. T. H.; Bassok, M.; Lewis, M. W.; Reimann, P.; and Glaser, R. 1988. *Self-explanations: How students study and use examples in learning to solve problems.* Pittsburgh: Learning Research and Development Center.

Chi, M. T. H.; Glaser, R.; and Farr, M. J. 1988. *The nature of expertise.* Hillsdale, NJ: Lawrence Erlbaum.

Chi, M. T. H.; Glaser, R.; and Rees, E. 1982. Expertise in problem solving.

In *Advances in the psychology of human intelligence*, ed. R. Sternberg, 1: 7-75. Hillsdale, NJ: Lawrence Erlbaum.

Chodorow, N. 1978. *The reproduction of mothering: Family structure and feminine personality*. Berkeley: University of California Press.

———. 1989. *Feminism and psychoanalytic theory*. New Haven, CT: Yale University Press.

Churchman, C. W. 1971. *The design of inquiring systems*. New York: Basic Books.

Cicourel, A. 1982. Interviews, surveys, and the problem of ecological validity. *American Sociologist* 17: 11-20.

———. 1987. The interpenetration of communicative contexts: Examples from medical encounters. *Social Psychology Quarterly* 50: 217-26.

Ciminero, A.. R.; Graham, L. E.; and Jackson, J. L. 1977. Reciprocal reactivity: Response-specific changes in independent observers. *Behavior Therapy* 8: 48-56.

Cirillo, L., and Wapner, S., eds. 1986. *Value suppositions in theories of human development.* Hillsdale, NJ: Lawrebce Erlbaum.

Claiborn, C. D., and Dixon, D. N. 1982. The acquisition of conceptual skills: An exploratory study. *Counselor Education and Supervision* 22: 274-81.

Clune, W. H. 1988. *Courts as cautious watchdogs: Constitutional and policy issues of standardized testing in education*. Berkeley, CA: National Commission on Testing and Public Policy.

Coan, R. 1979. *Psychologists: Personal and theoretical pathways*. New York: Irvington.

Cohen, S.; Evans, G. W.; Stokols, D.; and Krantz, D. S. 1986. *Behavior, health, and environmental stress.* New York: Plenum.

Cole, D. A.; Howard, G. S.; and Maxwell, S. E. 1981. The effects of mono versus multiple operationalization in construct validation efforts.

Journal of Consulting and Clinical Psychology 49: 395-405.

Cole, M. 1983. Society, mind, and development. In *The child and other cultural inventions,* ed. F. S. Kessel and A. W. Siegel, 89-114. New York: Praeger.

Cole, N. 1981. Bias in testing. *American Psychologist* 36: 1067-77.

Collins, A., and Stevens, A. L. 1982. Goals and strategies of inquiry teachers. In *Advances in instructional psychology,* ed. R. Glaser, 2: 65-119. Hillsdale, NJ: Lawrence Erlbaum.

Collins, H. M., and Pinch, T. J. 1982. *Frames of meaning: The social construction of extraordinary science.* Boston, MA: Routledge and Kegan Paul.

Collins, L. M., and Horn, J. L., eds. 1991. *Best methods for the analysis of change: Recent advances, unanswered questions, future directions.* Washington, D C: American Psychological Association.

Collins, S.; Barrett, M.; and Citrin, R. 1985. Models and mentors for the college campus: Developing community resources for women's career assistance. *Journal of College Student Personnel* 26: 368-69.

Colorado Psychological Association. 1982. *Guidelines for the use of computerized testing services.* Denver: Colorado Psychological Association.

Commons, M. L.; Richards, F. A.; and Armon, C. 1984. *Beyond formal operations: Late adolescent and adult cognitive development.* New York: Praeger.

Cone, J. D. 1988. Psychometric considerations and the multiple models of behavioral assessment. In *Behavioral assessment,* ed. A. S. Bellack and M. Hersen, 42-66. New York: Pergamon.

Connor, S. 1989. *Postmodernist culture.* Oxford: Basil Blackwell.

Conrad, C. F. 1978. A grounded theory of academic change. *Sociology of Education* 51: 101-12.

Converse, J. M., and Schuman, H. 1974. *Conversations at random: Survey research as interviewers see it.* New York: Wiley.

Cook, T. D. 1985. Postpositivist critical multiplism. In *Social science and social policy,* ed. R. L. Shotland and M. M. Mark, 21-62. Beverly Hills, CA: Sage.

Cook, T. D., and Campbell, D. T., eds. 1979. *Quasi-experimentation: Design and analysis issues for field settings.* Chicago: Rand McNally.

Cook, T. D., and Reichardt, C. S., eds. 1979. *Qualitative and quantitative methods in evaluation research.* Beverly Hills, CA: Sage.

Cooper, T. D., and Lewis, J. A. 1983. The crisis of relativism: Helping counselors cope with diversity. *Counselor Education and Supervision* 22: 290-95.

Corey, G. 1982. *A case approach to counseling and psychotherapy.* Belmont, CA: Brooks/Cole, Wadsworth International.

Cormier, W., and Cormier, L. 1991. *Interviewing strategies for helpers: Fundamental skills and cognitive behavioral interventions.* 3d ed. Pacific Grove, CA: Brooks/Cole.

Corsini, R., and Wedding, D. 1989. *Current psychotherapies.* 4th ed. Itasca, IL: F. E. Peacock.

Costello, E. J.;, Edelbrock, C. S.; and Costello, A. J. 1985. Validity of the NIMH Diagnostic Interview Schedule for children: A comparison between psychiatric and pediatric referrals. *Journal of Abnormal and Child Psychology* 13: 579-95.

Craik, F. I. M., and Lockhart, R. S. 1972. Levels of processing: A framework for memory research. *Journal of Verbal Learning and Verbal Behavior* 11: 671-84.

Crawford, M., and Gentry, M. 1989. *Gender and thought: Psychological perspectives.* New York: Springer-Verlag.

Crocker, L. M. 1986. *Introduction to classical and modern test theory.* New York: Holt, Rinehart & Winston.

Cronbach, L. J. 1975. Beyond the two disciplines of scientific psychology.

American Psychologist 30: 116-27.

———. 1982a. *Designing evaluations of educational and social programs.* San Francisco: Jossey-Bass.

———. 1982b. Prudent aspirations for social inquiry. In *The social sciences: Their nature and uses,* ed. W. H. Kruskal, 61-81. Chicago: University of Chicago Press.

———. 1986. Social inquiry by and for earthlings. In *Metatheory in social science,* ed. D. W. Fiske and R. A. Shweder, 83-10. Chicago: University of Chicago Press.

———. 1988. Five perspectives on validity argument. In *Test validity,* ed. H. Wainer and H. I. Braun, 3-17. Hillsdale, NJ: Lawrence Erlbaum.

———. 1989. Construct validation after thirty years. In *Intelligence: Measurement, theory, and public policy,* ed. R. J. Linn, 147-71. Urbana, IL: University of Illinois Press.

———. 1990. *Essentials of psychological testing.* 5th ed. New York: Harper & Row.

———. 1991. A moderate view: Response to Ellis and Blustein. *Journal of Counseling and Development,* 69: 556-57.

Cronbach, L. J.; Ambron, S. R.; Dornbusch, S. M.; Hess, R. D.; Hornick, R. C.; Phillips, D. C.; Walker, D. F.; and Weiner, S. S. 1980. *Toward reform of program evaluation.* San Francisco: Jossey-Bass.

Cronbach, L. J., and Snow, R. E. 1977. *Aptitudes and instructional methods.* New York: Irvington.

Csikszentimihalyi, M., and Beattie, O. 1979. Life themes: A theoretical and empirical explanation of their origins and effects. *Journal of Humanistic Psychology* 19: 45-63.

Cummings, T. G.; Mohrman, S. A.; Mohrman, A. M.; and Ledford, G. E. 1985. Organization design for the future: A collaborative research approach. In *Doing research that is useful for theory and practice,* ed. E. E. Lawler, A. M. Mohrman, S. A. Mohrman, G. E. Ledford, T. G. Cummings and Associates, 275-323. San Francisco: Jossey-Bass.

Cunningham, T. R., and Tharp, R. G. 1981. The influence of settings on accuracy and reliability of behavioral observation. *Behavioral Assessment* 3:67-78.

Cushman, P. 1990. Why the self is empty: Toward a historically situated psychology. *American Psychologist* 45: 599-611.

Dailey, J. G. 1971. *Assessment of lives: Personality evaluation in a bureaucratic society.* San Francisco: Jossey-Bass.

Dallmayr, F. R., and McCarthy, T. A., Eds. 1977. *Understanding and social inquiry.* Notre Dame, IN: University of Notre Dame Press.

Dana, R. H. 1987. Training for professional psychology: Science, practice, and identity. *Professional Psychology: Research and Practice* 18 (1): 9-16.

Dana, R. H., and Leech, S. 1974. Existential assessment. *Journal of Personality Assessment* 38: 428-35.

Dance, K. A., and Neufeld, R. W. J. 1988. Aptitude-treatment interaction research in the clinical setting: A review of attempts to dispel the "patient uniformity" myth. *Psychological Bulletin* 194: 192-213.

Danziger, K. 1987. Social context and investigative practice in early twentieth-century psychology. In *Psychology in twentieth-century thought and society,* ed. M. G. Ash and W. R. Woodward, 13-33. Cambridge: Cambridge University Press.

———. 1988. A question of identity: Who participated in psychological experiments? In *The rise of experimentation in American psychology,* ed. J. G. Morawski, 35-52. New Haven, CT: Yale University Press.

———. 1990. *Constructing the subject: Historical origins of psychological research.* Cambridge: Cambridge University Press.

Darlington, R. B., and Carlson, P. M. 1987. *Behavioral statistics: Logic and methods.* New York: Free Press.

Davidson, P. O., and Costello, C. G. N. 1969. *N=1: Experimental studies of single cases.* New York: Van Nostrand-Reinhold.

Davis, L. E., and Proctor, E. K. 1989. *Race, gender, and class: Guidelines for practice with individuals, families, and groups.* Englewood Cliffs, NJ: Prentice-Hall.

Dawes, R. M.; Faust, D.; and Meehl, P. E. 1988. Clinical versus actuarial judgment. *Science* 243: 1668-74.

Dawis, R. V. 1992. The individual differences tradition in counseling psychology. *Journal of Counseling Psychology* 39: 7-19.

DeCoster, D., and Brown, R. 1982. *Mentoring relationships in the educational process.* In *Mentoring transcript systems for promoting student growth,* ed. R. Brown and D. DeCoster, 5-17. San Francisco: Jossey-Bass.

Deegan, P. E. 1981. An empirical phenomenological study of failure to learn. *Journal of Phenomenological Psychology* 12: 231-44.

de Groot, A. D. 1969. *Methodology: Foundations of inference and research in the behavioral sciences.* The Hague: Mouton.

———. 1990. Unifying psychology: A European view. *New Ideas in Psychology* 8: 309-20.

DeLeon, P. H. 1986. Increasing the societal contribution of organized psychology. *American Psychologist* 41: 466-74.

DeMaster, B.; Reid, J.; and Twentyman, C. 1977. The effects of different amounts of feedback on observer's reliability. *Behavior Therapy* 8: 317-29.

Denmark, F.; Russo, N. F.; Frieze, I. H.; and Sechzer, J. A. 1988. Guidelines for avoiding sexism in psychological research. *American Psychologist* 43: 582-85.

Denzin, N. K. 1970. Symbolic interactionism and ethnomethodology. In *Understanding everyday life,* ed. J. Douglas, 261-287. Chicago: Aldine.

———. 1989. *Interpretive biography.* Beverly Hills, CA: Sage.

Dewey, J. 1929. *The quest for certainty.* New York: Minton, Balach.

———. 1933. *How we think.* Rev. ed. Lexington, MA: Heath

———. 1957. *Reconstruction in philosophy.* Boston, MA: Beacon.

Dewey, J., and Bentley, A. F. 1949. *Knowing and the known.* Boston: Beacon.

Diamond, S., and Royce, J. R. 1980. Cognitive abilities as expressions of three 'ways of knowing.' *Multivariate Behavioral Research* 15: 31-56.

Dijkstra, W., and van der Zouwen, J., 1982. *Response behavior in the survey interview.* New York: Academic Press.

Dingwall, R.; Eekelaar, J.; and Murray, T. 1983. *The protection of children.* Oxford: Basil Blackwell.

Dipboye, R. L., and Flanagan, M. F. 1979. Research settings in industrial and organizational psychology: Are findings in the field more generalizable than in the laboratory? *American Psychologist* 34:141-50.

Dokecki, P. R. 1990. On knowing the person as agent in caring relations. *Person-Centered Review* 5: 155-69.

Dorken, H., and Associates. 1986. *Professional psychology in transition: Meeting today's challenge.* San Francisco: Jossey-Bass.

Douglas, J. D. 1985. *Creative interviewing.* Beverly Hills, CA: Sage.

Dreyfus, H. L., and Dreyfus, S. E. 1986. *Mind over machine.* New York: Free Press.

Drum, D. J., and Lawler, A. C. 1988. *Developmental interventions.* Columbus, OH: Merrill.

Drummond, R. J. 1988. *Appraisal procedures for counselors and helping professionals.* Columbus, OH: Merrill.

Dunn, W. 1982. Reforms as arguments. *Knowledge: Creation, Diffusion, Utilization* 3: 293-326.

Ebel, R. L. 1964. The social consequences of educational testing. In *Proceedings of the 1963 Invitational Conference on Testing*

Problems. Princeton, NJ: Educational Testing Service.

Edelstein, W. 1983. Cultural constraints on development and the vicissitudes of progress. In *The child and other cultural inventions,* ed. F. S. Kessel and A. W. Siegel, 48-81. New York: Praeger.

Eells, K., and Guppy, W. 1963. Counselor's valuations of and preference for different types of counseling problem. *Journal of Counseling Psychology* 10: 146-55.

Egan, G. 1990. *The skilled helper: A systematic approach to effective helping.* 4th ed. Pacific Grove, CA: Brooks/Cole.

Eiduson, B. T. 1962. *Scientists: Their psychological world.* New York: Basic Books.

Eifert, G. H., and Evans, I. M. 1990. *Unifying behavior therapy: Contributions of paradigmatic behaviorism.* New York: Springer.

Einhorn, H. J. 1988. Diagnosis and causality in clinical and statistical prediction. In *Reasoning, inference, and judgment in clinical psychology,* ed. D. C. Turk & P. Salovey, 51-70. New York: The Free Press.

Einhorn, H. J., and Hogarth, R. M. 1981. Behavioral decision theory: Processes of judgment and choice. *Annual Review of Psychology,* 32: 53-88.

———. 1986. Judging probable cause. *Psychological Bulletin* 99: 3-19.

Eisler, I.; Dare, C.; and Szmukler, G. I. 1988. What's happened to family interaction research? An historical account and a family system viewpoint. *Journal of Marital and Family Therapy* 14: 45-65.

Elliott, R. 1983. Fitting process research to the practicing psychotherapist. *Psychotherapy: Theory, Research, and Practice* 20: 47-55.

Elliott, R.; James, E.; Reimschueseel, C.; Cislo, D.; and Sack, N. 1985. Significant events and the analysis of immediate therapeutic impacts. *Psychotherapy* 22: 620-30.

Elliott, R., and Shapiro, D. A. 1992. Client and therapist as analysts of significant events. In *Psychotherapy process research: Paradigmatic and narrative approaches,* ed. S. G. Toukmanian and D. L. Rennie, 163-86. Newbury Park, CA: Sage.

Ellis, M. V., and Blustein, D. L. 1991. Developing and using educational and psychological tests and measures: The unificationist perspective. *Journal of Counseling and Development* 69: 550-55.

Engestrom, Y.; Brown, K.; Engestrom R.; and Koistinen, K. 1990. Organizational forgetting: An activity-theoretical perspective. In *Collective remembering,* ed. D. Middleton and D. Edwards, 139-68. Newbury Park, CA: Sage.

Ennis, R. H. 1985. A logical basis for measuring critical thinking skills. *Educational Leadership* 43: 44-48.

— — —. 1987. Critical thinking and the curriculum. In *Thinking skills instruction: Concepts and techniques,* ed. M. Heiman and J. Slomianko, 40-48. Washington, D C: National Education Association.

Enns, C. Z. 1988. Dilemmas of power and equality in marital and family counseling: Proposals for a feminist perspective. *Journal of Counseling and Development* 67: 242-48.

— — —. 1993. Twenty years of feminist counseling and therapy: From naming biases to implementing multifaceted practice. *The Counseling Psychologist* 21: 3-87.

Epting, F. R., and Landfield, A. W., eds. 1985. *Anticipating personal construct psychology.* Lincoln, NB: University of Nebraska Press.

Epting, F. R., and Nazario, A. 1987. Designing a fixed role therapy. In *Personal construct therapy casebook,* ed. R. A. Neimeyer and G. J. Neimeyer, 277-89. New York: Springer.

Erdman, H. P.; Klein, M. H.; and Greist, J. H. 1985. Direct patient computer interviewing. *Journal of Consulting and Clinical Psychology* 53: 760-73.

Ericsson, K. A., and Simon, H. A. 1980. Verbal reports as data. *Psychological Review* 87: 215-51.

———. 1984. *Protocol analysis: Verbal accounts as data.* Cambridge, MA:

MIT Press.

Erikson, E. H. 1958. *Young man Luther: A study in psychoanalysis and history.* New York: Norton.

Erkut, S., and Mokros, J. 1984. Professors as models and mentors for college students. *American Educational Research Journal* 21: 399-417.

Evans, I. M. 1985. Building systems models as a strategy for target behavior selection in clinical assessment. *Behavioral Assessment* 7: 21-32.

Evans, I. M., and Wilson, F. E. 1983. Behavioral assessment as decision making: A theoretical analysis. In *Perspectives on behavior therapy in the eighties,* ed. M. Rosenbaum, C. M. Franks, and Y. Jaffe, 35-53. New York: Springer.

Eysenck, H. 1952. *The scientific study of personality.* London: Routledge & Kegan Paul.

———. 1976. *Case studies in behavior therapy.* London: Routledge & Kegan Paul.

Fass, P. S. 1980. The I.Q.: A cultural and historical framework. *American Journal of Education* 88: 431-58.

Fassinger, R. E. 1991. The hidden minority: Issues and challenges in working with lesbian women and gay men. *The Counseling Psychologist* 19: 157-76.

Feixas, G. 1990. Personal construct theory and systemic therapies: Parallel or convergent trends? *Journal of Marital and Family Therapy* 16: 1-20.

Feuerstein, R. 1979. *The dynamic assessment of the retarded performer.* Baltimore: University Park Press.

Feyerabend, P. 1975. *Against method.* London: New Left Books.

Fielding, N. G., and Lee, R. M., eds. 1991. *Using computers in qualitative research.* Newbury Park, CA: Sage.

Fieldstead, W. J., ed. 1970. *Qualitative methodology: Firsthand involvement with the social world.* Chicago: Markham.

Fine, M., and Turner, J. 1991. Tyranny and freedom: Looking at ideas in the practice of family therapy. *Family Process* 30: 307-20.

Firestone, W. A. 1987. Meaning in method: The rhetoric of quantitative and qualitative research. *Educational Researcher* 16: 16-21.

Firestone, W. A., and Herriott, R. E. 1983. The formalization of qualitative research: An application of 'soft' science to the policy world. *Evaluation Review* 7: 437-66.

Fischer, C. T. 1979. Individualized assessment and phenomenological psychology. *Journal of Personality Assessment* 43: 115-22.

———. 1987. The quality of qualitative research. *Theoretical and Philosophical Psychology* 7: 2-11.

Fischer, C. T., and Wertz, F. J. 1979. Empirical phenomenological analyses of being criminally victimized. In *Duquesne studies in phenomenological psychology,* ed. A. Giorgi, R. Knowles and D. L. Smith, 135-58. Vol. 3. Pittsburgh: Duquesne University Press.

Fiske, D. W. 1991. Macropsychology and micropsychology: Natural categories and natural kinds. In *Improving inquiry in social science: A volume in honor of Lee J. Cronbach,* ed. R. E. Snow and D. E. Wiley, 61-74. Hillsdale, NJ: Lawrence Erlbaum.

Fiske, S. T., and Taylor, S. E. 1984. *Social cognition.* New York: Random House.

Fitzgerald, L. F., and Osipow, S. H. 1986. An occupational analysis of counseling psychology: How special is the specialty? *American Psychologist* 41, 535-44.

Flanagan, J. C. 1954. The critical incidents technique. *Psychological Bulletin* 51: 327-58.

Flanagan, O. J. 1981. Psychology, progress, and the problem of reflexivity: A study in the epistemological foundations of psychology. *Journal of the History of the Behavioral Sciences* 17: 375-86.

Flowers, L. S., and Hayes, J. R. 1981. A cognitive process theory of writing. *College Composition and Communication* 32: 365-387.

Floyd, F. J., and Markman, H. J. 1983. Observational biases in spouse observation: Toward a cognitive/behavioral model of marriage. *Journal of Consulting & Clinical Psychology* 51: 450-57.

Forrest-Pressley, D. L.; MacKinnon, G. E.; and Waller, T. G., 1985. *Metacognition, cognition, and human performance.* Orlando, FL: Academic Press.

Forsyth, D. R., and Strong, S. R. 1986. The scientific study of counseling and psychotherapy: A unificationist view. *American Psychologist* 41: 113-19.

Forward, S. 1989. *Toxic parents.* New York: Bantam Books.

Foucault, M. 1980. *Language, counter-memory, and practice.* Ithaca, NY: Cornell University Press.

Fowler, F. J., Jr. 1984. *Survey research methods.* Newbury Park, CA: Sage.

Fowler, F. J. Jr., and Mangione, T. W. 1989. *Standardized survey interviewing.* Newbury Park, CA: Sage.

Francis, D. J.; Fletcher, J. M.; Stuebing, K. K.; Davidson, K. C.; and Thompson, N. M. 1991. Analysis of change: Modeling individual growth. *Journal of Consulting and Clinical Psychology* 59: 27-37.

Frank, G. 1984. The Boulder model: History, rationale, and critique. *Professional Psychology: Research and Practice* 15: 417-35.

Franks, V., and Rothblum, E. D. 1983. *Stereotyping of women: Its effects on mental health.* New York: Springer.

Freud, S. 1955. Analysis of a phobia in a five-year-old boy. In *The standard edition of the complete works of Sigmund Freud*, ed. J. Strachey, 10: 5-149. London: Hogarth.

Frey, R., and Adams-Webber, J. 1992. Mood-related changes in construing self and others. *International Journal of Personal Construct Psychology* 5: 367-76.

Friedlander, M. L., and Heatherington, L. 1989. Analyzing relational control in family therapy interviews. *Journal of Counseling Psychology* 36:139-48.

Furumoto, L. 1987. On the margins: Women and the professionalization of psychology in the United States, 1890-1940. In *Psychology in twentieth-century thought and society,* ed. M. G. Ash and W. R. Woodward, 93-113. Cambridge: Cambridge University Press.

Gail, J., and Newfield, N. 1992. A conversation analysis of a solution-focused marital therapy session. *Journal of Marital and Family Therapy* 18: 153-65.

Gallop, J. 1982. *The daughter's seduction: Feminism and psychoanalysis.* Ithaca, NY: Cornell University Press.

Gambrill, E. 1990. *Critical thinking in clinical practice.* San Francisco: Jossey-Bass.

Garb, H. N. 1984. The incremental validity of information used in personality assessment. *Clinical Psychology Review* 4: 641-55.

Gardner, H. 1983. *Frames of mind: The theory of multiple intelligences.* New York: Basic Books.

———. 1985. *The mind's new science.* New York: Basic Books.

———. 1988. *Assessment in context: The alternative to standardized testing.* Cambridge: Harvard Project Zero.

Garfield, S. L. 1991. Psychotherapy models and outcome research. *American Psychologist* 46: 1350-51.

———. 1992. Comments on "Retrospect: Psychology as a profession" by J. McKeen Cattell (1937). *American Psychologist* 60: 9-15.

Garfinkel, H. 1967. *Studies in ethnomethodology.* Englewood Cliffs, NJ: Prentice-Hall.

Gauld, A., and Shotter, J. 1977. *Human action and its psychological investigation.* London: Routledge and Kegan Paul.

Gauron, E. F., and Dickinson, J. K. 1969. The influence of seeing the patient first on diagnostic decision making in psychiatry. *American Journal of Psychiatry* 126: 199-205.

Gavelek, J. R., and Raphael, T. E. 1985. Metacognition, instruction, and questioning. In *Metacognition, cognition and human performance,* ed. D. L. Forrest-Pressley, G. E. MacKinnon, and T. G. Waller, 103-136. Orlando, FL: Academic Press.

Gavey, N. 1989. Feminist poststructuralism and discourse analysis. *Psychology of Women Quarterly* 13: 459-75.

Gawthrop, J., and Uhlemann, M. R. 1992. Effects of the problem-solving approach in ethics training. *Professional Psychology: Research and Practice* 23: 38-42.

Geertz, C. 1973. *The interpretation of culture.* New York: Basic Books.

———. 1983. *Local knowledge.* New York: Basic Books.

Geisinger, K. F. 1988. The golden rule in psychological testing: Please, please don't do it unto me. *Theoretical and Philosophical Psychology* 8: 15-23.

Geller, E. S. 1991. Where's the validity in social validity? *Journal of Applied Behavior Analysis* 24: 189-204.

Gelso, C. J. 1985. Rigor, relevance, and counseling research: On the need to maintain our course between Scylla and Charybdis. *Journal of Counseling and Development* 63: 551-53.

Gendlin, E. T. 1978. *Focusing.* New York: Everest House.

———. 1986. What comes after traditional psychotherapy research? *American Psychologist* 41: 131-36.

Gergen, K. J. 1973. Social psychology as history. *Journal of Personality and Social Psychology* 26: 309-20.

———. 1978. Toward generative theory. *Journal of Personality and Social Psychology* 36: 1344-60.

———. 1982. *Toward transformation in social knowledge.* New York: Springer-Verlag.

———. 1985. The social constructionist movement in modern psychology. *American Psychologist* 40: 266-75.

———. 1989. The possibility of psychological knowledge. In *Entering the circle: Hermeneutic investigation in psychology*, ed. M. J. Packer and R. B. Addison, 239-258. Albany: State University of New York Press.

———. 1991. *The saturated self.* New York: Basic Books.

Gergen, K. J., and Davis, K. E., eds. 1985. T*he social construction of the person.* New York: Springer-Verlag.

Gergen, K. J., and Gergen, M. M. 1986. Narrative form and the construction of psychological science. In *Narrative psychology: The storied nature of human conduct,* ed. T.R. Sarbin, 22-44. New York: Praeger.

———. 1988. Narrative and the self as relationship. *Advances in Experimental Social Psychology* 21: 17-56.

———. 1991. Toward reflexive methodologies. In *Research and reflexivity,* ed. F. Steier, 76-95. Newbury Park, CA: Sage.

Gergen, K. J., and Kaye, J. 1992. Beyond narrative in the negotiation of therapeutic meaning. In *Therapy as social construction,* ed. S. McNamee and K. J. Gergen, 166-85. Newbury Park, CA: Sage.

Gergen, M., ed. 1988. *Feminist thought and the structure of knowledge.* New York: New York University Press.

Germain, R. B. 1984. Implications of a person's level of cognitive development for cognitive approaches to counseling. *Personnel and Guidance Journal* 62: 585-87.

Getzels, J. W., and Csikszentmihalyi, N. 1967. Scientific creativity. *Science* 3: 80-84.

———. 1976. *The creative vision: A longitudinal study of problem finding in art.* New York: Wiley.

Gifford, B. R. 1988. *The allocation of opportunities and the politics of testing: A policy analytic perspective. Berkeley, CA: National* Commission on Testing and Public Policy.

Gilgun, J. F.; Daly, K.; and Handel, G., 1992. *Qualitative methods in family research.* Newbury Park, CA; Sage.

Gilligan, C. 1982. *In a different voice.* Cambridge: Harvard University Press.

———. 1990. Joining the resistance: Psychology, politics, girls, and women. *Michigan Quarterly Review* 29: 501-36.

Gilligan, C.; Ward, J. V.; and Taylor, J. M., 1988. *Mapping the moral domain: A contribution of women's thinking to psychological theory and education.* Cambridge: Harvard University Press.

Giorgi, A. 1975. An application of phenomenological method in psychology. In *Duquesne studies in phenomenological psychology*, ed. A. Giorgi, C.T. Fischer, and E. Murray, 2: 82-103. Pittsburgh: Duquesne University Press.

———. 1983. The importance of the phenomenological attitude for access to the psychological realm. In *Duquesne studies in phenomenological psychology*, ed. A. Giorgi, A. Barton, and C. Maes, 4: 72-79. Pittsburgh: Duquesne University Press.

———. 1985. *Phenomenology and psychological research.* Pittsburgh: Duquesne University Press.

Glaser, B. G., and Strauss, A. L. 1967. *The discovery of grounded theory: Strategies for qualitative research.* Mill Valley, CA: Sociology Press.

Glaser, R. 1984. Education and thinking: The role of knowledge. *American Psychologist* 39: 93-104.

Glass, G. V.; McGaw, B.; and Smith, M. L. 1981. *Meta-analysis in social research.* Beverly Hills, CA: Sage.

Gleick, J. 1987. *Chaos: Making of a new science.* New York: Viking Press.

Gluck, S., and Patai, D., 1991. *Women's words: The feminist practice of oral history.* New York: Routledge.

Goetz, J. P., and LeCompte, M. D. 1984. *Ethnographic and qualitative design in educational research.* New York: Academic Press.

Golay, K. 1982. *Learning patterns and temperament styles.* Newport Beach, CA: Manas-Systems.

Goldfried, M. 1984. Training the clinician as scientist-professional. *Professional Psychology: Research and Practice* 15: 477-81.

Goldman, L. 1977. Toward more meaningful research. *Personnel and Guidance Journal* 55: 363-68.

———. 1983. The Vocational Card Sort: A different view. *Measurement and Evaluation in Guidance* 16; 107-9.

———. 1989. Moving counseling research into the twenty-first century. *The Counseling Psychologist* 17; 81-86.

———. 1990. Qualitative assessment. *The Counseling Psychologist* 18: 205-13.

Goodman, N. 1978. *Ways of world making.* New York: Harvester.

Goodman, P. S. 1985. Critical issues in doing research that contributes to theory and practice. In *Doing research that is useful for theory and practice*, ed. E. E. Lawler, A. M. Mohrman, S. A. Mohrman, G. E. Ledford, T. G. Cummings, and Associates, 324-45. San Francisco: Jossey-Bass.

Goodyear, R. K. 1990. Research on the effects of test interpretation: A review. *The Counseling Psychologist* 18: 240-57.

Gordon, J., and Shontz, F. C. 1990. Living with the AIDS virus: A representative case. *Journal of Counseling and Development* 68: 287-92.

Goslin, D., 1969. *Handbook of socialization theory and research.* Chicago: Rand McNally.

Gowin, D. B. 1981. *Educating.* Ithaca, NY: Cornell University Press.

———. 1990. Epistemic elements in evaluation research. *Studies in Educational Evaluation* 16: 319-33.

Grady, K. 1981. Sex bias in research design. *Psychology of Women Quarterly* 5: 628-36.

Green, S. B.; McCoy, J. F.; Burns, K. P.; and Smith, A. C. 1982. Accuracy of observation data with whole interval, partial interval, and momentary time sampling recording techniques. *Journal of Behavioral Assessment* 4: 103-18.

Greenberg, L. S. 1986. Change process research. *Journal of Consulting and Clinical Psychology* 54: 4-9.

Greenberg, L. S., and Pinsof, W. M. 1986. Process research: Current trends and future perspectives. In *The therapeutic process: A research handbook,* ed. L. S. Greenberg and W. M. Pinsof, 3-20. New York: Guilford.

Greeno, J. G. 1989. A perspective on thinking. *American Psychologist,* 2: 131-41.

Greenwald, H., 1959. *Great cases in psychoanalysis.* New York: Ballantine Books.

Greenwood, J. D. 1991. *Relations and representations: An introduction to the philosophy of social psychological science.* New York: Routledge.

Groeben, N. 1990. Subjective theories and the explanation of human action. In *Everyday understanding: Social and scientific implications,* ed. G. R. Semin and K. J. Gergen, 19-44. Newbury Park, CA: Sage.

Gross, A. G. 1990. *The rhetoric of science.* Cambridge: Harvard University Press.

Guba, E. G. 1990. The alternative paradigm dialog. In *The paradigm dialog,* ed. E. G. Guba, 17-27. Newbury Park, CA: Sage.

Guba, E. G., and Lincoln, Y. S. 1989. *Fourth generation evaluation.* Newbury Park, CA: Sage.

———. 1990. Can there be a human science? Constructivism as an alternative. *Person-Centered Review* 5: 130-54.

Guidano, V. 1984. A constructivist outline of cognitive processes. In *Cognitive theory, research, and practice,* ed. M. A. Reda and M. J. Mahoney, 31-45. Cambridge: Ballinger.

———. 1987. *Complexity of the self: A developmental approach to psychology and therapy.* New York: Guilford.

Guidano, V. F., and Liotti, G. 1985. A constructivistic foundation for cognitive therapy. In *Cognition and psychotherapy*, ed. M. J. Mahoney and A. Freeman, 101-42. New York: Plenum.

Guion, R. M. 1980. On trinitarian conceptions of validity. *Professional Psychology,* 11: 385-98.

Gumperz, J. 1982. *Discourse strategies.* Cambridge: Cambridge University Press.

Gutting, G. 1980. *Paradigms and revolutions.* Notre Dame, IN: University of Notre Dame Press.

Haas, L. J.; Fennimore, D.; and Warburton, J. R. 1983. A bibliography on ethical and legal issues in psychotherapy, 1970-1982. *Professional Psychology: Research and Practice* 14: 771-79.

Habermas, J. 1971. *Knowledge and human interest.* Trans. Boston: Beacon.

———. 1973. *Theory and practice.* Boston: Beacon Press.

Hackman, J. R. 1985. Doing research that makes a difference. In *Doing research that is useful for theory and practice*, ed. E. E. Lawler, A. M. Mohrman, S. A. Mohrman, G. E. Ledford, T. G. Cummings, and Associates, 126-75. San Francisco: Jossey-Bass.

Hakel, M. D.; Sorcher, M.; Beer, M.; and Moses, J. L. 1982. *Making it happen: Designing research with implementation in mind.* Beverly Hills, CA: Sage.

Haley, J. 1976. *Problem-solving therapy.* San Francisco: Jossey-Bass.

Hall, R., and Sandler, B. 1983. *Academic mentoring for women students and faculty: A new look at an old way to get ahead.* Washington, DC: Association of American Colleges, Project on the Status and Education of Women.

Halpern, D. F. 1989. *Thought and knowledge: An introduction to critical thinking.* Hillsdale, NJ: Lawrence Erlbaum.

Hamacek, D. E. 1985. *Psychology in teaching, learning, and growth.* 3d ed. Boston: Allyn & Bacon.

Hamill, R.; Wilson, T. D.; and Nisbett, R. E. 1980. Insensitivity to sample bias: Generalizing from atypical cases. *Journal of Personality and Social Psychology* 39: 578-89.

Hamlyn, D. W. 1983. *Perception, learning, and the self: Essays in the philosophy of psychology.* London: Routledge & Kegan Paul.

Hammersley, M. 1992. *What's wrong with ethnography?* New York: Routledge.

Hand, D. J. 1981. Artificial intelligence. *Psychological Medicine* 11: 449-53.

Handel, G. 1991. Case study in family research. In *A case for the case study,* ed. J. R. Feagin, A. M. Orum, and G. Sjoberg, 244-68. Chapel Hill, NC: University of North Carolina Press.

Hanfling, O. 1981. *Logical positivism.* New York: Columbia University Press.

Hansen, N. R. 1958. *Patterns of discovery.* Cambridge: Cambridge University Press.

Harding, S. 1986. *The science question in feminism.* Ithaca, NY: Cornell University Press.

Harding, S., and Hintikka, M. 1983. *Discovering reality: Feminist perspectives on epistemology, metaphysics, methodology, and philosophy of science.* Boston: D. Reidel.

Hare-Mustin, R. T., and Maracek, J. 1988. The meaning of difference: Gender theory, postmodernism, and psychology. *American Psychologist* 43: 445-64.

Hare-Mustin, R. T., and Marecek, J., 1990. *Making a difference: Psychology and the construction of gender.* New Haven, CT: Yale University Press.

Harre, R. 1984. *Personal being: A theory for individual psychology.* Cambridge: Harvard University Press.

———. 1986. Social sources of mental content and order. In *Psychology: Redesigning the discipline,* ed. J. Margolis, P. T. Manicas, R. Harre, and P. F. Secord, 91-127. New York: Basil Blackwell.

———. 1987. Enlarging the paradigm. *New Ideas in Psychology* 5: 3-12.

Harre, R.; Clarke, D.; and DeCarlo, N. 1985. *Motives and mechanisms: An introduction to the psychology of action.* New York: Methuen.

Harre, R., and Secord, P. F. 1972. *The explanation of social behavior.* Oxford: Basil Blackwell.

Harriman, R. 1989. The rhetoric of inquiry and the professional scholar. In *Rhetoric in the human sciences,* ed. H. W. Simons, 211-32. Newbury Park, CA: Sage.

Hartmann, D. P., ed. 1982. *New direction for methodology of social and behavioral science: Using observers to study behavior.* San Francisco: Jossey-Bass.

Harvey, D. 1989. *The condition of postmodernity.* Oxford: Basil Blackwell.

Hawkins, R. P.; Peterson, R. F.; Schweid, E.; and Bijou, S. W. 1966. Behavior therapy in the home: Amelioration of problem parent-child relations with the parent in a therapeutic role. *Journal of Experimental Child Psychology* 4: 99-107.

Hay, L. R.; Nelson, R. O.; and Hay, W. M. 1977. The use of teachers as behavioral observers. *Journal of Applied Behavior Analysis* 10: 345-49.

———. 1980. Methodological problems in the use of participant observers. *Journal of Applied Behavior Analysis* 13: 501-4.

Hayakawa, S. I. 1978. *Language in thought and action.* 4th ed. New York: Harcourt Brace Jovanovich.

Hayes, S. C., and Nelson, R. O. 1981. Clinically relevant research: Requirements, problems, and solutions. *Behavioral Assessment* 3: 209-15.

Hayes, S. C.; Nelson, R. O.; and Jarrett, R. B. 1986. Evaluating the quality of behavioral assessment. In *Conceptual foundations of behavioral assessment,* ed. R. O. Nelson and S. C. Hayes, 463-504. New York: Guilford.

———. 1987. The treatment utility of assessment. *American Psychologist* 42: 963-74.

Hayes-Roth, B. 1977. Evolution of cognitive structures and processes. *Psychological Review* 84: 260-78.

Haynes, S. N.; Follingstad, D. R.; and Sullivan, J. 1979. Assessment of marital interaction and satisfaction. *Journal of Consulting and Clinical Psychology* 47: 789-91.

Haynes, S. N., and Horn, W. F. 1982. Reactivity in behavioral observation: A review. *Behavioral Assessment 4:* 369-86.

Healy, C. C. 1990. Reforming career appraisals to meet the needs of clients in the 1990s. *The Counseling Psychologist* 18: 214-26.

Heatherington, L., and Friedlander, M. L. 1990. Applying task analysis to structural family therapy. *Journal of Family Psychology* 4: 36-48.

Heelan, P. A. 1989. The new relevance of experiment: A postmodern problem. *Theoretical and Philosophical Psychology* 9: 11-19.

Heider, F. 1958. *The psychology of interpersonal relations.* New York: Wiley.

Heller, K. 1971. Laboratory interview research as an analogue to treatment. In *Handbook of psychotherapy and behavior change,* ed. A. E. Bergin and S. L. Garfield, 126-53. New York: Wiley.

Helmes, J. E. 1992. Why is there no study of cultural equivalence in standardized cognitive ability testing? *American Psychologist* 47: 1083-101.

Heppner, P. P.; Carter, J. A.; Claiborn, C. D.; Brooks, L.; Gelso, C. J.;

Fassinger, R. E.; Holloway, E. L.; Stone, G. L.; Wampold, B. E.; and Galassi, J. P. 1992. A proposal to integrate science and practice in counseling psychology. *The Counseling Psychologist* 20: 107-22.

Heppner, P. P.; Kivlighan, D. M.; and Wampold, B. E. 1992. *Research design in counseling.* Pacific Grove, CA: Brooks/Cole.

Heppner, P. P.; Rosenberg, J. I.; and Hedgespeth, J. 1992. Three methods in measuring the therapeutic process: Clients' and counselors' constructions of the therapeutic process versus actual therapeutic events. *Journal of Counseling Psychology* 39: 20-31.

Herbert, J. D., and Mueser, K. T. (1991). The proof is in the pudding: A commentary on Persons. *American Psychologist* 46: 1347-48.

Hermans, J. M., and Bonarius, H. 1991. The person as co-investigator in personality research. *European Journal of Personality* 5: 199-216.

Hermans, J. M.; Kempen, H. J. G.; and Van Loon, R. J. P. 1992. The dialogical self: Beyond individualism and rationalism. *American Psychologist* 47: 23-33.

Heron, J. 1981. Philosophical basis for a new paradigm. In *Human inquiry: A sourcebook of new paradigm research,* ed. P. Reason and J. Rowan, 19-35. New York: Wiley.

Hersen, M., and Barlow, D. H. 1976. *Single-case experimental designs: Strategies for studying behavior.* New York: Pergamon.

Hersen, M., and Turner, S. M., eds. 1985. *Diagnostic interviewing.* New York: Plenum.

Hesse, M. 1980. *Revolutions and reconstructions in the philosophy of science.* Bloomington, IN: Indiana University Press.

———. 1981. Theory and value in the social sciences. In *Conceptions of inquiry*, ed. S. Brown, J. Fauvel, and R. Finnegan, 309-26. New York: Methuen

Hettich, P. 1990. Journal writing: Old fare or nouvelle cuisine? *Teaching of Psychology* 17: 36-39.

Higgins, E. T., and Stangor, C. 1988. Context-driven social judgment and memory: When "behavior engulfs the field" in reconstructive memory. In *The social psychology of knowledge: Its scope and meaning,* ed. D. Bar-Tal and A. W. Kruglanski, 262-98. New York: Cambridge University Press.

Hill, C. E. 1989. *Therapist techniques and client outcomes: Eight cases of brief psychotherapy.* Newbury Park, CA: Sage.

———. 1990. Exploratory in-session process research in individual psychotherapy: A review. *Journal of Consulting and Clinical Psychology* 58: 288-94.

———. 1992. An overview of four measures to test the Hill process model: Therapist intentions, therapist response modes, client reaction, and client behaviors. *Journal of Counseling and Development* 70: 728-39.

Hill, C. E.; Carter, J. A.; and O'Farrell, M. K. 1983. A case study of the process and outcome of time-limited counseling. *Journal of Counseling Psychology* 58: 288-94.

Hill, T. E. 1961. *Contemporary theories of knowledge.* New York: Ronald Press.

Hillerbrand, E. 1989. Cognitive differences between experts and novices: Implications for group supervision. *Journal of Counseling and Development* 63: 545-47.

Hirsch, E. D. 1967. *Validity in interpretation.* New Haven, CT: Yale University Press.

Ho, D. Y. F. 1985. Prejudice, colonialism, and interethnic relations: An East-West dialogue. *Journal of Asian and African Studies* 20: 218-31.

—. 1988. Asian psychology: A dialogue on indigenization and beyond. In *Asian contributions to psychology,* ed. A. C. Paranjpe, D. Y. F. Ho, and R. W. Rieber, 53-77. New York: Praeger.

———. 1991. Relational orientation and methodological individualism. *Bulletin of the Hong Kong Psychological Society* 26/27: 1-15.

———. 1992. A metatheory of cross-cultural comparisons: Confronting culturocentrism. In *Psychology in international perspective,* ed. P. Gielen, L. L. Adler, and N. Milgram, 186-98. Amsterdam: Swets and Zeitlinger.

Hogarth, R. M. 1981. Beyond discrete biases: Functional and dysfunctional aspects of judgment heuristics. *Psychological Bulletin* 90: 197-217.

Hollinger, R., ed. 1985. *Hermeneutics and praxis.* South Bend, IN: Notre Dame University Press.

Hollis, F., and Woods, M. E. 1981. *Casework: A psychosocial therapy.* 3d ed. New York: Random House.

Hollon, S. D., and Flick, S. N. 1988. On the meaning and methods of clinical significance. *Behavioral Assessment* 10: 197-206.

Holloway, E. L., and Wolleat, P. L. 1980. Relationship of counselor conceptual level to clinical hypothesis formation. *Journal of Counseling Psychology* 27: 539-45.

Holt, R. R. 1958. Clinical and statistical prediction: A reformulation and some new data. *Journal of Abnormal and Social Psychology* 6: 1-12.

———. 1988. Judgment, inference, and reasoning in clinical perspective. In *Reasoning, inference, and judgment in clinical psychology,* ed. D. C. Turk and P. Salovey, 233-50. New York: Free Press.

Holton, G. 1973. *Thematic origins of scientific thought, Kepler to Einstein.* Cambridge: Harvard University Press.

Homans, G. A. 1978. What kind of myth is the myth of value-free social science? *Social Science Quarterly* 58: 530-41.

Honey, M. 1987. The interview as text: Hermeneutics considered as a model for analyzing the clinically informed research interview. *Human Development,* 30: 69-82.

Hooks, B. 1984. *Feminist theory: From margin to center.* Boston: South End.

Horley, J. 1987. The construal of events: Personal constructs versus personal projects. In *Experimenting with personal construct psychology,* ed. F.

Fransella and L. Thomas, 357-66. London: Routledge & Kegan Paul.

Horowitz, L. M.; Post, D. L.; French, R. S.; Wallis, K. D.; and Siegelman, E. Y. 1981. The prototype as a construct in abnormal psychology: 2. Clarifying disagreement in psychiatric judgments. *Journal of Abnormal Psychology* 90: 575-85.

Horowitz, L. M.; Wright, J. C.; Lowenstein, E.; and Parad, H. W. 1981. The prototype as a construct in abnormal psychology: 1. A method for deriving prototypes. *Journal of Abnormal Psychology* 90: 568-74.

Hoshmand, L. T. 1989. Alternate research paradigms: A review and teaching proposal. *The Counseling Psychologist* 17: 3-79.

———. 1991. Clinical inquiry as scientific training. *The Counseling Psychologist* 19: 431-53.

———. 1993. The personal narrative in the communal construction of self and life issues. In *Constructivist assessment,* ed. G. J. Neimeyer, 179-205. Newbury Park, CA: Sage.

———. 1994. Supervision of pre-doctoral graduate research: A practice-oriented approach. *The Counseling Psychologist* 22: 147-61.

Hoshmand, L. T., and Martin, J. 1992. Can methodological pluralism contribute to research on practice? Paper presented at the American Psychological Association Conference, Washington, D C, August.

Hoshmand, L. T., and Martin, J., in press. *Method choice and inquiry process: Lessons from programmatic research in therapeutic psychology.* New York: Teachers College Press.

Hoshmand, L. T., and Polkinghorne, D. E. 1992. Redefining the science-practice relationship and professional training. *American Psychologist* 47: 55-66.

Houts, A. C., and Galante, M. 1985. The impact of evaluative disposition and subsequent information on clinical impression. *Journal of Social and Clinical Psychology* 3: 201-12.

Howard, G. S. 1982. Improving methodology via research on research methods. *Journal of Counseling Psychology* 29: 318-26.

———. 1984a. A modest proposal for a revision of strategies for counseling research. *Journal of Counseling Psychology* 31: 430-41.

———. 1984b. On studying humans. *The Counseling Psychologist* 12: 101-9.

———. 1985a. Can research in the human sciences become more relevant to practice? *Journal of Counseling and Development* 63: 539-44.

———. 1985b. The role of values in the science of psychology. *American Psychologist* 40: 255-65.

———. 1991. Culture tales: A narrative approach to thinking, cross-cultural psychology, and psychotherapy. *American Psychologist* 46: 187-97.

Howard, G. S., and Conway, C. G. 1986. Can there be an empirical science of volitional action? *American Psychologist* 41: 1241-51.

———. 1987. The next steps toward a science of agency. *American Psychologist* 42: 1034-35.

Howard, G. S.; Maerlender, A. C.; Myers, P. R.; and Curtin, T. 1992. In stories we trust: Studies of the validity of autobiographies. *Journal of Counseling Psychology* 39: 398-405.

Howard, G. S.; Maxwell, S. E.; Weiner, R. L.; Boynton, K. S.; and Rooney, W. M. 1980. Is a behavioral measure the best estimate of behavioral parameters? Perhaps not. *Applied Psychological Measurement* 4: 293-311.

Howard, G. S.; Myers, P. R.; and Curtin, T. D. 1991. Can science furnish evidence of human freedom? Self-determination versus conformity in human action. *International Journal of Personal Construct Psychology* 4: 371-95.

Howard, G. S.; Youngs, W. H.; and Siatczynski, A. M. 1988. Reforming methodology in psychological research. *Journal of Mind and Behavior* 10: 393-412.

Hsu, F. L. K. 1983. *Rugged individualism reconsidered: Essays in psycho-*

logical anthropology. Knoxville, TN: University of Tennessee Press.

———. 1985. The self in cross-cultural perspective. In *Culture and self: Asian and Western perspectives,* ed. A. J. Marsella, G. de Vos, and F. L. K. Hsu, 24-55. New York: Tavistock.

Huitema, B. E. 1986. Statistical analysis and single-subject designs: Some misunderstandings. In *Research methods in applied behavior analysis: Issues and advances,* ed. A. Poling and R. W. Fuqua, 209-232. New York: Plenum.

Hunt, D. 1966. A conceptual system change model and its application to education. In *Experience, structure, and adaptability,* ed. O. J. Harvey, 68-84. New York: Springer.

———. 1970. A conceptual level matching model for coordinating learner characteristics with educational approaches. *Interchange* 1: 68-82.

Hunter, J. E., and Schmidt, F. L. 1990. *Methods of meta-analysis: Correcting error and bias in research findings.* Newbury Park, CA: Sage.

Hutt, S. J., and Hutt, C. 1970. *Direct observation and measurement of behavior.* Springfield, IL: C. C. Thomas.

Ibrahim, F. A. 1986. Reflections on the cultural encapsulation of the APA Ethical Principles: Recommendations for revisions. Paper presented at symposium, Are the APA Ethical Principles Culturally Encapsulated? Annual meeting of the American Psychological Association, Washington, DC, August.

Ibrahim, F. A., and Arredondo, P. M. 1986. Ethical standards for cross-cultural counseling: Preparation, practice, assessment, and research. *Journal of Counseling and Development* 64: 349-51.

Imber, S. D.; Glanz, L. M.; Elkin, I.; Sotsky, S. M.; Boyer, J. L.; and Leber, W. R. 1986. Ethical issues in psychotherapy research. *American Psychologist* 41: 137-46.

Ingram, R. E., ed. 1986. *Information processing approaches to clinical psychology.* New York: Academic Press.

Inhelder, B., & Piaget, J. 1958. *The growth of logical thinking from childhood to adolescence.* London: Routledge & Kegan Paul.

Ivey, A. E. 1988. *Intentional interviewing and counseling: Facilitating client development.* 2d ed. Pacific Grove, CA: Brooks/Cole.

———. 1993. On the need for reconstruction of our present practice of counseling and psychotherapy. *The Counseling Psychologist* 21: 225-28.

Ivey, A. E., and Authier, J. 1978. *Microcounseling: Innovations in interviewing, counseling, psychotherapy, and psychoeducation.* 2d ed. Springfield, IL: C. C. Thomas.

Ivey, A.; Ivey, M.; and Simek-Morgan, L. 1993. *Counseling and psychotherapy: A multicultural perspective.* Needham Heights, MA: Allyn & Bacon.

Jack, D.C. 1991. *Silencing the self: Women and depression.* Cambridge: Harvard University Press.

Jacklin, C. N., and McBride-Chang, C. 1991. The effects of feminist scholarship on developmental psychology. *Psychology of Women Quarterly* 15: 549-56.

Jackson Lears, T. J. 1983. From salvation to self-realization. In *The culture of consumption,* ed. R. Wightman Fox and T. J. Jackson Lears, 1-38. New York: Pantheon.

Jacobs, D. F. 1983. Standards of professional practice: The development and application of practice for professional psychologists. In *The professional psychologist handbook,* ed B. D. Sales, 19-75. New York: Plenum.

Jacobs, J. 1985. "In the best interests of the child": Official court reports as an artifact of negotiated reality in children's assessment centers. *Clinical Sociology Review* 3: 88-108.

Jacobson, N. S. 1985a. The role of observational measures in behavior therapy outcome research. *Behavioral Assessment* 7: 297-308.

———. 1985b. Uses versus abuses of observational measures. *Behavioral Assessment* 7: 323-30.

Jacobson, N. S., ed. 1988. Defining clinically significant change. Special issue. *Behavioral Assessment* 10.

Jacobson, N. S.; Follette, W. C.; and Revenstorf, D. 1984. Psychotherapy outcome research: Methods for reporting variability and evaluating clinical significance. *Behavior Therapy* 15: 336-52.

Jacobson, N. S., and Moore, D. 1981. Spouses as observers of the events in their relationship. *Journal of Consulting and Clinical Psychology* 40: 269-77.

Jacobson, N. S., and Revenstorf, D. 1988. Statistics for assessing the clinical significance of psychotherapy techniques: Issues, problems, and new developments. *Behavioral Assessment,* 10: 133-45.

Jacobson, N. S., and Truax, P. 1991. Clinical significance: A statistical approach to defining meaningful change in psychotherapy research. *Journal of Consulting and Clinical Psychology* 1: 12-19.

James, W. 1907. *Pragmatism.* New York: Meridian.

Janoff-Bulman, R. 1989. Assumptive worlds and the stress of traumatic events: Applications of the schema construct. *Social Cognition* 7: 113-36.

Jason, L. A.; Felner, R. D.; Moritsugu, J. N.; and Farber, S. S. 1983. Future directions for preventive psychology. In *Preventive psychology: Theory, research, and practice,* ed. R. D. Felner, L. A. Jason, J. N. Moritsugu, and S. S. Farber, 297-309. New York: Pergamon.

Johnson-Laird, P. N. 1983. *Mental models: Towards a cognitive science of language, inference, and consciousness.* Cambridge: Harvard University Press.

Jones, E. E., and Nisbett, R. E. 1971. *The actor and the observer: Divergent perceptions of the causes of behavior.* Morristown, NJ: General Learning Press.

Jones, J.; Levine, I. S.; and Rosenberg, A. P., eds. 1991. Special issue: Homelessness. *American Psychologist* 46: 1108-252.

Jorgensen, D. L. 1989. *Participant observation: A methodology for human studies.* Newbury Park, CA: Sage.

Joyce Monitz, L. 1985. Epistemological therapy and constructivism. In *Cognition and psychotherapy,* ed. M. J. Mahoney and A. Freeman, 143-79. New York: Plenum.

Jung, C. G. 1923. *Psychological types.* New York: Harcourt Brace.

Kagan, S. 1989/1990. The structural approach to cooperative learning. *Educational Leadership* 47 (Dec./Jan.): 12-15.

Kahneman, D.; Slovic, P.; and Tversky, A., eds. 1982. *Judgment under uncertainty: Heuristics and biases.* Cambridge: Cambridge University Press.

Kahneman, D., and Tversky, A. 1973. On the psychology of prediction. *Psychological Review* 80: 237-51.

Kamin, L. 1974. *The science and politics of I.Q.* Potomac, MD: Lawrence Erlbaum.

Kanfer, F. H. 1985. Target selection for clinical change programs. *Behavioral Assessment* 7: 7-19.

———. 1990. The scientist-practitioner connection: A bridge in need of constant attention. *Professional Psychology: Research and Practice* 21: 264, 270.

Kantor, D., and Andreozzi, L. 1985. The cybernetics of family therapy and family therapy research. In *Integrating research and clinical practice,* ed. L. Andreozzi, 37-50. Rockville, MD: Aspen.

Kantor, D., and Neal, J. 1985. Integrative shifts for the theory and practice of family systems therapy. *Family Process* 24: 13-30.

Kaplan, A. 1964. *The conduct of inquiry: Methodology for behavioral science.* New York: Harper & Row.

Kaplan, M. 1983. A woman's view of DSM-III. *American Psychologist* 38: 786-92.

Katzner, D. W. 1983. *Analysis without measurement.* Cambridge:

Cambridge University Press.

Kazdin, A. E. 1977. Assessing the clinical or applied importance of behavior change through social validation. *Behavior Modification* 1: 427-52.

———. 1982. *Single-case research designs: Methods for clinical and applied settings.* New York: Oxford University Press.

———. 1985. Selection of target behaviors: The relationship of the treatment focus to clinical dysfunction. *Behavioral Assessment* 7:, 33-47.

———. 1992. *Methodological issues and strategies in clinical research.* Washington, D C: American Psychological Association.

Kazdin, A. E.; Siegel, T. C.; and Bass, D. 1990. Drawing on clinical practice to inform research on child and adolescent psychotherapy. *Professional Psychology: Research and Practice* 21: 189-98.

Keeney, B. P., and Morris, J. P. 1985a. Family therapy practice and research: A dialogue. In *Integrating research and clinical practice*, ed. L. Andreozzi, 98-107. Rockville, MD: Aspen.

———. 1985b. Implications of cybernetic epistemology for clinical research: A reply to Howard. *Journal of Counseling and Development* 63: 548-50.

Keirsey, D., and Bates, M. 1978. *Please understand me: Character and temperament types.* Del Mar, CA: Prometheus Nemesis.

Keller, E. 1985. *Reflections on gender and science.* New Haven, CT: Yale University Press.

Kelly, G. A. 1955. *The psychology of personal constructs,* vols. 1 and 2. New York: Norton.

———. 1970. A brief introduction to personal construct theory. In *Perspectives in personal construct theory*, ed. D. Bannister, 1-29. New York: Academic Press.

Kelly, H. H. 1973. The process of causal attribution. *American Psychologist* 28: 107-28.

Kelman, H. C. 1972. The rights of the subject in social research: An analysis in terms of relative power and legitimacy. *American Psychologist* 27: 989-1016.

Kendall, P. C., and Butcher, J. N., eds. 1982. *Handbook of research methods in clinical psychology.* New York: Wiley.

Kendall, P. C., and Grove, W. M. 1988. Normative comparisons in therapy outcome. *Behavioral Assessment* 10: 147-58.

Kendler, H. H. 1987. *Historical foundations of modern psychology.* Pacific Grove, CA: Brooks/Cole.

Kenny, D. A. 1975. A quasi-experimental approach to assessing treatment effects in the nonequivalent group design. *Psychological Bulletin* 68: 345-62.

Kent, R. N.; O'Leary, K. D.; Diament, C.; and Dietz, A. 1974. Expectation biases in observational evaluation of therapeutic change. *Journal of Consulting and Clinical Psychology* 42: 774-80.

Kessen, W. 1983. The child and other cultural inventions. In *The child and other cultural inventions,* ed. F. S. Kessel and A. W. Siegel, 26-39. New York: Praeger.

Kidder, L. H. 1981. *Research methods in social relations.* 4th ed. New York: Holt, Rinehart & Winston.

Kidder, L. H., and Judd, C. M. 1986. *Research methods in social relations.* 5th ed. New York: Holt, Rinehart & Winston.

Kiesler, C. A., and Morton, T. L. 1988. Psychology and public policy in the "health care revolution." *American Psychologist* 43: 993-1003.

Kiesler, D. J. 1966. Some myths of psychotherapy research and the search for a paradigm. *Psychological Bulletin* 65: 110-36.

Kim, U., and Berry, J., eds. 1993. *Indigenous psychologies: Experience and research in cultural context.* Cambridge: Cambridge University Press.

Kimble, G. A. 1984. Psychology's two cultures. *American Psychologist* 39: 833-39.

King, P. M. 1978. The development of reflective judgment and formal operational thinking in adolescents and young adults. Ph.D. diss., University of Minnesota. *Dissertation Abstracts International* 38: 7233A.

———. 1983. *Reflective Judgment Questionnaire.* Technical Report no. 1. Bowling Green, OH: Bowling Green State University.

———. 1986. Formal reasoning in adults: A review and critique. In *Adult cognitive development: Methods and models*, ed. R. A. Mines and K. S. Kitchener, 1-2. New York: Praeger.

King, P. M.; Kitchener, K. S.; Davison, M. L.; Parker, C. A.; and Wood, P. K. 1983. The justification of beliefs in young adults: A longitudinal study. *Human Development* 26: 106-16.

Kirk, J., and Miller, M. L. 1986. *Reliability and validity in qualitative research.* Beverly Hills, CA: Sage.

Kitchener, K. S. 1978. Holistic and the organismic model in human developmental psychology. *Human Development* 25: 233-49.

———. 1983. Cognition, metacognition and epistemic cognition: A three-level model of cognitive processing. *Human Development* 4: 222-32.

———. 1984. Intuition, critical evaluation, and ethical principles: The foundation for ethical decisions in counseling psychology. *The Counseling Psychologist* 12: 43-57.

———. 1986. The reflective judgment model: Characteristics, evidence, and measurement. In *Adult cognitive development: Methods and models*, ed. R. A. Mines and K. S. Kitchener, 76-91. New York: Praeger.

Kleiman, L. S., and Faley, R. H. 1985. The implications of professional and legal guidelines for court decisions involving criterion-related validity: A review and analysis. *Personnel Psychology* 38: 803-33.

Kleinmuntz, B. 1963. MMPI decision rules for the identification of college maladjustments. *Psychological Monographs* 77: 1-22.

———. 1968. The processing of clinical information by man and machine.

In *Formal representation of human judgment*, ed. B. Kleinmuntz, 149-86. New York: Wiley.

———. 1984. The scientific study of clinical judgment in psychology and medicine. *Clinical Psychological Review* 4: 111-26.

Klinger, E. 1978. Modes of normal conscious flow. In *The stream of consciousness,* ed. K. S. Pope, and J. L. Singer, 225-57. New York: Plenum.

Klonoff, E. A.; Revis, E. S.; and Tice, D. M. 1985. The effect of stimulus presentation of order and observational method on ratings of performance anxiety. *Behavioral Assessment* 7: 185-96.

Knapp, M. 1978. *Nonverbal communication in human interaction.* New York: Holt, Rinehart & Winston.

Koch, S. 1981a. The nature and limits of psychological knowledge: Lessons of a century qua "science." *American Psychologist* 36: 257-69.

———. 1981b. Psychology and its human clientele: Beneficiaries or victims? In *Psychology and society: In search of symbiosis*, ed. R. A. Kasschau and F. S. Kessel, 30-60. New York: Holt, Rinehart & Winston.

Koch, S., ed. 1959-1963. *Psychology: A study of a science.* Vols. 1-6. New York: McGraw-Hill.

Koch, S., & Leary, D. E., eds. 1992. *A century of psychology as science.* (1985.) Washington, D C: American Psychological Association.

Koester, A., and Smythies, J. R., eds. 1969. *Beyond reductionism.* New York: Macmillan.

Koester, G. A. 1954. A study of the diagnostic process. *Educational and Psychological Measurement* 14: 473-86.

Kohlberg, L. 1984. *Essays on moral development:* Vol. 2. *The psychology of moral development.* New York: Harper & Row.

Kopta, S. M.; Newman, F. L.; McGovern, M. P.; and Sandrock, D. 1986. Psychological orientations: A comparison of conceptualizations, interventions, and treatment plan costs. *Journal of Consulting and Clinical Psychology* 54: 369-74.

Krantz, D. L. 1987. Psychology's search for unity. *New Ideas in Psychology* 5:329-39.

Krasner, L., and Houts, A. C. 1984. A study of the "value" systems of behavioral scientists. *American Psychologist* 39: 840-50.

Kratochwill, T. R. 1985a. Selection of target behaviors: Issues and directions. *Behavioral Assessment* 7: 3-5.

———. 1985b. Selection of target behaviors in behavioral consultation. *Behavioral Assessment* 7: 49-61.

Kratochwill, T. R., ed. 1978. *Single-subject research.* New York: Academic Press.

Kratwohl, D. R. 1985. *Social and behavioral science research.* San Francisco: Jossey-Bass.

Krippendorff, K. 1980. *Content analysis : An introduction to its methodology.* Beverly Hills, CA: Sage.

Krippner, S.; Ruttenber, A. J.; Engelman, S.; and Granger, D. 1985. Toward the application of general systems theory in humanistic psychology. *Systems Research* 2: 105-15.

Kuehl, B. P.; Newfield, N. A.; and Joanning, H. 1990. A client-based description of family therapy. *Journal of Family Psychology* 3: 310-21.

Kuhn, D.; Amsel, E.; and O'Laughlin, M. 1988. *The development of scientific thinking skills.* San Diego: Academic Press.

Kuhn, T. 1970. *The structure of scientific revolutions.* 2d ed. Chicago: University of Chicago Press.

Kukla, A. 1989. Nonempirical issues in psychology. *American Psychologist* 44: 785-94.

Kuncel, R. B., and Fiske, D. W. 1974. Stability of response process and response. *Educational and Psychological Measurement* 34:743-55.

Kvale, S. 1983. The qualitative research interview: A phenomenological and a hermeneutical mode of understanding. *Journal of Phenomenological Psychology* 14: 171-96.

———. Kvale, S. 1986. Psychoanalytic therapy as qualitative research. In *Qualitative research in psychology,* ed. P.D. Ashworth, A. Giorgi, and A. J. de Konig, 155-84. Pittsburgh, PA: Duquesne University Press.

———. 1987a. Interpretation of the qualitative research interview. In *Advances in qualitative psychology: Themes and variations,* ed. F. J. van Zuuren, F. J. Wertz, & B. Mook, 25-40. Sweden: Swets North American/Berwyn.

———. 1987b. Validity in the qualitative interview. *Methods* 1(2): 37-72.

Kvale, S., ed. 1992. *Psychology and postmodernism.* Newbury Park, CA: Sage.

Lakatos, I. 1978. *The methodology of scientific research programs.* Cambridge: Cambridge University Press.

Lambert, M. J. 1983. Comments on "A case study of the process and outcome of time-limited counseling." *Journal of Counseling Psychology* 30: 22-25.

Landfield, A. W., and Leitner, L., eds. 1980. *Personal construct psychology: Psychotherapy and personality.* New York: Academic Press.

Lang, P. J.; Levin, D. N.; Miller, G. A.; and Kozak, M. J. 1983. Fear behavior, fear imagery, and the psychophysiology of emotion: The problem of affective response integration. *Journal of Abnormal Psychology* 92: 276-306.

Langer, E. J., and Abelson, R. P. 1974. A patient by any other name...: Clinician group differences in labeling bias. *Journal of Consulting and Clinical Psychology* 42: 4-9.

La Rossa, R.; Gordon, B. A.; Wilson, R. J.; Bairan, A.; and Jaret, C. 1991. The fluctuating image of the twentieth century American father. *Journal of Marriage and the Family* 53: 987-97.

La Rossa, R., and Wolf, J. H. 1985. On qualitative family research. *Journal of Marriage and the Family* 47: 531-41.

Larry P. v. Riles, 495 F. Supp. 926 (N.D. Cal. 1979), *Appeal docketed,* No. 80-4027 (9th Cir. Jan. 17, 1980).

Lasch, C. 1979. *The culture of narcissism.* New York: Norton.

Laslett, B., and Rapoport , R. 1985. Collaborative interviewing and interactive research. *Journal of Marriage and the Family* 47: 968-77.

Lather, P. 1986. Research as praxis. *Harvard Educational Review* 56: 257-77.

Laudan, L. 1990. *Science and relativism: Some key controversies in the philosophy of science.* Chicago: University of Chicago Press.

Lawler, E. E.; Mohrman, A. M.; Mohrman, S. A.; Ledford, G. E., Jr.; Cummings, T. G.; and Associates. 1985. *Doing research that is useful for theory and practice.* San Francisco: Jossey-Bass.

Lawson, H. 1985. *Reflexivity: A postmodern predicament.* La Salle, IL: Open Court.

Leahey, T. H. 1987. *A history of psychology: Main currents in psychological thought.* 2d ed. Englewood Cliffs, NJ: Prentice-Hall.

———. 1991. *A history of modern psychology.* Englewood Cliffs, NJ: Prentice-Hall.

———. 1992. The mythical revolutions of American psychology. *American Psychologist* 47: 308-18.

LeCompte, M. D., and Goetz, J. P. 1982. Problems of reliability and validity in ethnographic research. *Review of Educational Research* 52: 31-60.

Lefebvre, V. A.; Lefebvre, V. D.; and Adams-Webber, J. 1986. Modeling an experiment on construing self and others. *Journal of Mathematical Psychology* 13: 119-330.

Lenski, G., and Leggett, J. 1960. Caste, class, and deference in the research interview. *American Journal of Sociology* 65: 463-67.

Lerman, H. 1986. From Freud to feminist personality theory: Getting here from there. *Psychology of Women Quarterly* 10: 1-18.

Lerman, H., and Porter, N., eds. 1990. *Feminist ethics in psychotherapy.* New York: Springer-Verlag.

Lerner, B. 1978. The Supreme Court and the APA, AERA, NCME test standards: Past references and future possibilities. *American Psychologist* 33: 915-19.

Lesche, C. 1962. *A metascientific study of psychosomatic theories and their application in medicine.* New York: Humanities Press.

———. 1973. On the metascience of psychoanalysis. *The Human Context,* 5, 268-84.

———. 1978. Some metascientific reflections on the differences between psychoanalysis and psychotherapy. *Scandinavian Psychoanalytic Review* 1: 147-81.

———. 1981. The relation between metapsychology and clinical psychoanalysis. *Scandinavian Psychoanalytic Review* 4: 59-74.

———. 1985. Is psychoanalysis therapeutic technique or scientific research? A metascientific investigation. In *Annals of theoretical psychology,* ed K. B. Madsen and L. P. Mos, 3: 157-187. New York: Plenum.

Lesgold, A. M.; Feltovich, P. J.; Glaser, R.; and Wang, Y. 1981. *The acquisition of perceptual diagnostic skills in radiology.* Technical Report PDS-1. Pittsburgh: Learning Research & Development Center, University of Pittsburgh.

Leventhal, T.; Slepian, H. J.; Gluck, M. R.; and Rosenblatt, B. P. 1962. The utilization of the psychologist-patient relationship in diagnostic testing. *Journal of Projective Techniques* 26: 66-79.

Levine, A., and Levine, M. 1977. The social context of evaluative research: A case study. *Evaluation Quarterly* 1: 515-42.

Levine, H. G.; Gallimore, R.; Weisner, T. S.; and Turner, J. L. 1980. Teaching participant-observation research methods: A skills-building approach. *Anthropology and Education Quarterly* 11: 38-54.

Levine, M., and Levine, A. 1992. *Helping children: A social history.* New York: Oxford University Press.

Levinson, D.; Darrow, C.; Klein, E.; Levinson, M.; and McKee, B. 1978. *The seasons of a man's life.* New York: Knopf.

Leviton, L. C.; and Hughes, E. F. X. 1981. Research on the utilization of evaluations: A review and synthesis. *Evaluation Review* 5: 535-48.

Levy, L. H. 1963. *Psychological interpretation.* New York: Holt, Rinehart & Winston.

Levy, S. M. 1981. The experience of undergoing a heart attack: The construction of a new reality. *Journal of Phenomenological Psychology* 12:153-71.

Lewin, K., ed. 1948. *Resolving social conflicts.* New York: Harper & Row.

Lidz, C. S. 1983. Dynamic assessment and the preschool child. *Journal of Psychoeducational Assessment* 1: 59-72.

Liljestrom, R. 1983. The public child, the commercial child, our child. In *The child and other cultural inventions*, ed. F. S. Kessel and A. W. Siegel, 124-52. New York: Praeger.

Lincoln, Y. S., ed. 1985. *Organizational theory and inquiry: The paradigm revolution.* Beverly Hills, CA: Sage.

Lincoln, Y. S., and Guba, E. G. 1985. *Naturalistic inquiry.* Beverly Hills, CA: Sage.

———. 1986. But is it rigorous? Trustworthiness and authenticity in naturalistic evaluation. In *Naturalistic evaluation,* ed. D. D. Williams, 73-83. San Francisco: Jossey-Bass.

———. 1989. Ethics: The failure of positivistic science. *Review of Higher Education* 12: 221-24.

———. 1990. Judging the quality of case study reports. *Qualitative Studies in Education* 3: 53-59.

Linde, C. 1983. *The creation of coherence in life stories.* Norwood, NJ: Ablex.

Linn, R. L. 1986. Educational testing and assessment: Research needs and policy issues. *American Psychologist* 41: 1153-60.

Linville, P. W., and Clark, L. F. 1989. Production systems and social problem solving: Specificity, flexibility, and expertise. In *Advances in social cognition*, ed. R. S. Wyer Jr., and T. K. Srull, 2: 131-52. Hillsdale, NJ: Lawrence Erlbaum.

Lipinski, D., and Nelson, R. 1974. Problems in the use of naturalistic observation as a means of behavioral assessment. *Behavior Therapy* 5: 341-51.

Locander, W.; Sudman, S.; and Bradburn, N. 1976. An investigation of interview method, threat and response distortion. *Journal of the American Statistical Association* 71: 269-75.

Loevinger, J. 1976. *Ego development: Conceptions and theories.* San Francisco: Jossey-Bass.

Lofland, J. 1971. *Analyzing social settings.* Belmont, CA: Wadsworth.

Loftus, E. F. 1993. The reality of repressed memories. *American Psychologist* 48: 518-37.

London, P. 1986. Major issues in psychotherapy integration. *International Journal of Eclectic Psychotherapy* 5: 211-16.

Loos, V. E., and Epstein, E. S. 1989. Conversational construction of meaning in family therapy: Some evolving thoughts on Kelly's sociality corollary. *International Journal of Personal Construct Psychology* 2: 149-67.

Lord, C. G.; Ross, L.; and Lepper, M. R. 1979. Biased assimilation and attitude polarization: The effects of prior theories on subsequent evidence. *Journal of Personality and Social Psychology* 37: 2098-110.

Lorion, R. P. 1991. Psychology's response to the nation's health care crisis. *American Psychologist* 46: 516-19.

Lott, B. 1991. Social psychology: Humanist roots and feminist future. *Psychology of Women Quarterly* 15: 505-20.

Lubek, I. 1986. Fifty years of frustration and aggression: Some historical notes on a long-lived hypothesis. In *Dialectics and ideology*, ed. K. S. Larsen, 30-84. Norwood, NJ: Ablex.

Luria, A. R. 1976. *Cognitive development: Its cultural and social foundations.* Cambridge: Harvard University Press.

Lyddon, W. J. 1989a. Personal epistemology and preference for counseling. *Journal of Counseling Psychology* 36: 423-29.

———. 1989b. Root metaphor theory: A philosophical framework for counseling and psychotherapy. *Journal of Counseling and Development* 67: 442-48.

Lykes, M. B., and Stewart, A. 1986. Evaluating the feminist challenge to research in personality and social psychology: 1963-1983. *Psychology of Women Quarterly* 10: 393-412.

Lyotard, J. F. 1984. *The postmodern condition: A report on knowledge.* Minneapolis: University of Minnesota Press.

McAdams, D. P. 1988. *Power, intimacy, and the life story: Personological inquiries into identity.* New York: Guilford.

McAdams, D. P., and Ochberg, R. 1988. Psychobiography and life narratives. Special issue. *Journal of Personality* 56 (1): 1-326.

McCracken, G. 1988. *The long interview.* Newbury Park, CA: Sage.

McCullough, J. P. 1984. Single-case investigative research and its relevance for the nonoperant clinician. *Psychotherapy* 21: 382-88.

Mace, F. C., and Kratochwill, T. R. 1986. The individual subject in behavior analysis research. In *The individual subject and scientific psychology,* ed. Valsiner, J., 153-80. New York: Plenum.

McFall, R. M. 1986. Theory and method in assessment: The vital link. *Behavioral Assessment* 8: 3-10.

McGoldrick, M.; Pearce, J. K.; and Giordano, J., eds. 1982. *Ethnicity and family therapy.* New York: Guilford.

McGovern, M. P.; Newman, F. L.; and Kopta, S. M. 1986. Metatheoretical assumptions and psychotherapy orientation: Clinician attributions of patients' problem causality and responsibility for treatment outcome. *Journal of Consulting and Clinical Psychology* 54: 476-81.

McGuire, W. J. 1973. The yin and yang of progress in social psychology: Seven koan. *Journal of Personality and Social Psychology* 26:446-51.

MacIntyre, A. 1981. *After virtue.* Notre Dame, IN: University of Notre Dame Press.

———. 1988. *Whose justice? Which rationality?* Notre Dame, IN: University of Notre Dame Press.

McKay, D. G. 1988. Under what conditions can theoretical psychology survive and prosper? Integrating the rational and empirical epistemologies. *Psychological Review* 95: 559-65.

MacKenzie, B. D. 1977. *Behaviorism and the limits of scientific method.* Atlantic Highlands, NJ: Humanities Press.

Mackie, D., and Cooper, J. 1984. Attitude polarization: Effects of group membership. *Journal of Personality and Social Psychology* 46: 575-85.

MacKinnon, L. K., and Miller, D. 1987. The new epistemology and the Milan approach: Feminist and sociopolitical considerations. *Journal of Marital and Family Therapy* 13: 139-55.

McLeroy, K. R.; Bibeau, D.; Steckler, A.; and Glanz, K. 1988. An ecological perspective on health promotion programs. *Health Education Quarterly* 15: 351-78.

McMullin, E. 1984. A case for scientific realism. In *Essays on scientific realism,* ed. J. J. Leplin, 53-71. Berkeley: University of California Press.

McNamee, S., and Gergen, K. J. 1992. *Therapy as social construction.*

Newbury Park, CA: Sage.

McReynolds, P. 1989. Diagnosis and clinical assessment: Current status and major issues. In *Annual Review of Psychology,* ed. M. R. Rosenzweig and L. W. Porter, 40: 83-108. Palo Alto, CA: Annual Reviews.

Maddux, J. E.; Stoltenberg, C. D.; Rosenwein, R., eds. 1987. *Social processes in clinical and counseling psychology*. New York: Springer-Verlag.

Madsen, K. B. 1985. Psychological metatheory. In *Annals of theoretical psychology,* ed. K. B. Madsen and L. P. Mos, 3: 1-16. New York: Plenum.

Magnusson, D., ed. 1981. *Toward a psychology of situations: An interactional perspective.* Hillsdale, NJ: Lawrence Erlbaum.

Mahoney, M. J. 1976. *Scientist as subject: The psychological imperative.* Cambridge: Ballinger.

———. M. J. 1979. Psychology of the scientist: An evaluative review. *Social Studies of Science* 9: 349-75.

———. 1988a. Rationalism and constructivism in clinical judgment. In *Reasoning, inference, and judgment in clinical psychology*, ed. D. C. Turk and P. Salovey, 155-81. New York: Free Press.

———. 1988b. The cognitive sciences and psychotherapy: Patterns in a developing relationship. In *Handbook of cognitive-behavioral therapies,* ed. K. S. Dobson, 357-86. New York: Guilford.

———. 1989. Scientific psychology and radical behaviorism: Important distinctions based in scientism and objectivism. *American Psychologist* 44: 1372-77.

———. 1991. *Human change processes: The scientific foundations of psychotherapy*. New York: Basic Books.

Mahoney, M. J., and DeMonbreun, B. G. 1977. Psychology of the scientist: An analysis of problem-solving bias. *Cognitive Therapy and Research* 1: 229-38.

Mahoney, M. J., and Lyddon, W. J. 1988. Recent developments in cognitive approaches to counseling and psychotherapy. *The Counseling Psychologist* 16: 190-234.

Mahrer, A. R. 1970. Interpretation of patient behavior through goals, feelings, and context. *Journal of Individual Psychology* 26: 186-95.

———. 1978. The therapist-patient relationship: Conceptual analysis and a proposal for a paradigm shift. *Psychotherapy: Theory, Research, and Practice* 15: 201-15.

———. 1979. An invitation to theoreticians and researchers from an applied experiential practitioner. *Psychotherapy: Theory, Research, and Practice* 16: 409-18.

———. 1985. *Psychotherapeutic change: An alternative approach to meaning and measurement.* New York: Norton.

———. 1986. *Therapeutic experiencing: The process of change.* New York: Norton.

———. 1988. Discovery-oriented psychotherapy research: Rationale, aims, and methods. *American Psychologist* 43: 694-702.

Mahrer, A. R., and Nadler, W. P. 1986. Good moments in psychotherapy: A preliminary review, a list, and some promising research avenues. *Journal of Consulting and Clinical Psychology* 54:10-15.

Mair, M. M. 1988. Psychology as storytelling. *International Journal of Personal Construct Psychology* 1: 125-38.

Malcolm, N. 1967. Wittgenstein. In *The encyclopedia of philosophy,* ed. P. Edwards, 8: 327-39.

Manicas, P. T. 1986. Whitter psychology. In *Psychology: Designing the discipline,* ed. J. Margolis, P. T. Manicas, R. Harre, and P. F. Secord, 52-90. New York: Basil Blackwell.

——— . 1987. *A history and philosophy of the social sciences.* New York: Basil Blackwell.

Manicas, P. T., and Rosenberg, A. 1985. Naturalism, epistemological individualism and "The Strong Program" in the sociology of knowledge. *Journal for the Theory of Social Behavior* 15: 76-102.

Manicas, P. T., and Secord, P. F. 1983. Implications for psychology of the new philosophy of science. *American Psychologist* 39: 399-413.

Margolin, G.; Hattem, D.; John, R. S.; and Yost, K. 1985. Perceptual agreement between spouses and outside observers when coding themselves and a stranger dyad. *Behavioral Assessment* 7: 235-47.

Margolin, G.; Michelli, J.; and Jacobson, N. 1988. Assessment of marital dysfunction. In *Behavioral assessment,* ed. A. S. Bellack and M. Hersen, 441-89. New York: Pergamon.

Margolis, J. 1980. The trouble with homunculus theories. *Philosophy of Science* 47: 244-59.

———. 1986a. *Pragmatism without foundations: Reconciling realism and relativism.* New York: Basil Blackwell.

———. 1986b. Psychology and its methodological options. In *Psychology: Designing the discipline*, ed. J. Margolis, P. T. Manicas, R. Harre, and P. F. Secord, 12-51. New York: Basil Blackwell.

Margolis, J.; Manicas, P. T.; Harre, R.; and Secord, P. F., eds. 1986. *Psychology: Designing the discipline.* New York: Basil Blackwell.

Markman, E. M. 1979. Realizing you don't understand: Elementary school children's awareness of inconsistencies. *Child Development* 50: 643-55.

Markus, H., and Nurius, P. 1986. Possible selves. *American Psychologist* 41: 954-69.

Markus, H.; Smith, J.; and Moreland, R. 1985. Role of the self-concept in the perception of others. *Journal of Personality and Social Psychology* 49:1495-512.

Marsella, A.; DeVos, G.; and Hsu, F. L. K., eds. 1985. *Culture and self: Asian and Western perspectives.* New York: Tavistock.

Marsella, A., and Pedersen, P., eds. 1981. *Cross-cultural counseling and psychotherapy: Foundations, evaluation, and ethnocultural considerations.* Elmsford, NY: Pergamon.

Martin, J. 1984. The cognitive mediational paradigm for research on counseling. *Journal of Counseling Psychology* 31: 559-72.

——— 1988. A proposal for researching possible relationships between scientific theories and the personal theories of counselors and clients. *Journal of Counseling and Development* 66: 261-65.

———. 1989. A rationale and proposal for cognitive-mediational research on counseling and psychotherapy. *The Counseling Psychologist* 17: 111-35.

———. 1991. To theorize or not to theorize. *American Psychologist* 46: 651-52.

———. 1992. Cognitive-mediational research on counseling and psychotherapy. In *Psychotherapy process research: Paradigmatic and narrative approaches,* ed. S. G. Toukmanian and D. L. Rennie, 108-33. Newbury Park, CA: Sage.

Martin, J.; Feldman, M. S.; Hatch, M. J.; and Sim, S. 1983. The uniqueness paradox in organizational stories. *Administrative Science Quarterly* 28:438-53.

Martin, J.; Martin, W.; and Slemon, A. G. 1989. Cognitive-mediational models of action-act sequences in counseling. *Journal of Counseling Psychology* 36: 8-16.

Martin, J., and Stelmaczonek, K. 1988. Participants' identification and recall of important events in counseling. *Journal of Counseling Psychology* 35: 385-90.

Maruyama, M. 1963. The second cybernetics: Deviation-amplifying mutual causal processes. *American Scientist* 51: 164-79.

Mash, E. J. 1985. Some comments on target selection in behavior therapy. *Behavioral Assessment* 7: 63-78.

Masling, L. 1961. The effect of warm and cold interaction on the administration and scoring of an intelligence test. *Journal of Consulting*

Psychology 23: 336-41.

Maslow, A. 1966. *The psychology of science: A reconnaissance.* Chicago: Henry Regnery.

Masters, J. 1984. Psychology, research, and social policy. *American Psychologist* 39: 851-62.

Masters, J.; Burish, T.; Hollon, S.; and Rimm, D. 1987. *Behavior therapy: Techniques and empirical findings.* 3d ed. San Diego: Harcourt Brace Jovanovich.

Masterson, J. F., and Klein, R., eds. 1988. *Psychotherapy of the disorders of the self: The Masterson approach.* New York: Brunner/Mazel.

Matarazzo, J. D. 1971. The practice of psychotherapy is art and not science. In *Creative developments in psychotherapy,* ed. A. R. Mahrer and L. Pearson, 364-92. Cleveland: The Press of Case Western Reserve University.

———. 1983. The reliability of psychiatric and psychological diagnosis. *Clinical Psychology Review* 3: 103-45.

———. 1986. Computerized clinical psychological test interpretation: Invalidated plus all mean and no sigma. *American Psychologist* 41: 14-25.

Mayer, R. E. 1981. *The promise of cognitive psychology.* San Francisco: Freeman.

Mead, G. H. 1962. *Mind, self, and society.* Chicago: University of Chicago Press.

Meehl, P. E. 1954. *Clinical versus statistical prediction.* Minneapolis: University of Minnesota.

———. 1960. The cognitive activity of the clinician. *American Psychologist* 15: 19-27.

———. 1978. Theoretical risks and tabular asterisks: Sir Karl, Sir Ronald, and the slow progress of soft psychology. *Journal of Consulting and Clinical Psychology* 46: 806-34.

———. 1991. Why summaries of research on psychological theories are often uninterpretable. In *Improving inquiry in social science,* ed. R. E. Snow and D. E. Wiley, 13-59. Hillsdale, NJ: Lawrence Erlbaum.

Meehl, P. E., ed. 1973. *Psychodiagnosis: Selected papers.* Minneapolis: University of Minnesota Press.

Meichenbaum, D., and Butler, L. 1980. Cognitive ethology: Assessing the streams of cognition and emotion. In *Advances in the study of communication and affect: Assessment and modification of emotional behavior,* ed. K. Blankstein, P. Pliner, and J. Polivy, 6: 139-63. New York: Plenum.

Meichenbaum, D., and Cameron, R. 1981. Issues in cognitive assessment: An overview. In *Cognitive assessment,* ed. T. Merluzzi, C. Glass, and M. Genest, 3-15. New York: Guilford.

Merleau-Ponty, M. 1962. *Phenomenology of perception.* Trans. C. Smith. New York: Humanities Press.

Merluzzi, T.; Glass, C.; and Genest, M., eds. 1981. *Cognitive assessment.* New York: Guilford.

Merton, R. K. 1973. *Science and the sociology of knowledge.* London: Allen & Unwin.

Messer, S. B. 1991. The case formulation approach: Issues of reliability and validity. *American Psychologist* 46: 1348-49.

Messick, S. 1980. Test validity and the ethics of assessment. *American Psychologist* 35: 1012-27.

———. 1981. Evidence and ethics in the evaluation of tests. *Educational Researcher* 10:9-20.

———. 1984. The psychology of educational measurement. *Journal of Educational Measurement* 21: 215-37.

———. 1988. The once and future issues of validity: Assessing the meaning and consequences of measurement. In *Test validity,* ed. H. Wainer and H. I. Braun, 33-45. Hillsdale, NJ: Lawrence Erlbaum.

———. 1989. Validity. In *Educational measurement,* ed. R. L. Linn, 13-103. 3d ed. New York: Macmillan.

Meyers, C. 1987. *Teaching students to think critically.* San Francisco: Jossey-Bass.

Middleton, D., and Edwards, D., eds. 1990. *Collective remembering.* Newbury Park, CA: Sage.

Miles, M. B. 1990. New methods for qualitative data collection and analysis: Vignettes and prestructured cases. *International Journal of Qualitative Studies in Education* 3: 37-51.

Miles, M. B., and Huberman, A. M. 1984. *Qualitaive data analysis: A sourcebook of new methods.* Beverly Hills, CA: Sage.

Miles, M. B., and Huberman, A. M. 1994. *Qualitative data analysis: An expanded sourcebook.* Newbury Park, CA: Sage.

Miller, J. B. 1986. *Toward a new psychology of women.* 2d ed. Boston: Beacon.

Miller, M. J. 1985. Counselor as hypothesis tester: Some implications of research. *Journal of Counseling and Development* 63: 276-78.

Miller-Jones, D. 1989. Culture and testing. *American Psychologist* 44: 360-66.

Mio, J., and Iwamasa, G. 1993. To do, or not to do: That is the question for white cross-cultural researchers. *The Counseling Psychologist* 21: 197-212.

Mirkin, M. P., and Koman, S. L., eds. 1985. *Handbook of adolescents and family therapy.* Boston: Allyn & Bacon.

Mirman, J., and Tishman, S. 1988. Infusing thinking through "connections." *Educational Leadership* 45: 64-65.

Mischel, T., ed. 1969. *Human action.* New York: Academic Press.

Misgeld, D., and Jardine, D. W. 1989. Hermeneutics as the undisciplined child: Hermeneutic and technical images of education. In *Entering the circle: Hermeneutic investigation in psychology,* ed. M. J. Packer and R. B. Addison, 259-73. New York: State University of New York Press.

Mishler, E. G. 1984. *The discourse of medicine: Dialectics of medical interviews.* Norwood, NJ: Ablex.

———. 1986a. The analysis of interview-narratives. In *Narrative psychology: The storied nature of human conduct,* ed. T. R. Sarbin, 233-55. New York: Praeger.

———. 1986b. *Research interviewing: Context and narrative.* Cambridge: Harvard University Press.

Misiak, H., and Sexton, V. S. 1983. *Phenomenological, existential, and humanistic psychologies: A historical survey.* New York: Grune & Stratton.

Mitroff, I. I., and Kilmann, R. H. 1975. Stories managers tell: A new tool for organizational problem solving. *Management Review* 64: 18-28.

———. 1978. *Methodological approaches to social science.* San Francisco: Jossey-Bass.

Moerman, M. 1988. *Talking culture: Ethnography and conversation analysis.* Philadelphia: University of Pennsylvania Press.

Moll, L., ed. 1990. *Vygotsky and education: Instructional implications and applications of sociohistorical psychology.* New York: Cambridge University Press.

Montemayor, R., and Van Komen, R. 1980. Age segregation of adolescents in and out of school. *Journal of Youth and Adolescence* 9: 371-81.

Montgomery, J. P. 1982. A phenomenological investigation of the premenstruum. *Journal of Phenomenological Psychology* 13: 45-72.

Moon, S. M.; Dillon, D. R.; and Sprenkle, D. H. 1990. Family therapy and qualitative research. *Journal of Marital and Family Therapy* 16: 357-73.

——— 1991. On balance and synergy: Family therapy and qualitative research revisited. *Journal of Marital and Family Therapy* 17: 173-78.

Moos, R. H. 1979. Social ecological perspectives on health. In *Health psychology: A handbook*, ed. G. C. Stone, F. Cohen, and N. E. Adler, 523-47. San Francisco: Jossey-Bass.

Morawski, J. G. 1982. Assessing psychology's moral heritage through our neglected utopias. *American Psychologist* 37: 1082-95.

Morawski, J. G., ed. 1988. *The rise of experimentation in American psychology*. New Haven, CT: Yale University Press.

Morawski, J. G., and Agronick, G. 1991. A restive legacy: The history of feminist work in experimental and cognitive psychology. *Psychology of Women Quarterly* 15: 567-80.

Morgan, D. L. 1988. *Focus groups as qualitative research*. Newbury Park, CA: Sage.

Morgan, E. 1991. Levels of analysis and the received view—hermeneutics controversy. *Theoretical and Philosophical Psychology* 11: 43-55.

Morgan, G., ed. 1983. *Beyond method*. Beverly Hills, CA: Sage.

Morganstern, K. P. 1988. Behavioral interviewing. In *Behavioral assessment: A practical handbook*, ed. A. S. Bellack and M. Hersen, 86-118. 3d ed. New York: Pergamon.

Morley, S. and Adams, M. 1989. Some simple statistical tests for exploring single-case time-series data. *British Journal of Clinical Psychology* 28: 1-18.

Morris, S. B.; Turner, C. W.; and Szykula, S. A. 1988. Psychotherapy outcome research: An application of a new method for evaluating research methodology. *Psychotherapy* 25: 18-26.

Morrison, R. L. 1988. Structured interviews and rating scales. In *Behavioral assessment: A practical handbook*, ed. A. S. Bellack and M. Hersen, 252-77. 3d ed. New York: Pergamon.

Morrow-Bradley, C., and Elliott, R. 1986. Utilization of psychotherapy research by practicing psychotherapists. *American Psychologist* 41: 188-97.

Mos, L. P.; Wardell, D.; and Royce, J. R. 1974. A factor analysis of some measures of cognitive style. *Multivariate Research* 9: 47-58.

Moustakas, C. 1990. Heuristic research: Design and methodology. *Person-Centered Review* 5: 170-90.

Mulkay, M. 1979. *Science and the sociology of knowledge.* London: Allen & Unwin.

Munley, P. H. 1974. A review of counseling analogue research methods. *Journal of Counseling Psychology* 21: 320-30.

Murphy, J. M., and Gilligan, C. 1980. Moral development in late adolescence and adulthood: A critique and reconstruction of Kohlberg's theory. *Human Development* 10: 311-33.

Murphy, K. R. 1986. When your top choice turns you down: Effect of rejected offers on the utility of selection tests. *Psychological Bulletin* 99: 133-38.

Murphy, K. R., and Davishofer, C. O. 1988. *Psychological testing: Principles and applications.* Englewood Cliffs, NJ: Prentice-Hall.

Myers, I. 1962. *Manual: The Myers-Briggs Type Indicator.* Palo Alto, CA: Consulting Psychologists Press.

Myers, H. F. 1992. Overview and historical perspectives on ethnic minority clinical training in psychology. *The Clinical Psychologist* 45: 5-12.

National Research Council. 1979. *Privacy and confidentiality as factors in survey response.* Washington, D C: National Academy of Sciences.

Neilsen, J. ed. 1990. *Feminist research methods.* Boulder, CO: Westview Press.

Neimeyer, G. J., ed. 1993. *Constructivist assessment: A casebook.* Newbury Park, CA: Sage.

Neimeyer, G. J., and Neimeyer, R. A. 1993. Defining the boundaries of constructivist assessment. In *Constructivist assessment: A casebook,* G. J. Neimeyer, ed. 1-30. Newbury Park, CA: Sage.

Neimeyer, G. J., and Resnikoff, A. 1982. Qualitative strategies in counseling research. *The Counseling Psychologist 10:* 75-85.

Neimeyer, R. A. 1988a. Clinical guidelines for conducting interpersonal transaction groups. *International Journal of Personal Construct Psychology* 1: 181-90.

———. 1988b. Integrative directions in personal construct therapy. *International Journal of Personal Construct Psychology* 1: 283-97.

Neimeyer, R. A., and Feixas, G. 1990. Constructivist contributions to psychotherapy integration. *Journal of Integrative and Eclectic Psychotherapy* 9: 4-20.

Neisser, U. 1967. *Cognitive psychology.* New York: Appleton-Century-Crofts.

———. 1976. *Cognition and reality: Principles and implications of cognitive psychology*. San Francisco: Freeman.

———. 1982. *Memory observed.* Oxford: W. H. Freeman.

Nelson, J. S.; Megill, A.; and McClosky, D. N. 1987. *The rhetoric of the human sciences: Language and argument in scholarship and human affairs.* Madison, WI: University of Wisconsin Press.

Neuringer, A. 1981. Self-experimentation. *Behaviorism* 9: 79-94.

Newell, A., and Simon, H. A. 1972. *Human problem solving.* Englewood Cliffs, NJ: Prentice-Hall.

Newman, F. L., and Howard, K. I. 1991. Introduction to the special section on seeking new clinical research methods. *Journal of Consulting and Clinical Psychology* 59: 8-11.

Nickerson, R. S.; Perkins, D. N.,; and Smith, E. E. 1985. *The teaching of thinking.* Hillsdale, NJ: Lawrence Erlbaum.

Nickles, T. 1980. *Scientific discovery, logic, and rationality*. London: D. Reidel.

Nietzel, M. T., and Trull, T. J. 1988. Meta-analytic approaches to social comparisons: A method for measuring clinical significance. *Behavioral Assessment* 10: 159-69.

Nisbett, R. E.; Caputo, C.; Legant, P.; and Maracek, J. 1973. Behavior as seen by the actor and as seen by the observer. *Journal of Personality and Social Psychology* 27: 154-65.

Nisbett, R. E.; Krantz, D. H.; Jepson, C.; and Kunda, Z. 1983. The use of statistical heuristics in everyday inductive reasoning. *Psychological Review* 90: 339-63.

Nisbett, R. E., and Ross, L. 1980. *Human inference: Strategies and short comings of social judgment.* Englewood Cliffs, NJ: Prentice-Hall.

Nisbett, R., and Wilson, T. 1976. Telling more than we can know: Verbal reports on mental processes. *Journal of Personality and Social Psychology* 34: 641-53.

———. 1977. Verbal reports about causal inferences on social judgment: Private versus public theories. *Journal of Personality and Social Psychology* 35: 613-24.

Norcross, J. C. 1986. Eclectic psychotherapy: An introduction and overview. In *Handbook of eclectic psychotherapy,* ed. J. C. Norcross, 3-24. New York: Brunner/Mazel.

Norwood, R. 1985. *Women who love too much.* New York: Pocket Books.

Novak, J. D. 1985. Metalearning and metaknowledge strategies to help students learn how to learn. In *Cognitive structure and conceptual change,* ed. L. H. T. West and A. L. Pines, 189-209. New York: Academic Press.

Nuttall, E. V., and Ivey, A. E. 1978. Research for action: The tradition and its implementation. In *Research methods for counselors: Practical approaches in field settings,* ed. L. Goldman, 79-116. New York: Wiley.

O'Connell, A. N., and Russo, N. F., eds. 1991. Women's heritage in psychology: Origins, development, and future directions. Special issue. *Psychology of Women Quarterly* 15(4).

O'Dell, J. W., and Bahmer, A. J. 1981. Rogers, Lazarus, and Shostrom in content analysis. *Journal of Clinical Psychology* 37: 507-10.

O'Donnell, J. 1979. E. G. Boring and the uses of history. *American Psychologist* 34: 289-95.

———. 1985. *The origins of behaviorism.* New York: New York University Press.

O'Donohue, W. 1989. The (even) bolder model: The clinical psychologist as metaphysician-scientist-practitioner. *American Psychologist,* 44: 1460-68.

Ohio Psychological Association. 1983. *Principles for dealing with ethics cases involving computerized assessment.* Columbus: Ohio Psychological Association.

Okrent, M. 1988. *Heidegger's pragmatism.* Ithaca, NY: Cornell University Press.

O'Leary, K. D., and Borkovec, T. D. 1978. Conceptual, methodological, and ethical problems of placebo groups in psychotherapy research. *American Psychologist* 33: 821-30.

Ollendick, T. H., and Hersen, M., ed. 1984. *Child behavioral assessment: Principles and procedures.* New York: Pergamon.

Oltmans, T. F.; Neale, J. M.; and Davison, G. C. 1991. *Case studies in abnormal psychology.* 3d ed. New York: Wiley.

Oskamp, S. 1965. Overconfidence in case-study judgments. *Journal of Consulting Psychology* 29: 270-76.

Ossorio, P. G. 1974. *Meaning and symbolism.* LRI Report no. 10. Boulder, CO: Institute for Linguistic Research.

Othmer, E. 1989. *The clinical interview using DSM-IIIR.* Washington, D C: American Psychiatric Press.

Packer, M. J. 1985. Hermeneutic inquiry in the study of human conduct. *American Psychologist* 40: 1081-93.

Packer, M. J., and Addison, R. B. 1989a. Evaluating an interpretive account.

In *Entering the circle: Hermeneutic investigation in psychology* ed. M. J. Packer and R. B. Addison, 275-92. New York: State University of New York Press.

Packer, M. J., & Addison, R. B., eds. 1989b. *Entering the circle: Hermeneutic investigation in psychology.* New York: State University of New York Press.

Palinscar, A. S., and Brown, A. L. 1984. Reciprocal teaching of comprehension-monitoring activities. *Cognition and Instruction* 2: 117-75.

Panksepp, J. 1990. Can "mind" and behavior be understood without understanding the brain? *New Ideas in Psychology* 8: 139-49.

Paradise, L. V., and Siegelwaks, B. 1982. Ethical training for group leaders. *Journal for Specialists in Group Work* 7: 162-66.

Paranjpe, A. C. 1988a. A personality theory according to Vedanta. In *Asian contributions to psychology,* ed. A. C. Paranjpe, D. Y. F. Ho, & R. W. Rieber, 185-213. New York: Praeger.

———. 1988b. Introduction to *Asian contributions to psychology,* ed. A. C. Paranjpe, D. Y. F. Ho, and R. W. Rieber, 1-50. New York: Praeger.

Parker, I. 1989. *The crisis in modern social psychology—and how to end it.* London: Routledge & Kegan Paul.

Parker, I., and Shotter, J., eds. 1990. *Deconstructing social psychology.* London: Routledge.

Patterson, C. H. 1985a. New light for counseling theory. *Journal of Counseling and Development* 63: 349-50.

———. 1985b. *The therapeutic relationship: Foundations for an eclectic psychotherapy.* Pacific Grove, CA: Brooks/Cole.

Patterson, G. R. 1986. Performance models for antisocial boys. *American Psychologist* 41: 432-44.

Patton, M. Q. 1978. *Utilization-focused evaluation.* Beverly Hills, CA: Sage.

———. 1990. *Qualitative evaluation and research methods.* 2nd ed.

Newbury Park, CA: Sage.

Paul, G. L. 1967. Strategy of outcome research in psychotherapy. *Journal of Consulting Psychology* 31: 109-18.

Paul, R. W. 1984. Critical thinking: Fundamental to education for a free society. *Educational Leadership* 42: 4-14.

———. 1990. Critical and reflective thinking: A philosophical perspective. In *Dimensions of thinking and cognitive instruction,* ed. B. F. Jones and L. Idol, 445-94. Hillsdale, NJ: Lawrence Erlbaum.

Pearce, W. B., and Cronen, V. E. 1980. *Communication, action, and meaning: The creation of social realities.* New York: Praeger.

Pedersen, P., ed. 1985. *Handbook of cross-cultural counseling and therapy.* Westport, CT: Greenwood.

Pellegrino, J. W., and Glaser, R. 1982. Analyzing aptitudes for learning inductive reasoning. In *Advances in instructional psychology*, ed. R. Glaser, 2: 269-345. Hillsdale, NJ: Lawrence Erlbaum.

Pepper, S. C. 1942. *World hypothesis: A study in evidence.* Berkeley: University of California Press.

Perkins, D. N., and Salomon, G. 1989. Are cognitive skills context bound? *Educational Researcher* 18: 16-24.

Perry, W. 1970. *Forms of intellectual and ethical development in the college years.* New York: Holt, Rinehart & Winston.

Persons, J. B. 1989. *Cognitive therapy in practice: A case formulation approach.* New York: Norton.

———. 1991. Psychotherapy outcome studies do not accurately represent current models of psychotherapy. *American Psychologist* 46: 99-106.

Peterson, D. R. 1985. Twenty years of practitioner training in psychology. *American Psychologist* 40: 441-51.

———. 1991. Connection and disconnection of research and practice in the education of professional psychologists. *American Psychologist* 46:

422-29.

Pettigrew, A. M. 1985. Contextualist research: A natural way to link theory and practice. In *Doing research that is useful for theory and practice,* ed. E. E. Lawler, A. M. Mohrman, S. A. Mohrman, G. E. Ledford, T. G. Cummings and Associates, 222-48, 271-74. San Francisco: Jossey-Bass.

Phelan, J. G. 1964. Rationale employed by clinical psychologists in diagnostic judgment. *Journal of Clinical Psychology* 20: 454-59.

Phillips, B. N. 1989. Role of the practitioner in applying science to practice. *Professional Psychology: Research and Practice* 20: 3-8.

Piaget, J. 1952. *The origins of intelligence in children.* New York: Norton.

———. 1969. *The mechanisms of perception.* London: Routledge.

———. 1970. Piaget's theory. In *Carmichael's manual of child psychology,* ed. P. H. Mussen, 703-32. 3d ed. New York: Wiley.

Pine, F. 1989. Motivation, personality organization, and the four psychologies of psychoanalysis. *Journal of the American Psychoanalytic Association* 37: 31-64.

Pinsof, W. M. 1989. A conceptual framework and methodological criteria for family therapy process research. *Journal of Consulting and Clinical Psychology* 57: 53-59.

Plous, S., and Zimbardo, P. G. 1986. Attributional biases among clinicians: A comparison of psychoanalysts and behavior therapists. *Journal of Clinical and Consulting Psychology* 54: 568-70.

Polanyi, M. 1962. Tacit knowledge and its bearing on some problems in philosophy. *Review of Modern Physics* 34: 601-15.

———. 1964. *Personal knowledge.* New York: Harbor Torchbooks.

———. 1966. *The tacit dimension.* Garden City, N Y: Doubleday.

Polkinghorne, D. E. 1983. *Methodology for the human sciences: Systems of inquiry.* Albany: State University of New York.

———. 1986. Conceptual validity in a nontheoretical human science. *Journal of Phenomenological Psychology* 17: 129-49.

———. 1988. *Narrative knowing and the human sciences.* Albany: State University of New York Press.

Pollner, M., and Goode, D. 1990. Ethnomethodology and person-centering practices. *Person-Centered Review* 5: 203-20.

Ponterotto, J. G., and Casas, J. M. 1991. *Handbook of racial/ethnic minority counseling research.* Springfield, IL: C. C. Thomas.

Popkewitz, T. S. 1990. Whose future? Whose past? Notes on critical theory and methodology. In *The paradigm dialog,* ed. E. G. Guba, 31-45. Newbury Park, CA: Sage.

Pople, H. E. 1982. Heuristic methods for imposing structure on ill-structure: The structuring of medical diagnostics. In *Artificial intelligence in medicine,* ed. P. Szolovits, 119-90. Boulder, CO: Westview.

Popper, K. R. 1962. *Conjectures and refutations.* New York: Basic Books.

———. 1972. *Objective knowledge: An evolutionary approach.* Oxford: Clarendon.

———. 1983. *Realism and the aim of science.* Totowa, NJ: Rowman & Littlefield.

Potter, J., and Wetherell, M. 1987a. *Discourse and social psychology: Beyond attitudes and behavior.* London: Sage.

———. 1987b. How to analyze discourse. In *Discourse and social psychology,* ed. J. Potter, and M. Wetherell, 158-76. Newbury Park, CA: Sage.

Presser, S. 1983. Review essay: Survey research methodology versus survey research practice. *Contemporary Sociology* 12: 636-39.

Pressley, M., and Levin, J. 1983. *Cognitive strategy research: Educational applications.* New York: Springer-Verlag.

Prilleltensky, I. 1989. Psychology and the status quo. *American Psychologist*

44: 795-802.

———. 1990. Enhancing the social ethics of psychology: Toward a psychology at the service of social change. *Canadian Psychology* 31: 310-19.

Prochaska, J. O., and Norcross, J. C. 1986. Exploring paths toward integration: Ten ways not to get there. *International Journal of Eclectic Psychotherapy* 5: 136-39.

Rabin, A. I.; Aronoff, J.; Barclay, A. M.; and Zucker, R. A. eds. 1981. *Further explorations in personality*. New York: Wiley.

Rabin, A. I.; Zucker, R. A.; Emmons, R. A.; and Frank, S. eds. 1990. *Studying persons and lives.* New York: Springer.

Radnitzky, G. 1970 *Contemporary schools of metascience.* 2 vols. Goteborg: Akademiforlaget.

Raimy, V., ed. 1950. *Training in clinical psychology*. New York: Prentice-Hall. (Written by the staff of the Conference on Graduate Education in Clinical Psychology, Boulder, CO, August 1949.)

Ravn, I. 1991. What should guide reality construction? In *Research and reflexivity,* ed. F. Steier, 96-114. Newbury Park, CA: Sage.

Reason, P. 1981. Issues of validity in new paradigm research. In *Human inquiry: A sourcebook of new paradigm research,* ed. P. Reason & J. Rowan, 239-50. New York: Wiley.

Reason, P., and Rowan, J., eds. 1981. *Human inquiry: A sourcebook of new paradigm research.* New York: Wiley.

Redfield, J. P., and Paul, G. L. 1976. Bias in behavioral observation as a function of observer familiarity with subjects and typicality of behavior. *Journal of Consulting and Clinical Psychology* 44: 156.

Regan, D. T.; Straus, E.; and Fazio, R. 1974. Liking and the attribution process. *Journal of Experimental Social Psychology* 10: 385, 397.

Reichenbach, H. 1938. *Experience and prediction.* Chicago: University of Chicago Press.

———. 1951. *The rise of scientific philosophy.* Berkeley: University of California Press.

Reilly, R. R., and Smither, J. W. 1985. An examination of two alternative techniques to estimate the standard deviation of job performance in dollars. *Journal of Applied Psychology* 70: 651-61.

Rennie, D. L. 1990. Toward a representation of the client's experience of the psychotherapy hour. In *Client-centered and experiential therapy in the nineties,* ed. G. Lietaer, J. Rombauts, and R. Van Balen, 155-72. Leuven, Belgium: Leuven University Press.

———. 1992. Qualitative analysis of the client's experience of psychotherapy. In *Psychotherapy process research,* ed. S. G. Toukmanian and D. L. Rennie, 211-33. Newbury Park, CA: Sage.

Rennie, D. L.; Phillips, J. R.; and Quartaro, G. K. 1988. Grounded theory: A promising approach to conceptualization in psychology. *Canadian Psychology* 29: 139-50.

Rennie, D. L., and Toukmanian, G. S. 1992a. Explanation in psychotherapy process research. In *Psychotherapy process research: Narrative and paradigmatic approaches*, ed. S. Toukmanian and D. L. Rennie, 234-51. Newbury Park, CA: Sage.

Rest, J. R. 1986. Moral development in young adults. In *Adult cognitive development: Methods and models,* ed. R. A. Mines and K. S. Kitchener, 92-111. New York: Praeger.

Reynolds, C. 1984. Critical measurement issues in learning disabilities. *Journal of Special Education* 18(4): 451-76.

Rice, L. N. 1992. From naturalistic observation of psychotherapy process to microtheories of change. In *Psychotherapy process research: Narrative and paradigmatic approaches,* ed. S. Toukmanian and D. L. Rennie, 1-21. Newbury Park, CA: Sage.

Rice, L. N., and Greenberg, L. S., eds. 1984. *Patterns of change: Intensive analysis of psychotherapy process.* New York: Guilford.

Ricketts, M. 1989. Epistemological values of feminists in psychology. *Psychology of Women Quarterly* 13: 401-15.

Riger, S. 1992. Epistemological debates, feminist voices: Science, social values, and the study of women. *American Psychologist* 47: 730-40.

Ricoeur, P. 1983, 1985. *Narrative and time,* Vols 1 and 2. Chicago: University of Chicago Press.

Ricoeur, P. 1984. *Hermeneutics and the human sciences.* New York: Cambridge University Press.

Roberts, P., and Newton, P. M. 1987. Levinsonian studies of women's adult development. *Psychology and Aging* 2: 154-63.

Robins, L. N.; Helzer, J. E.; Ratcliff, K. S.; and Seyfried, W. 1982. Validity of the Diagnostic Interview Schedule, version II: DSM-III diagnosis. *Psychological Medicine* 12: 855-70.

Robinson, C. A., and Hayes, J. R. 1978. Making inferences about relevance in understanding problems. In *Human reasoning,* ed. R. Revlin and R. E. Mayer, 195-206. Washington, D C: Winston.

Robinson, J. K., and Woodward, W. R. 1989. The convergence of behavioral biology and operant psychology: Toward an interlevel and interfield science. *The Behavior Analyst* 12: 131-41.

Roe, A. 1952. *The making of a scientist.* New York: Dodd, Mead.

Rogers, C. 1961. *On becoming a person.* Boston: Houghton Mifflin.

Rogers, C. 1980. *A way of being.* Boston: Houghton Mifflin.

———. 1985. Toward a more human science of the person. *Journal of Humanistic Psychology* 25: 7-24.

Rogers, W.; Ryack, B.,; and Moeller, G. 1979. Computer-aided medical diagnosis: Literature review. *International Journal of Bio-Medical Computing* 10: 267-89.

Rogoff, B. 1985. Childhood as culturally construed: Review of F. S. Kessel and A. W. Siegel, *The child and other cultural inventions. Contemporary Psychology* 30: 444-46.

———. 1990. *Apprenticeship in thinking: Cognitive development in social context*. New York: Oxford University Press.

Rokeach, M. 1960. *The open and closed mind.* New York: Basic Books.

Rondal, J. A. 1985 *Adult-child interaction and the process of language interaction.* New York: Praeger.

Rorty, R. 1991. *Objectivity, relativism, and truth.* Cambridge: Cambridge University Press.

Rose, D. 1990. *Living the ethnographic life.* Newbury Park, CA: Sage.

Rose, S., and Rose, H. 1980. The myth of the neutrality of science. In *Science and liberation,* ed. R. Arditti, P. Brennan, and S. Cavrak, 17-32. Boston: South End Press.

Rosen, S. I. 1981. One researcher's self-questioning. In *Human inquiry: A sourcebook of new paradigm research,* ed. P. Reason and J. Rowan, 401-11. New York: Wiley.

Rosenblatt, P. C. 1981. Ethnographic case studies. In *Scientific inquiry and the social sciences: A volume in honor of Donald T. Campbell,* ed. M. B. Brewer and B. E. Collins, 194-225. San Francisco: Jossey-Bass.

Rosenthal, R. 1988. *Experimenter effects in behavioral research.* 2d ed. New York: Irvington.

———. 1991. *Meta-analytic procedures for social research.* Newbury Park, CA: Sage.

Rosenthal, R., and Rosnow, R. L., eds. 1969. *Artifact in behavioral research.* New York: Academic Press.

Ross, A. O. 1981. Of rigor and relevance. *Professional Psychology* 12: 319-27.

Rouse, J. 1987. *Knowledge and power: Toward a political philosophy of science.* Ithaca, NY: Cornell University Press.

Rowan, J. 1981. A dialectical paradigm for research. In *Human inquiry: A sourcebook of new paradigm research*, ed. P. Reason and J. Rowan, 93-112. New York: Wiley.

Royce, J. R. 1964. *The encapsulated man: An interdisciplinary essay on the search for meaning.* Princeton, NJ: Van Nostrand.

———. 1975. Epistemic styles, individuality and world view. In *Perspectives in information science,* ed. A. Debous and W. J. Cameron, 259-95. Leyden, The Netherlands: International Publishing.

———. 1978. How can we best advance the construction of theory in psychology? *Canadian Psychological Review* 19: 259-76.

———. 1985. The problem of theoretical pluralism in psychology. In *Annals of theoretical psychology,* ed. K. B. Madsen and L. P. Mos, 3: 297-315. New York: Plenum.

Royce, J. R.; Coward, H.; Egan, E.; Kessel, F.; and Mos, L. 1978. Psychological epistemology: A critical review of the empirical literature and the theoretical issues. *Genetic Psychology Monographs* 97: 265-353.

Royce, J. R., and Mos, L. P. 1980. *Psycho-Epistemological Profile manual.* Edmonton, Canada: University of Alberta Press.

Rumelhart, D. E. 1981. *Understanding understanding.* La Jolla, CA: University of California, Center for Human Information Processing.

———. 1984. Schemata and the cognitive system. In *Handbook of social cognition,* ed. S. R. Wyer and T. K. Srull, 161-68. Hillsdale, NJ: Lawrence Erlbaum.

Runyan, W. McK. 1982. *Life histories and psychobiography: Explorations in theory and method.* New York: Oxford University Press.

———. 1983. Idiographic goals and methods in the study of lives. *Journal of Personality* 51: 413-37.

Rustemeyer, A. 1977. Measuring interviewer performance in mock interviews. *Proceedings of the American Statistical Association (Social Statistics Section), 1977:* 341-46.

Rutter, M., & Graham, P. 1968. The reliability and validity of the psychiatric assessment of the child: I. Interview with the child. *British Journal of Psychiatry* 114: 563-79.

Ryan, W. 1971. *Blaming the victim.* New York: Pantheon.

Rychlak, J. F. 1969. Lockean vs. Kantian theoretical models and the "cause" of therapeutic change. *Psychotherapy: Theory, Research, and Practice* 6: 214-22.

———. 1981. *A philosophy of science for personality theory.* Malabar, FL: Krieger.

———. 1985. Eclecticism in psychological theorizing: Good and bad. *Journal of Counseling and Development* 63: 351-53.

———. 1988. *The psychology of rigorous humanism.* 2d ed. New York: New York University Press.

Sackett, G. P. 1978. *Observing behavior.* Vol. 2. Baltimore: University Park Press.

Sadler, W. A., and Whimbey, A. 1985. A holistic approach to improving thinking skills. *Phi Delta Kappan,* 67: 199-203.

Safran, J. D.; Vallis, T. M.; Segal, Z. V.; and Shaw, B. F. 1986. Assessment of core cognitive processes in cognitive therapy. *Cognitive Therapy and Research* 10: 509-26.

Sahlins, M. 1982. Individual experience and cultural order. In *The social sciences: Their nature and uses,* ed. W. H. Kruskal, 35-48. Chicago: University of Chicago Press.

Salner, M. 1985. Women, graduate education, and feminist knowledge. *Journal of Education* 167: 46-58.

———. 1988. Epistemic beliefs and their developmental relationship to postpositivist psychology. In *Recent trends in theoretical psychology,* ed. W. J. Baker, L. P. Mos, H. V. Rappard, and H. J. Stam, 65-76. New York: Springer-Verlag.

Samelson, F. 1979. Putting psychology on the map: Ideology and intelligence testing. In *Psychology in social context,* ed. A. R. Buss, 103-68. New York: Irvington.

Sampson, E. E. 1977. Psychology and the American ideal. *Journal of*

Personality and Social Psychology 35: 767-82.

———. 1985. The decentralization of identity: Toward a revised concept of personal and social order. *American Psychologist* 40: 1203-11.

———. 1988. The debate on individualism: Indigenous psychologies of the individual and their role in personal and societal functioning. *American Psychologist* 43: 15-22.

———. 1989a. The challenge of social change for psychology: Globalization and psychology's theory of the person. *American Psychologist,* 44: 914-21.

———. 1989b. The deconstruction of self. In *Texts of identity,* ed, J. Shotter and K. J. Gergen, 1-19. Newbury Park, CA: Sage.

———. 1993. Identity politics: Challenges to psychology's understanding. *American Psychologist* 48: 1219-30.

Sampson, J. P. 1986. Computer applications in testing and assessment. Special issue. *Measurement and Evaluation in Counseling and Development* 19: 4-61.

———. 1990. Computer-assisted testing and the goals of counseling. *The Counseling Psychologist* 18: 227-39.

Sanday, P. R. 1983. The ethnographic paradigm. In *Qualitative methodology,* ed. J. Van Mannen, 19-36. Beverly Hills, CA: Sage.

Sandifer, M. G.; Hordern, A.; and Green, L. M. 1970. The psychiatric interview: The impact of the first three minutes. *American Journal of Psychiatry* 126: 968-73.

Sanford, N. 1981a. A model for action research. In *Human inquiry: A sourcebook of new paradigm research*, ed. P. Reason and J. Rowan, 173-81. New York: Wiley.

———. 1981b. Will psychologists study human problems? *American Psychologist* 20: 192-202.

Sappington, A. A. 1990. Recent psychological approaches to the free will versus determinism issue. *Psychological Bulletin* 108: 19-29.

Sarason, S. B. 1974. *The psychological sense of community.* San Francisco: Jossey-Bass

———. 1978. The nature of problem solving in social action. *American Psychologist* 33: 370-80.

———. 1981a. An asocial psychology and a misdirected clinical psychology. *American Psychologist* 36: 827-36.

———. 1981b. *Psychology misdirected.* New York: Free Press.

———. 1984. If it can be studied or developed, should it be? *American Psychologist* 39: 477-85.

———. 1985. *Caring and compassion in clinical practice.* San Francisco: Jossey-Bass.

———. 1986. And what is the public interest? *American Psychologist* 41: 899-905.

Sarbin, T. R. 1940. The case record in psychological counseling. *Journal of Applied Psychology* 24: 184-97.

———. 1977. Contextualism: A world view for modern psychology. In *1976 Nebraska Symposium on motivation,* ed. A. W. Landfield, 1-42. Lincoln, NE: University of Nebraska Press.

———. 1986a. The narrative as a root metaphor for psychology. In *Narrative psychology: The storied nature of human conduct,* ed. T. R. Sarbin, 3-21. New York: Praeger.

Sarbin, T. R., ed. 1986b. *Narrative psychology: The storied nature of human conduct*. New York: Praeger.

Sarbin, T. R.; Taft, R.; and Bailey, D. E. 1960. *Clinical inference and cognitive theory.* New York: Holt, Rinehart & Winston.

Satir, V. 1983. *Conjoint family therapy.* Rev. ed. Palo Alto, CA: Science & Behavior Books.

Saunders, S. M.; Howard, K. I.; and Newman, F. L. 1988. Evaluating the clinical significance of treatment effects: Norms and normality.

Behavioral Assessment 10: 207-18.

Scarr, S. 1985. Constructing psychology: Making facts and fables for our times. *American Psychologist* 40: 499-512.

———. 1988. Race and gender as psychological variables. *American Psychologist* 43: 56-59.

Schacht, T. E. 1991. Formulation-based psychotherapy research: Some further considerations. *American Psychologist* 46: 1346-47.

Schaeffer, N. C. 1980. Evaluating race-of-interviewer effects in a national survey. *Sociological Methods and Research* 8: 400-19.

Schank, R., and Abelson, R. 1977. *Scripts, plans, goals, and understanding: An inquiry into human knowledge.* Hillsdale, NJ: Lawrence Erlbaum.

Scheff, T. J. 1984. *Labeling madness.* 2d ed. Englewood Cliffs, NJ: Prentice-Hall.

Scheflen, A. E. 1966. Natural history method in psychotherapy: Communicational research. Reprinted in *Creative developments in psychotherapy,* ed. A. R. Mahrer and L. Pearson, 393-422, Cleveland: The Press of Case Western Reserve University.

Scheper-Hughes, N., and Lovell, A. M., eds. 1987. *Psychiatry inside out: Selected writings of Franco Basaglia.* New York: Columbia University Press.

Schlipp, P., ed. 1951. *The philosophy of John Dewey.* 2d ed. New York: Tudor.

Schmidt, F. L. 1992. What do data really mean? Research findings, meta-analysis, and cumulative knowledge in psychology. *American Psychologist* 47: 1173-81.

Schneider, S. F. 1990. Psychology at a crossroads. *American Psychologist* 45: 521-29.

Schneider, W., and Shiffrin, R. M. 1977. Controlled and automated human information processing: Detection, search and attention. *Psychological Review* 84: 1-66.

Schon, D. 1963. *The displacement of concepts.* Cambridge: Tavistock Press.

———. 1983. *The reflective practitioner: How professionals think in action.* New York: Basic Books.

———. 1987. *Educating the reflective practitioner.* San Francisco: Jossey-Bass.

Schuller, D. Y., and McNamara, J. R. 1976. Expectancy factors in behavioral observation. *Behavior Therapy* 7: 519-27.

Schuman, H., and Presser, S. 1981. *Questions and answers in attitude surveys: Experiments on question form, wording, and content.* New York: Academic Press.

Schur, E. 1976. *The awareness trap: Self-absorption instead of social change.* New York: McGraw-Hill.

Schutz, A. 1970. *On phenomenology and social relations.* Chicago: University of Chicago Press.

Schwartz, G. E. 1982. Testing the biopsychosocial model: The ultimate challenge facing behavioral medicine? *Journal of Consulting and Clinical Psychology* 50: 1040-53.

Schwartzman, H. B. 1992. *Ethnography in organizations.* Newbury Park: Sage.

Scott, J.; Williams, J. M. G.; and Beck, A. T, eds. 1989. *Cognitive therapy in clinical practice: An illustrative casebook.* New York: Routledge.

Scriven, M. 1980. *The logic of evaluation.* Inverness, CA: Edgepress.

———. 1986a. Evaluation as a paradigm for educational research. In *New directions in educational evaluation,* ed. E. R. House, 53-67. London: Falmer.

———. 1986b. New frontiers of evaluation. *Evaluation Practice* 7: 7-44.

Seashore, S. E. 1985. Institutional and organizational issues in doing useful research. In *Doing research that is useful for theory and practice,* ed. E. E. Lawler, A. M. Mohrman, S. A. Mohrman, G. E. Ledford, T. G.

Cummings and Associates, 45-78. San Francisco: Jossey-Bass.

Sechrest, L. 1992. The past future of clinical psychology: A reflection on Woodworth (1937). *American Psychologist* 60: 18-23.

Seligman, M. E. P. 1975. Helplessness: *On depression, development, and death.* San Francisco: Freeman.

———. 1991. *Learned optimism.* New York: Knopf.

Semin, G. R., and Gergen, K. J. 1990a. *Everyday understanding: Social and scientific implications.* Newbury Park, CA: Sage.

———. 1990b. Everyday understanding in science and daily life. In *Everyday understanding: Social and scientific implications,* ed. G. R. Semin and K. J. Gergen, 1-18. Newbury Park, CA: Sage.

Serlin, R. C. 1987. Hypothesis testing, theory building, and the philosophy of science. *Journal of Counseling Psychology* 34: 365-71.

Serlin, R. C., and Lapsley, D. K. 1985. Rationality in psychological research: The good-enough principle. *American Psychologist* 40: 73-83.

Shadish, W. R. Jr. 1986. Planned critical multiplism: Some elaborations. *Behavioral Assessment* 8: 75-103.

Shadish, W. R., Jr.; Cook, T. D.; and Leviton, L. C. 1991. *Foundations of program evaluation.* Newbury Park, CA: Sage.

Shafer, R. 1970. An overview of Heinz Hartmann's contribution to psychoanalysis. *International Journal of Psychoanalysis* 51: 425-46

Shakow, D. 1978. Clinical psychology seen some fifty years later. *American Psychologist* 33: 148-58.

Shapiro, M. B. 1961. The single case in fundamental clinical psychological research. *British Journal of Medical Psychology* 34: 255-62.

———. 1966. The single case in clinical psychological research. *Journal of General Psychology* 74: 3-23.

Shiffrin, R. M., and Schneider, W. 1977. Controlled and automated human information processing: II. Perceptual learning, automatic attending, and a general theory. *Psychological Review* 84: 127-50.

Shneidman, E. S., ed. 1981. *Endeavors in psychology: Selections from the personology of Henry A. Murray*. New York: Harper & Row.

Shoham-Salomon, V. 1990. Interrelating research processes of process research. *Journal of Consulting and Clinical Psychology* 58: 295-303.

Shoham-Salomon, V., and Hannah, M. T. 1991. Client-treatment interaction in the study of differential change processes. *Journal of Consulting and Clinical Psychology* 59: 217-25.

Shontz, F. C. 1985. A personologic approach for health psychology research. *American Behavioral Scientist* 28: 510-24.

Shontz, F. C., and Rosenak, C. M. 1985. Models for clinically relevant research. *Professional Psychology: Research and Practice* 16: 296-304.

Shotter, J. 1975. *Images of man in psychological research*. London: Methuen.

Shotter, J., and Gergen, K. J., eds. 1989. *Texts of identity*. Newbury Park, CA: Sage.

Shrewsbury, C. M. 1987. What is feminist pedagogy? *Women's Studies Quarterly* 15(3/4): 6-13.

Shuller, D. Y., and McNamara, J. R. 1976. Expectancy factors in behavioral observation. *Behavior Therapy* 7: 519-27.

Sieber, J. E. 1992. *Planning ethically responsible research*. Newbury Park, CA: Sage.

Sieber, J. E., and Stanley, B. 1988. Ethical and professional dimensions of socially sensitive research. *American Psychologist* 43: 49-55.

Siegel, I. E. 1984. A constructivist perspective for teaching thinking. *Educational Leadership* 42: 18-21.

Siegel, S., and Castellan, J. N. 1988. *Nonparametric statistics for the behavioral sciences*. 2d ed. New York: McGraw-Hill.

Silverman, D. 1993. *Interpreting qualitative data: Methods for analyzing talk, text, and interaction.* Newbury Park, CA: Sage.

Silverman, H. J. 1990. *Postmodernism: Philosophy and the arts.* New York: Routledge.

Simon, A., and Bayer, E. G. 1974. *Mirrors for behavior III: An anthology of observation instruments.* Wyncote, PA: Communication Material Center.

Sinha, J. N. 1958. *Indian psychology: Cognition.* Vol. 1. 2d ed. Calcutta: Sinha Publishing.

Skinner, B. F. 1963. Behaviorism at fifty. *Science* 140: 951.

———. 1987. Whatever happened to psychology as the science of behavior? *American Psychologist* 42: 780-86.

Skodol, A. E. 1987. *Problems in differential diagnosis: From DSM III to DSM III-R in clinical practice.* Washington, DC: American Psychiatric Press.

Skrtic, T. M. 1985. Doing naturalistic research into educational organizations. In *Organizational theory and inquiry,* ed. Y. S. Lincoln, 185-220. Beverly Hills, CA: Sage.

Slosson, S. W., and Callisto, T. A. 1984. *Observational analysis.* East Aurora, NY: Slosson Educational Publications.

Sluzki, C. E. 1992. Transformations: A blueprint for narrative changes in therapy. *Family Process* 31: 217-30.

Smith, E., and Miller, F. 1978. Limits on perception of cognitive processes: A reply to Nisbett and Wilson. *Psychological Review* 85: 355-62.

Smith, J., and Heshusius, L. 1986. Closing down the conversation: The end of the quantitative-qualitative debate among educational enquirers. *Educational Researcher* 15: 4-12.

Smith, M. B. 1985. The metaphorical basis of selfhood. In *Culture and self: Asian and western perspectives,* ed. A. J. Marsella, G. Devos, and F. L. K. Hsu, 56-88. New York: Tavistock.

———. 1990. Psychology in the public interest. *American Psychologist* 45: 530-36.

Smith, M. L.; Glass, C. V.; and Miller, T. I. 1980. *The benefits of psychotherapy*. Baltimore: Johns Hopkins University Press.

Snow, R. E. 1991. Aptitude-treatment interaction as a framework for research on individual differences in psychotherapy. *Journal of Consulting and Clinical Psychology* 59: 205-16.

Snyder, M. 1976. Attribution and behavior: Social perception and social causation. In *New directions in attribution research,* ed J. H. Harvey, W. J. Likes, & R. F. Kidd, 1: 53-72. Hillsdale, NJ: Lawrence Erlbaum.

Snyder, M., and Thomsen, C. J. 1988. Interactions between therapists and clients: Hypothesis testing and behavioral confirmation. In *Reasoning, inference, and judgment in clinical psychology,* ed. D. C. Turk and P. Salovey, 124-52. New York: Free Press.

Soldz, S. 1989. Do psychotherapists use distinct construct subsystems for construing clients and personal acquaintances? A repertory grid study. *Journal of Social and Clinical Psychology* 8: 97-112.

———. 1992. Negativity in psychotherapists' evaluations of clients and personal acquaintances. *International Journal of Personal Construct Psychology* 5: 393-411.

Spence, D. P. 1989. Rhetoric vs. evidence as a source of persuasion. In *Entering the circle: Hermeneutic investigation in psychology,* ed. M. J. Packer and R. B. Addison, 205-21. Albany: State University of New York Press.

Spence, J. T. 1985. Achievement American style. *American Psychologist* 40: 1285-95.

Sperry, R. W. 1988. Psychology's mentalistic paradigm and the religion/ science tension. *American Psychologist* 43: 607-13.

———. 1990. Structure and significance of the consciousness revolution. *Person-Centered Review* 5: 120-29.

Spindler, G. D., ed. 1970 *Being an anthropologist: Fieldwork in eleven cultures.* New York: Holt, Rinehart and Winston.

Spitzer; R. L., Endicott, J.; Cohen, J.; and Fleiss, J. L. 1974. Constraints on the validity of computer diagnosis. *Archives of General Psychiatry* 31: 197-203.

Spitzer, R. L., and Williams, J. B. W. 1985. *Structured clinical interview for DSM-III.* New York: Biometrics Research Department, New York State Psychiatric Institute.

Spitzer, R. L.; Williams, J. B. W.; and Gibbon, M. 1987. *The structured clinical interview for DSM-III-R (SCID).* New York: Biometrics Research Department, New York State Psychiatric Institute.

Spradley, J. P. 1979. *The ethnographic interview.* New York: Holt, Rinehart & Winston.

———. 1980. *Participant observation.* New York: Holt, Rinehart & Winston.

Staats, A. W. 1971. Linguistic-mentalistic theory versus an explanatory S-R theory of language development. In *The ontogenesis of grammar,* ed. D. I. Slobin, 103-50. San Diego: Academic Press.

———. 1981. Paradigmatic behaviorism, unified theory, unified theory construction methods, and the zeitgeist of separatism. *American Psychologist* 36: 239-56.

———. 1983. *Psychology's crisis of disunity: Philosophy and method for a unified science.* New York: Praeger.

———. 1991. Unified positivism and unification psychology: Fad or new field? *American Psychologist* 46: 899-912.

Staats, A. W., and Eifert, G. H. 1990. The paradigmatic behaviorism theory of emotions: Basis for unification. *Clinical Psychology Review* 10: 539-66.

Staats, A. W., and Heiby, E. M. 1985. The paradigmatic behaviorism theory of depression: Unified, explanatory, and heuristic. In *Theoretical issues in behavior therapy,* ed. S. Reiss and R. R. Bootzin, 279-330. San Diego: Academic Press.

Stadler, H. A. 1986. Making hard choices: Clarifying controversial ethical issues. *Journal of Counseling and Human Development* 19: 1-10.

Stake, R. E. 1978. The case study method in social inquiry. *Educational Researcher* 7: 5-8.

———. 1986. *Quieting reform.* Urbana: University of Illinois Press.

Stam, H. J.; Rogers, S. T. B.; and Gergen, K. J., eds. 1987. *The analysis of psychological theory: Metapsychological perspectives.* Washington, D C: Hemisphere and Harper & Row.

Stanfield, J. H., and Dennis, R. M., eds. 1993. *Race and ethnicity in research methods.* Newbury Park, CA: Sage.

Stangl, D.; Pfohl, B.; Zimmerman, M.; Bowers, W.; and Corenthal, C. 1985. A structured interview for the DSM-III personality disorders. *Archives of General Psychiatry* 42: 591-96.

Steenbarger, B. N. 1991. Root metaphors and parables: A comment on Van Hesteren and Ivey. *Journal of Counseling and Development* 69: 380-81.

Steier, F. 1985. Toward a cybernetic methodology of family therapy research: Fitting research methods to family practice. In *Integrating Research and practice,* ed. L. Andreozzi, 27-36. Rockville, MD: Aspen.

———. 1991a. Reflexivity and methodology: An ecological constructionism. In F. Steier, *Research and reflexivity,* ed. 163-85. Newbury Park, CA: Sage.

———. 1991b. Research as self-reflexivity, self-reflexivity as social process. In *Research and reflexivity,* ed. F. Steier, 1-11. Newbury Park: Sage.

Steier, F., ed. 1991c. *Research and reflexivity.* Newbury Park, CA: Sage.

Sternberg, R. J. 1983. Components of human intelligence. *Cognition* 15:1-48.

———.1985a. *Beyond I.Q.: A triarchic theory of human intelligence.* New York: Cambridge University Press.

———. 1985b. Teaching critical thinking, Part 2: Possible solutions. *Phi Delta Kappan* 67: 277-80.

Sternberg, R. J., and Davidson, J. E. 1983. Insight in the gifted. *Educational Psychology* 18: 51-57.

Sternberg, R. J., and Kagan, J. 1986. *Intelligence applied: Understanding and increasing your intellectual skills.* San Diego: Harcourt Brace Jovanovich.

Sternberg, R. J., and Wagner, R. K., eds. 1986. *Practical intelligence: Nature and origins of competence in the everyday world.* Cambridge: Cambridge University Press.

Stevenson, H. 1972. *Children's learning.* New York: Appleton-Century-Crofts.

Stewart, A. J. 1989. Social intelligence and adaptation to life changes. In *Advances in social cognition,* ed. R. S. Wyer and T. K. Srull, 2: 187-96. Hillsdale, NJ: Lawrence Erlbaum.

Stewart, D. W., and Shandasani, P. N. 1990. *Focus groups.* Newbury Park, CA: Sage.

Stiles, W. B., and Schneider, C. K. 1992. Assessing qualitative research for publication and practice. Paper presented at the American Psychological Association Meeting, Washington, DC, August.

Stiles, W. B.; Shapiro, D. A.; and Elliott, R. 1986. Are all psychotherapies equivalent? *American Psychologist* 41: 165-80.

Stokols, D. 1987. Conceptual strategies of environmental psychology. In *Handbook of environmental psychology,* ed. D. Stokols, and I. Altman, 41-70. New York: Wiley.

———. 1992. Establishing and maintaining healthy environments: Toward a social ecology of health promotion. *American Psychologist* 47: 6-22.

Stokols, D., and Altman, I, eds. 1987. *Handbook of evironmental psychology.* New York: Wiley.

Straker, G. 1987. Conflicts of theory and views of human nature: The case of Kernberg versus Kohut. *South African Journal of Psychology* 17: 76-78.

Strange, C. C., and King, P. M. 1981. Intellectual development and its relationship to maturation during the college years. *Journal of Applied Developmental Psychology* 2: 281-95.

Strauss, A. L. 1987. *Qualitative analysis for social scientists.* Cambridge: Cambridge University Press.

Stricker, G., and Keisner, R. H., eds. 1985. *From research to clinical practice.* New York: Plenum.

Strickland, B. 1983. Responding to current concerns in clinical psychology. *The Clinical Psychologist* 37: 25-27.

Strong, S. 1991. Theory-driven science and naive empiricism in counseling psychology. *Journal of Counseling Psychology* 38: 204-10.

Strong, S. R., and Claiborn, C. D. 1982. *Change through interaction: Social psychological processes of counseling and psychotherapy.* New York: Wiley.

Strong, S. R.; Welsh, J. A.; Corcoran, J. L.; and Hoyt, W. T. 1992. Social psychology and counseling psychology: The history, products, and promise of an interface. *Journal of Counseling Psychology* 39: 139-57.

Strupp, H. H. 1981. Clinical research, clinical practice, and the crisis of confidence. *Journal of Consulting and Clinical Psychology* 49: 216-19.

———. 1986. Psychotherapy: Research, practice, and public policy (How to avoid dead ends). *American Psychologist* 41: 120-30.

———. 1989. Psychotherapy: Can the practitioner learn from the researcher? *American Psychologist* 44: 717-24.

Sudman, S., and Bradburn, N. M. 1974. *Response effects in surveys.* Chicago: Aldine.

Sue, D. W.; Arredondo, P.; and McDavis, R. J. 1992. Multicultural counseling competencies and standards: A call to the profession. *Journal of*

Counseling and Development 70: 477-86.

Sue, D. W, and Sue, S. 1987. Cultural factors in the clinical assessment of Asian Americans. *Journal of Consulting and Clinical Psychology* 55: 479-87.

———. 1990. *Counseling the culturally different: Theory and practice.* 2d ed. New York: Wiley.

Sugarman, J. 1992. Round the epistemological bend: A comment on "Levels of analysis and the received view—hermeneutics controversy." *Theoretical and Philosophical Psychology* 12: 27-37.

Sullivan, E. V. 1984. *A critical psychology.* New York: Plenum.

Sullivan, H. S. 1954. *The psychiatric interview.* New York: Norton.

Sumprer, G., and Walfish, S., eds. 1988. *Clinical, counseling, and com--munity psychology: A student guide to graduate training and professional practice.* New York: Irvington.

Sundberg, N. D.; Taplin, J. R.; and Tyler, L. E. 1983. *Introduction to clinical psychology.* New York: Prentice-Hall.

Suppe, F. 1977. *The structure of scientific theories.* 2d. ed. Urbana, IL: University of Illinois Press.

Taggart, M. 1985. The feminist critique in epistemological perspective: Questions of context in family therapy. *Journal of Marital and Family Therapy* 11: 113-26.

Tajfel, H., ed. 1984. *The social dimension: European developments in social psychology.* Vols. 1 & 2. Cambridge: Cambridge University Press.

Tallent, N. 1988. *Psychological report writing.* 3d ed. Englewood Cliffs, NJ: Prentice-Hall.

Taplin, J. R. 1980. Implications of general systems theory for assessment and intervention. *Professional Psychology* 11: 722-27.

Taplin, P. S., and Reid, J. B. 1973. Effects of instructional set and experimental influence on observer reliability. *Child Development* 44: 547-54.

Tarule, J. M. 1989. The voices of connected knowing and collaborative learning. Paper presented at Ways of Knowing Conference, Olympia, WA, November.

Task Force on Psychology and Public Policy. 1986. Psychology and public policy. *American Psychologist* 41: 914-21.

Taylor, C. 1985. *Human agency and language: Philosophical Papers 1.* Cambridge: Cambridge University Press.

Taylor, S. E., and Crocker, J. 1981. Schematic basis of social information processing. In *Social cognition: The Ontario Symposium in Personality and Social Psychology,* ed. E. T. Higgins, A. P. Herman, and M. P. Zenna, 89-134. Hillsdale, NJ: Lawrence Erlbaum.

Tesch, R. 1990. *Qualitative research: Analysis types and software tools.* New York: Falmer.

Tharp, R. G., and Gallimore, R. L. 1982. Inquiry process in program development. *Journal of Community Psychology* 10: 103-18.

———. 1988. *Rousing minds to life.* Cambridge: Cambridge University Press.

Thomas, L. E., and Chambers, K. O. 1989. Phenomenology of life satisfaction among elderly men: Quantitative and qualitative views. *Psychology and Aging* 4: 284-89.

Thompson, P. 1978. *The voice of the past: Oral history.* Oxford: Oxford University Press.

Tomm, K. 1986. On incorporating the therapist in a scientific theory of family therapy. *Journal of Marital and Family Therapy* 12: 373-78.

Torbert, W. R. 1976. *Creating a community of inquiry: Conflict, collaboration, transformation.* New York: Wiley.

———. 1981. Why educational research has been so uneducational: The case for a new model of social science based on collaborative inquiry. In *Human inquiry: A sourcebook of new paradigm research,* ed. P. Reason and J. Rowan, 141-51. New York: Wiley.

Toukmanian, S. G. 1990. A schema-based information processing perspective on client change in experiential psychotherapy. In *Client-centered and experiential psychotherapy in the nineties,* ed. G. Lietaer, J. Rombaus, and R. Van Balen, 309-26. Leuven, Belgium: Leuven University Press.

———. 1992. Studying the client's perceptual processes and their outcomes in psychotherapy. In *Psychotherapy process research: Paradigmatic and narrative approaches,* ed. S. G. Toukmanian and D. L. Rennie, 77-106. Newbury Park, CA: Sage.

Toukmanian, S. G., and Rennie, D. L, eds. 1992. *Psychotherapy process research: Paradigmatic and narrative approaches*. Newbury Park, CA: Sage.

Toulmin, S. E. 1969. Concepts and the explanation of human behavior. In *Human action: Conceptual and empirical issues,* ed. T. Mischel, 35-104. New York: Academic Press.

———. 1972. *Human understanding.* Vol. 1. Princeton, NJ: Princeton University Press.

———. 1983. The construal of reality in modern and postmodern science. In *The politics of interpretation,* ed. W. J. T. Mitchell, 99-117. Chicago: University of Chicago Press.

Triandis, H. C.; Lisansky, J.; Setiadi, B.; Chang, B. H.; Marin, G.; and Betancourt, H. 1982. Stereotyping among Hispanics and Anglos: The uniformity, intensity, direction, and quality of auto- and heterostereotypes. *Journal of Cross-Cultural Psychology* 13: 409-26.

Treisman, M., and Williams, T. C. 1984. A theory of criterion setting with an application to sequential dependencies. *Psychological Review* 91: 68-111.

Trimbur, J. 1989. Consensus and difference in collaborative learning. *College English* 51: 602-16.

Trow, G. W. S. 1981. *Within the context of no context.* Boston: Little, Brown.

Turk, D. C., and Salovey, P., eds. 1988. *Reasoning, inference, and judgment in clinical psychology*. New York: Free Press.

Turk, D. C.; Salovey, P.; and Prentice, D. A. 1988. Psychotherapy: An information processing perspective. In *Reasoning, inference, and judgment in clinical psychology,* ed. D. C. Turk and P. Salovey, 1-14. New York: Free Press.

Turkat, I. D. 1985. *Behavioral case formulation.* New York: Plenum.

Turner, C. F., and Martin, E., eds. 1984. *Surveying subjective phenomena.* 2 vols. New York: Russell Sage Foundation.

Tversky, A., and Kahneman, D. 1971. Belief in the law of small numbers. *Psychological Bulletin* 76: 105-10.

———. 1974. Judgment under uncertainty: Heuristics and biases. *Science* 185: 1124-31.

Tymchuk, A. J. 1981. Ethical decision-making and psychological treatment. *Journal of Psychiatric Treatment and Evaluation* 3: 507-13.

Uhr, L. 1966. *Pattern recognition.* New York: Wiley.

Uhr, L., and Vossler, C. 1963. Pattern-recognition program that generates, evaluates, and adjusts its own operators. In *Computers and thought,* ed. E. A. Feigenbaum and F. Feldman, 251-68. New York: McGraw-Hill.

Ullman, L. P., and Krasner, L., eds. 1965. *Case studies in behavior modification.* New York: Holt, Rinehart & Winston.

Uniform Guidelines on Employee Selection Procedures. 1978. *Federal Register* 43: No. 166, 38290-28309.

Vallacher, R. R., and Wegner, D. M. 1987. What do people think that they're doing? Action identification and human behavior. *Psychological Review* 94: 3-15.

Valle, R. S., and Halling, S., eds. 1989. *Existential-phenomenological perspectives in psychology.* New York: Plenum.

Valsiner, J., ed. 1986. *The individual subject and scientific psychology.* New York: Plenum

Van Hesteren, F.; Sawatzky, D. D.; and Zingle, H. W. 1982. Conceptual complexity and the helping relationship. *Canadian Counselor* 17: 4-13.

Van Maanen, J., ed. 1983. *Qualitative methodology.* Beverly Hills, CA: Sage.

Van Maanen, M. 1990. *Researching lived experience.* Albany: State University of New York Press.

Van Strien, P. J. 1987. Model discipline, research traditions, and the theoretical unification of psychology. In *Current issues in theoretical Psychology*, ed. W. J. Baker, M. E. Hyland, H. Van Rappard, and A. W. Staats, 333-44. Amsterdam: Elsevier.

Van Wormer, K. 1989. Co-dependency: Implications for women and therapy. *Women and Therapy* 8: 51-63.

Vega, W. A., and Murphy, J. W. 1990. *Culture and the restructuring of community mental health.* New York: Greenwood Press.

Veroff, J. 1983. Contextual determinants of personality. *Personality and Social Psychology Bulletin* 9: 331-44.

Viney, L. 1983. The assessment of psychological states through content analysis of verbal communications. *Psychological Bulletin* 84: 542-63.

———. 1993. Listening to what my clients and I say: Content analysis categories and scales. In *Constructivist assessment: A casebook,* ed. G. J. Neimeyer, 104-42. Newbury Park, CA: Sage.

Vitz, P. 1977. *Psychology as religion: The cult of self-worship.* Grand Rapids, MI: Eerdmans.

von Bertalanffy, L. 1968. *General system theory.* New York: Brazilier.

von Foerster, H. 1981. *Observing systems.* Seaside, CA: Intersystems.

von Glasersfeld, E. 1984. An introduction to radical constructivism. In *The invented reality,* ed. P. Watzlawick, 17-40. New York: Norton.

Vygotsky, L. S. 1962. *Thought and language.* Trans. E. Haufman and G. Vakar. Cambridge: MIT Press.

———. 1978. *Mind in society.* ed. M. Cole. Cambridge: Harvard University Press.

Wachtel, P. L. 1983. *The poverty of affluence: A psychological portrait of the American way of life.* New York: Free Press/Macmillan.

Wallace, C. J., and Elder, J. P. 1980. Statistics to evaluate measurement accuracy and treatment effects in single-subject designs. In *Progress in behavior modification,* ed. M. Hersen, R. M. Eisler, and P. M. Miller, 12: 40-79. New York: Academic Press.

Wallach, M. A., and Wallach, L. 1983. *Psychology's sanction for selfishness: The error of egoism in theory and therapy.* San Francisco: Freeman.

Wallston, B. 1981. What are the questions in psychology of women: A feminist approach to research. *Psychology of Women Quarterly* 5: 597-617.

Walsh, R. 1989. Do research reports in mainstream feminist psychology journals reflect feminist values? *Psychology of Women Quarterly* 13: 433-44.

Walsh, W. M. 1991. *Case studies in family therapy.* Boston: Allyn & Bacon.

Walters, M.; Carter, B.; Papp, P.; and Silverman, O. 1988. *The invisible web: Gender patterns in family relationships.* New York: Guilford.

Wampold, B. E. 1991. Root metaphor versus square root: Research evidence for a contextualist theme. *Journal of Counseling and Development* 70: 297-99.

Wampold, B. E., and Jenson, W. R. 1986. Clinical significance revisited. *Behavior Therapy* 17: 302-05.

Warwick, D. P. 1980. *The teaching of ethics in the social sciences.* New York: The Hastings Center.

———. 1983a. On methodological integration in social research. In *Social research in developing countries,* ed. M. Bulmer and D. P. Warwick, 275-97. New York: Wiley.

———. 1983b. The politics and ethics of field research. In *Social research in developing countries,* ed. M. Bulmer and D. P. Warwick, 315-30. New York: Wiley.

Wason, P. C. 1960. On the failure to eliminate hypotheses in a conceptual task. *Quarterly Journal of Experimental Psychology* 12: 129-40.

Wason, P. C., and Johnson-Laird, P. N. 1972. *Psychology of reasoning.* Cambridge: Harvard University Press.

Wason, P. C., and Johnson-Laird, P. N., eds. 1968. *Thinking and reasoning.* Baltimore: Penguin.

Watson, D. L., and Tharp, R. G. 1993. *Self-directed behavior: Self-modification for personal adjustment.* Pacific Grove, CA: Brooks/Cole.

Watzlawick, P.; Beavin: J.; and Jackson, D. 1967. *Pragmatics of human communication.* New York: Norton.

Watzlawick, P.; Weakland, J.; and Fisch, R. 1974. *Change: Principles of problem formulation and problem resolution.* New York: Norton.

Weary, G., and Mirels, H. L., eds. 1982. *Integration of clinical and social psychology.* New York: Oxford University Press.

Webb, E. J.; Campbell, D. T.; Schwartz, R. D.; and Sechrest, L. 1966. *Unobtrusive measures: Nonreactive research in the social sciences.* Stokie, IL: Rand McNally.

Webb, E. J.; Campbell, D. T.; Schwartz, R. D.; Sechrest, L.; and Grove, J. B. 1981. *Nonreactive measures in the social sciences.* 2d ed. Boston: Houghton Mifflin.

Weber, R. P. 1990. *Basic content analysis.* 2d ed. Newbury Park, CA: Sage.

Wedding, D. and Corsini, R. J. eds. 1989. *Case studies in psychotherapy.* Itasca, IL: F. E. Peacock.

Weimer, W. B. 1974. Overview of a cognitive conspiracy: Reflections on the volume. In *Cognition and the symbolic processes,* ed. W. B. Weimer and D. S. Palermo, 1: 415-42. Hillsdale, NJ: Lawrence Erlbaum.

———. 1977a. A conceptual framework for cognitive psychology: Motor theories of the mind. In *Perceiving, acting, and knowing: Toward an ecological psychology,* ed. R. Shaw and J. Bransford, 267-311. Hillsdale, NJ: Lawrence Erlbaum.

———. 1977b. Scientific inquiry, assessment, and logic: Comments on Bowers and Mahoney-DeMonbreun. *Cognitive Therapy and Research* 1: 247-55.

———. 1980. Psychotherapy and philosophy of science. In *Psychotherapy process: Current issues and future directions,* ed. M. J. Mahoney, 369-93. New York: Plenum.

Weinberg, H., and Hire, A. W. 1962. *Case book in abnormal psychology.* New York: Knopf.

Weiner, B. 1991. Metaphors in motivation and attribution. *American Psychologist* 46: 921-30.

Weinstein, G. 1981. Self science education. In *New directions for student services: Education for student development,* ed. J. Fried, 73-78. San Francisco: Jossey-Bass.

Weinstein, G., and Alschuler, A. S. 1985. Educating and counseling for self-knowledge development. *Journal of Counseling and Development* 64: 19-25.

Weinstein, G.; Hardin, J.; and Weinstein, M. 1976. *Education of the self.* Amherst, MA: Mandala.

Weiss, C. 1968. Validity of welfare mothers' interview responses. *Public Opinion Quarterly* 32: 622-33.

Welfel, E. R. 1982. How students make judgments: Do educational level and academic major make a difference? *Journal of College Student Personnel* 23: 430-97.

Werner, H., and Kaplan, B. 1963. *Symbol formation.* New York: Wiley.

Werry, J. S., and Quay, H. C. 1969. Observing the classroom behavior of elementary school children. *Exceptional Children* 2: 461-70.

Wertsch, J. V. 1986. *Vygotsky and the social formation of mind.* Cambridge: Harvard University Press.

Wertz, F. J. 1983. From everyday to psychological description: Analyzing the moments of a qualitative data analysis. *Journal of Phenomenological Psychology* 14: 197-242.

Westcott, M. R. 1968. *Toward a contemporary psychology of intuition.* New York: Holt, Rinehart & Winston.

Westermeyer, J. 1987. Cultural factors in clinical assessment. *Journal of Consulting and Clinical Psychology* 55: 471-78.

Wexler, P. 1983. *Critical social psychology.* Boston: Routledge & Kegan Paul.

Whipple, W. R. 1987. Collaborative learning: Recognizing it when we see it. *American Association of Higher Education Bulletin* (October): 3-6.

White, P. 1980. Limitations on verbal reports on internal events: A refutation of Nisbett and Wilson and of Bem. *Psychological Review* 87: 105-12.

White, P. A. 1990. Ideas about causation in philosophy and psychology. *Psychological Bulletin* 108: 3-18.

White, S. H. 1983. Psychology as a moral science. In *The child and other cultural inventions,* ed. F. S. Kessel and A. W. Siegel, 1-25. New York: Praeger.

Widick, C. 1977. The Perry scheme: A foundation for developmental practice. *The Counseling Psychologist* 16: 35-38.

Wilcox, R. R. 1987. New designs in analysis of variance. *Annual Review of Psychology* 38: 29-60.

Wilkins, W. 1986. Rhetoric and irrelevant criteria that disguise behavior therapy efficacy: Historical and contemporary notes. *Journal of Behavior Therapy and Experimental Psychiatry* 17: 83-89.

Williams, F. 1979. *Reasoning with statistics.* New York: Holt, Rinehart and Winston.

Williams, R. N. 1992. The human context of agency. *American Psychologist* 47: 752-60.

Willingham, W. W. 1988. Testing handicapped people: The validity issue. In *Test validity,* ed. H. Wainer and H. I. Braun, 89-103. Hillsdale, NJ: Lawrence Erlbaum.

Wills, T. A. 1978. Perceptions of clients by professional helpers. *Psychological Bulletin* 85: 968-1000.

Wills, T. A., ed. 1982. *Basic processes in helping relationships.* Orlando, FL: Academic Press.

Winkler, R. L. 1972. *An introduction to Bayesian inference and decision.* New York: Holt, Rinehart & Winston.

Winnett, R. A.; King, A. C.; and Altman, D. G. 1989. *Health psychology and public health: An integrative approach.* New York: Pergamon.

Winnett, R. A.; Moore, J. F.; and Anderson, E. S. 1991. Extending the concept of social validity: Behavior analysis for disease prevention and health promotion. *Journal of Applied Behavior Analysis* 24: 215-30.

Wittgenstein, L. 1968. *Philosophical investigations.* Trans. G. E. M. Anscombe. 3d ed. New York: Macmillan.

Wittrock, M. C. 1974. Learning as a generative process. *Educational Psychologist* 11: 87-95.

Wolf, A. 1983. Simplicity and universality in the transition to chaos. *Physical Review Letters* 46: 933.

Wolf, M. M. 1978. Social validity: The case for subjective measurement or how behavior analysis is finding its heart. *Journal of Applied Behavior Analysis* 11: 203-14.

Wolpe, J. 1990. *The practice of behavior therapy.* 4th ed. New York: Pergamon.

Wolpe, J., and Rachman, S. 1960. Psychoanalytic evidence: A critique based on Freud's case of little Hans. *Journal of Nervous and Mental Disease,* 130: 135-48.

Wood, P. 1983. Inquiring systems and problem structure: Implications for cognitive development. *Hunan Development* 26: 249-265.

Woodward, W. R. 1980. Toward a critical historiography of psychology. In *Historiography of contemporary psychology,* ed. J. Brozek, 29-67. Toronto: Hogrefe.

Woodward, W. R., and Ash, M. G. 1982. *The problematic science: Psychology in nineteenth-century thought.* New York: Praeger.

Woolgar, S., ed. 1988. *Knowledge and reflexivity.* London: Sage.

Wrenn, C. G. 1962. The culturally encapsulated counselor. *Harvard Educational Review* 32: 444-49.

———. 1985. Afterword: The culturally encapsulated counselor revisited. In *Handbook of cross-cultural counseling and therapy,* ed. P. Pedersen, 323-29. Westport, CT: Greenwood.

Wyer, S. R., and Srull, T. K., eds. 1984. *Handbook of social cognition.* Hillsdale, NJ: Lawrence Erlbaum.

Yanow, S. 1987. Ontological and interpretive logics in organizational studies. *Methods* 1: 73-90.

Yin, R. K. 1989. *Case study research: Design and methods.* 2d ed. Newbury Park, CA: Sage.

Young-Eisendrath, P., and Hall, J. A., eds. 1987. *The book of the self: Person, pretext, and process.* New York: New York University Press.

Zimpfer, D. G., and DeTrude, J. 1990. Follow-up of doctoral graduate students in counseling. *Journal of Counseling and Development* 69: 51-56.

Ziskin, J. 1981. Coping with psychiatric and psychological testimony. Vols. 1 & 2. 3d ed. Venice, CA: Law and Psychology Press.

Index